SALVATORE FERRAGAMO 1898–1960

Southern
ARGONAUT
Pacific

HOLLYWOOD BOOT SHOP

P. 2
SALVATORE FERRAGAMO WITH ACTRESS KATHLEEN KEY ON THE *ARGONAUT* TRAIN, WHICH WAS OFTEN USED AS THE PERFECT SET FOR MANY HOLLYWOOD PROMOTIONAL PHOTOS, 1926

SUEDE AND KIDSKIN SANDAL, 1924

KIDSKIN AND VELVET SANDAL, 1930–35; EMBROIDERED CANVAS AND KIDSKIN SANDAL, 1926–28

SILK SATIN AND KIDSKIN SANDAL, 1924; KIDSKIN AND SILK SATIN SANDAL, 1927

KIDSKIN AND SILK SATIN SANDAL, 1924

RUDOLPH VALENTINO,
1925

DOUGLAS FAIRBANKS
AND JOHN BARRYMORE,
FERRAGAMO'S CLIENTS,
1924

GLORIA SWANSON
WEARING FERRAGAMO
SHOES IN THE FILM *SADIE THOMPSON*, DIRECTED
BY RAOUL WALSH, 1928

ACTRESS LOLA TODD
IN A TOTAL LOOK
DESIGNED BY SALVATORE
FERRAGAMO, 1925

SILK SATIN PUMP WITH RHINESTONE BUCKLE, 1927–30. MODEL DESIGNED FOR ACTRESS MARY PICKFORD

MARY PICKFORD, 1920s

ACTRESS JOAN CRAWFORD AT THE HOLLYWOOD BOOT SHOP, 1925–26

RAFFIA MULE WITH BRASS HEEL, 1927. MODEL WORN BY JOAN CRAWFORD

SILK SATIN PUMP WITH RHINESTONE DUST, 1927. MODEL DESIGNED FOR ACTRESS MARION DAVIES

MARION DAVIES, 1928

ACTRESS OLIVE HASBROUCK WITH SALVATORE FERRAGAMO, MEASURING HER MEDIAN LINE, 1927

VETIA, SUEDE AND CROCODILE, 1927–30. MODEL DESIGNED FOR OLIVE HASBROUCK

SUEDE AND CALFSKIN CLOSED SHOE, 1927–30; CALFSKIN CLOSED SHOE, 1927–30. BOTH MODELS WERE DESIGNED FOR ACTRESS POLA NEGRI

POLA NEGRI AND CHARLIE CHAPLIN, BOTH SALVATORE FERRAGAMO'S CLIENTS, 1923

WRITER AND SCREENWRITER ANITA LOOS, FERRAGAMO'S CLIENT, 1926

SUEDE AND CALFSKIN LACED SHOE, 1928–30. MODEL DESIGNED FOR ANITA LOOS

KIDSKIN SHOE WITH EASTERN-STYLE TOE. MODEL DESIGNED FOR DOUGLAS FAIRBANKS IN *THE THIEF OF BAGDAD*, DIRECTED BY RAOUL WALSH, 1924

DOUGLAS FAIRBANKS IN *THE THIEF OF BAGDAD*, 1924

SCENE FROM *THE TEN COMMANDMENTS*, DIRECTED BY CECIL B. DEMILLE, 1923. SALVATORE FERRAGAMO DESIGNED SHOES FOR THE LEADING ACTORS

CALFSKIN SHOE WITH EASTERN-STYLE TOE DESIGNED FOR *THE TEN COMMANDMENTS*, 1923

CALFSKIN SANDALS DESIGNED FOR *THE KING OF KINGS*, DIRECTED BY CECIL B. DEMILLE, 1927

SCENES FROM *THE KING OF KINGS*, 1927. SALVATORE FERRAGAMO MADE SOME OF THE FOOTWEAR FOR THE FILM

PHARAOH TUTANKHAMUN'S GOLD MASK, DISCOVERED IN EGYPT IN 1922

KIDSKIN SANDAL WITH BRASS HEEL, 1930

KIDSKIN LACED SHOE
WITH HAND-PAINTED
HEEL, 1927

MATERIALS AND INSPIRATION

P. 34
SUEDE PUMP WITH
GLOVED ARCH AND MICA
HEEL, 1955–56

ADVERT FOR THE SALP COMPANY, IN *RIVISTA ITALIANA CALZATURE*, JUNE 1939. BIBLIOTECA NAZIONALE CENTRALE DI FIRENZE, FLORENCE

SNAPPER SKIN PUMP, 1930–35

SEA LEOPARD AND CALFSKIN LACED SHOE WITH LAYERED WEDGE HEEL IN COVERED CORK, 1939

SEA LEOPARD SKIN (ANARHICHAS LUPUS)

SUEDE, LIZARD,
AND KIDSKIN CLOSED SHOE
WITH LAYERED WEDGE
HEEL IN COVERED CORK,
1942–44

MATA, CROCODILE, 1949;
BUBIA, ACROCHORDUS (SEA
SNAKE), 1927–30

SEVRES, SEALSKIN,
1959

INUIT CRAFTSMANSHIP (GREENLAND), *CEREMONIAL GARMENTS (THONG AND SHORT PANTS)*, EARLY TWENTIETH CENTURY, SEALSKIN. SISTEMA MUSEALE DI ATENEO, UNIVERSITÀ DEGLI STUDI DI FIRENZE, FLORENCE

KANIANIGMIUT CRAFTSMANSHIP (ALASKA), *NARRATIVE SEQUENCE*, SECOND HALF OF THE NINETEENTH CENTURY, WALRUS TUSK IVORY. SISTEMA MUSEALE DI ATENEO, UNIVERSITÀ DEGLI STUDI DI FIRENZE, FLORENCE

CALFSKIN AND TOAD
SKIN LACED SHOE, 1940

BOARSKIN LACED SHOE, 1954–55; *CAMPIA*, OSTRICH AND CALFSKIN, 1949–50

INDA, LLAMA SKIN, 1959; *DURIA*, ANTELOPE AND CALFSKIN, 1953

FLORENCE

KIDSKIN, CALFSKIN, AND SUEDE BALLERINA SHOES, 1955–56. THESE MODELS WERE INSPIRED BY TRADITIONAL NATIVE AMERICAN FOOTWEAR

ANTELOPE LACED SHOE
WITH TOE SHAPED LIKE A
RHINOCEROS HORN, 1938

MAX ERNST, *HISTOIRE NATURELLE* (PARIS, 1926), PLATE XXVIII, PRINT (COLLOTYPE). BIBLIOTECA NAZIONALE CENTRALE DI FIRENZE, FLORENCE

KIDSKIN SANDAL, 1930

LUCIO VENNA, *COTURNO FERRAGAMO*, 1930, PENCIL AND WATERCOLOR ON CARDBOARD. MUSEO FERRAGAMO, FLORENCE

ROMAN ART, *STATUE FOOT WITH SANDAL*, IMPERIAL AGE, FIRST–SECOND CENTURY, BRONZE. MUSEO ARCHEOLOGICO NAZIONALE (DIREZIONE REGIONALE MUSEI DELLA TOSCANA), FLORENCE

KIDSKIN AND SILK SATIN SANDAL WITH LAYERED WEDGE HEEL IN COVERED CORK, 1938

VOGUE USA, FEBRUARY 15, 1939. MUSEO FERRAGAMO, FLORENCE

ENEA, SUEDE AND KIDSKIN, 1936–38

SUEDE AND KIDSKIN SANDALS WITH LAYERED WEDGE HEEL IN COVERED CORK, 1936–38

JAPANESE CRAFTSMANSHIP, *TOSEI GUSOKU* (MODERN ARMOR), LATE EIGHTEENTH CENTURY, LACQUERED STEEL, COPPER, AND SILK. MUSEO STIBBERT, FLORENCE

SILK SOUTACHE AND CELLOPHANE SANDAL, 1957–58

PROCESSED KIDSKIN SANDAL WITH ORIENTAL-STYLE DECORATION AND WEDGE HEEL COVERED IN CORK, 1956

SIRIANO, KIDSKIN WITH DAMASK DECORATION AND SHAPED WEDGE HEEL IN COVERED WOOD, 1947–50

L'ETRUSCO (FERNANDO BALDI), *ADVERTISING POSTER FOR SALVATORE FERRAGAMO*, 1951, ACRYLIC AND TEMPERA ON CANVAS. MUSEO FERRAGAMO, FLORENCE

GUIDO GIANNINI, *LIBRO BIANCO*, 1906–07, MOROCCAN LEATHER BINDING, THREADED FRAME WITH SMALL IRON INSERT DECORATION IN DERÔME STYLE. ATELIER DEGLI ARTIGIANELLI COLLECTION – FONDAZIONE CR FIRENZE, FLORENCE

JOHANN WILHELM MEYER COMPANY (AUGSBURG), *EDITORIAL COVER*, FIRST HALF OF THE EIGHTEENTH CENTURY, LAID, EMBOSSED PAPER WITH A FLORAL PATTERN IN RELIEF. ATELIER DEGLI ARTIGIANELLI COLLECTION – FONDAZIONE CR FIRENZE, FLORENCE

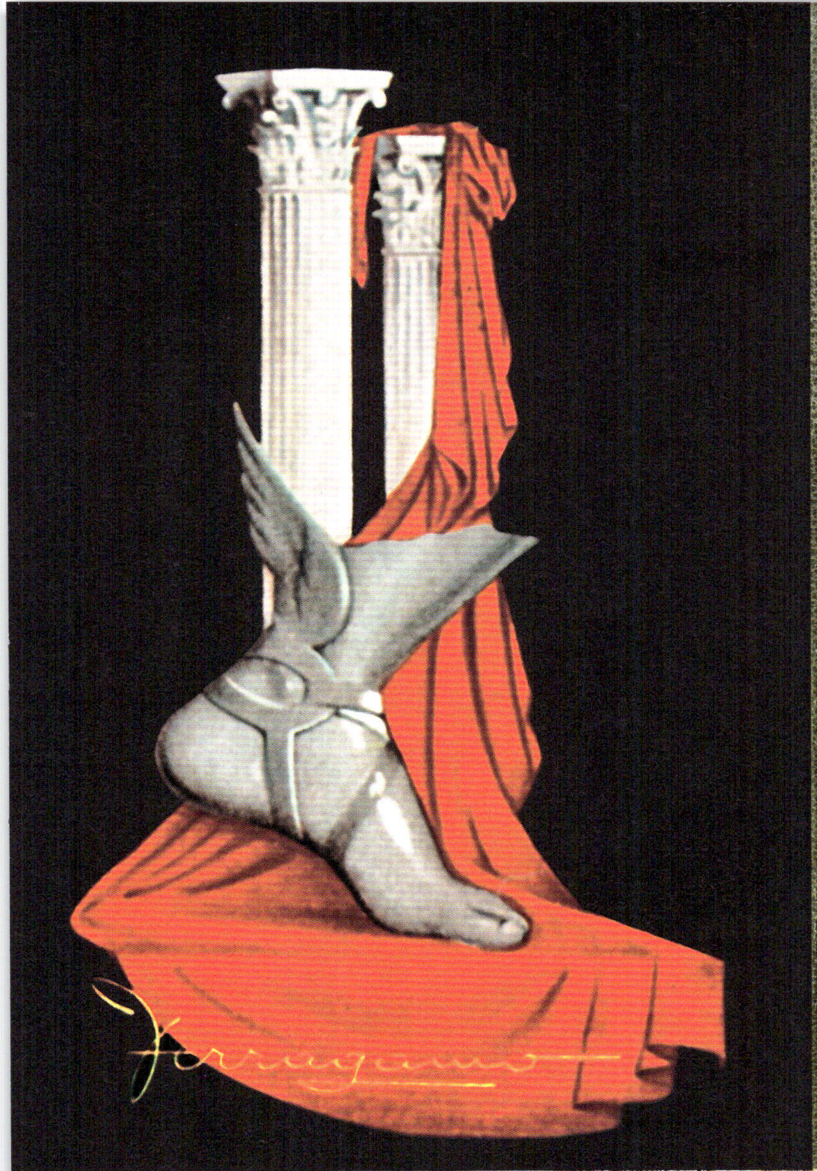
Ferragamo

SUEDE AND KIDSKIN PUMP, 1958–59

ETRUSCAN ART, *OVOIDAL COOKING POT*, SEVENTH CENTURY BC, CLAY CERAMIC PAINTED WITH GEOMETRIC PATTERNS, FROM POGGIO BUCO (GROSSETO). MUSEO ARCHEOLOGICO NAZIONALE (DIREZIONE REGIONALE MUSEI DELLA TOSCANA), FLORENCE

VOGUE USA, FEBRUARY 1, 1939

TOP TO BOTTOM: *WODKA*, SUEDE AND KIDSKIN, 1940; SUEDE AND KIDSKIN LACED SHOE, 1940; *STRADA*, SUEDE AND KIDSKIN, 1940; *ATTICA*, CALFSKIN AND KIDSKIN, 1941. WEDGE HEELS IN COVERED CORK

KIDSKIN AND METAL HEELS DECORATED WITH RHINESTONES AND STONES, 1950s

CASSANDRA, SILK SATIN AND HEEL DECORATED WITH RHINESTONES, 1956

SALVATORE FERRAGAMO
LOOKS THROUGH
THE VINYLITE SOLE
OF HIS SANDAL, 1955

DAMASK SILK FABRIC
SANDAL WITH VINYLITE
SOLE AND MICA HEEL,
1955

NYLON THREAD NET
AND KIDSKIN SANDAL,
1947–49

ASTRAPIA NIGRA,
NINETEENTH CENTURY,
NATURALIZED
TAXIDERMIC SPECIMEN.
SISTEMA MUSEALE DI
ATENEO, UNIVERSITÀ
DEGLI STUDI DI FIRENZE,
FLORENCE

JACKIE, SILK SATIN WITH
SILVER ORNAMENT,
RHINESTONES, AND
FEATHERS, 1960

JACKIE, SILK SATIN WITH SILVER ORNAMENT, RHINESTONES, AND FEATHERS, 1960

PARADISEA REGGIANA, NINETEENTH CENTURY, NATURALIZED TAXIDERMIC SPECIMEN. SISTEMA MUSEALE DI ATENEO, UNIVERSITÀ DEGLI STUDI DI FIRENZE, FLORENCE

IRIDE, TAVARNELLE LACE
WITH SILK THREAD CHAIN
STITCH EMBROIDERY
AND KIDSKIN, 1930–36

TAVARNELLE LACE AND KIDSKIN SANDAL WITH APPLICATION OF SEQUINS AND HEEL DECORATED IN RHINESTONE, 1950–52

ITALIAN CRAFTSMANSHIP (TAVARNELLE VAL DI PESA, FLORENCE), *BASKET*, 1930s, TAVARNELLE LACE. LORETTA CAPONI COLLECTION, FLORENCE

CENERENTOLA,
TAVARNELLE LACE
WITH SILK THREAD FLAT
STITCH EMBROIDERY
AND SILK SATIN, 1930–35

TWO-PIECE SHOE IN SILK SATIN, KIDSKIN, AND TAVARNELLE LACE WITH SILK THREAD FLAT STITCH EMBROIDERY, 1930–35; TAVARNELLE LACE AND SILK SATIN SANDAL, 1955–59

SANDAL IN SILK
THREAD FLAT STITCH
EMBROIDERED CANVAS
AND KIDSKIN, 1938

SUEDE LACED SHOE, 1938

ENRICO PRAMPOLINI,
COMPOSIZIONE GEOMETRICA,
C. 1930, TAPESTRY IN
INTERTWINED INLAY
WITH WOOLEN THREAD.
FONDAZIONE MASSIMO E
SONIA CIRULLI, SAN LAZZARO
DI SAVENA (BOLOGNA)

CALFSKIN AND SUEDE PUMP, 1939

KIDSKIN SANDAL, 1935

ENRICO PRAMPOLINI, *COMPOSIZIONE GEOMETRICA*, C. 1930, TAPESTRIES IN INTERTWINED INLAY WITH WOOLEN THREAD. FONDAZIONE MASSIMO E SONIA CIRULLI, SAN LAZZARO DI SAVENA (BOLOGNA)

E.P

E.P

LACED SHOE IN COTTON
THREAD HALF STITCH
CANVAS, 1935–38

SONIA DELAUNAY, *SONIA DELAUNAY: SES PEINTURES, SES OBJETS, SES TISSUS SIMULTANÉS, SES MODES* (PARIS: LIBRAIRIE DES ARTS DÉCORATIFS, 1925), PLATE XX, STENCIL ON PAPER. BIBLIOTECA NAZIONALE CENTRALE DI FIRENZE, FLORENCE

SONIA DELAUNAY, *PROJET DE TISSU, GOUACHE F 1544 – VARIANT OF NO. 61 "BLACK BOOK I" AND NO. 160 "BLACK BOOK II,"* 1924, GOUACHE ON PAPER. PRIVATE COLLECTION, MILAN. COURTESY GIÒ MARCONI

SONIA DELAUNAY, *UNTITLED*, 1929, GOUACHE ON PAPER. PRIVATE COLLECTION, MILAN. COURTESY GIÒ MARCONI

PUMP IN SILK
THREAD CHAIN
STITCH EMBROIDERY
AND CALFSKIN, 1930–35

TULLIO D'ALBISOLA,
"BAKER" PITCHER, 1929,
CERAMIC DECORATED
UNDER GLAZE. PRIVATE
COLLECTION

ARCOBALENO, SUEDE AND SILK THREAD CHAIN STITCH EMBROIDERY, 1935

DETAIL OF CEILING OF THE CAR SHOW AT THE *EXPOSITION INTERNATIONALE DES ARTS ET DES TECHNIQUES APPLIQUÉS À LA VIE MODERNE*, GRAND PALAIS, PARIS, 1937

SONIA DELAUNAY, *UNTITLED*, 1930, GOUACHE ON PAPER. PRIVATE COLLECTION, MILAN. COURTESY GIÒ MARCONI

SONIA DELAUNAY, *UNTITLED*, 1931, GOUACHE ON PAPER. PRIVATE COLLECTION, MILAN. COURTESY GIÒ MARCONI

IVAN PUNI, *R.F.O.*, 1916, OIL, WOOD, AND OBJECTS ON PANEL. FONDAZIONE MASSIMO E SONIA CIRULLI, SAN LAZZARO DI SAVENA (BOLOGNA)

THEO VAN DOESBURG, *STUDY FOR COUNTER COMPOSITION XIII*, C. 1925, OIL ON PANEL. FONDAZIONE MASSIMO E SONIA CIRULLI, SAN LAZZARO DI SAVENA (BOLOGNA)

KURT SCHWITTERS, *RAPHAËL*, 1928, COLLAGE ELEMENTS AND MIXED MEDIA ON CARDBOARD. FONDAZIONE MASSIMO E SONIA CIRULLI, SAN LAZZARO DI SAVENA (BOLOGNA)

KURT SCHWITTERS, *UNTITLED*, 1941, OIL, COLLAGE ELEMENTS, FABRICS, AND OBJECTS ON CARDBOARD. FONDAZIONE MASSIMO E SONIA CIRULLI, SAN LAZZARO DI SAVENA (BOLOGNA)

SUEDE LACED SHOE
WITH WEDGE HEEL
IN COVERED CORK,
1938–40

BICE LAZZARI, *TAPESTRY*, 1928, COLORED LENCI CLOTH INLAY. ARCHIVIO BICE LAZZARI, ROME

HEMP SANDAL WITH WOVEN COTTON CORD, 1936–38

ANITA PITTONI, *DRESS FOR JULIA BANFI BERTOLOTTI*, 1939, BROOM FIBER. JULIA & GIANGIO BANFI COLLECTION

FELT SABOT WITH COTTON RIBBONS, 1938

HEMP AND KIDSKIN LACED SHOE WITH LAYERED CORK HEEL COVERED WITH SUEDE, 1936–38

MARISA BRONZINI WITH GEGIA AND MICHELA BRONZINI, *VARIANTE CERCHI* DRESS, 1938, HANDMADE HEMP CLOTH WITH SILK BORDER, CIRCLE DECORATION MADE USING THE "SPOLINATO" TECHNIQUE. PRIVATE COLLECTION

POLLICINO, HEMP WITH
SUEDE DECORATIONS
AND WEDGE HEEL IN
CORK COVERED WITH
CALFSKIN, 1940

EMBROIDERED HEMP
SANDAL WITH CORK
HEEL, 1935–38

EMBROIDERED HEMP
AND KIDSKIN
SANDAL WITH LAYERED
WEDGE HEEL IN
COVERED CORK, 1944

PIGSKIN LACED SHOE
WITH SOLE IN RUBBER
DERIVATIVE, 1944

FUSTIAN ANKLE-BOOT
SANDAL WITH PAINTED
WOODEN WEDGE, 1944

ANTELOPE AND
GROSGRAIN SANDAL
WITH LAYERED WEDGE
HEEL IN COVERED CORK,
1940

SUEDE SANDAL WITH
CORK WEDGE HEEL
AND SOLE IN RUBBER
DERIVATIVE, 1941

FILIPINO GRASS SANDALS
IN A WOVEN MAT FINISH,
1936–38

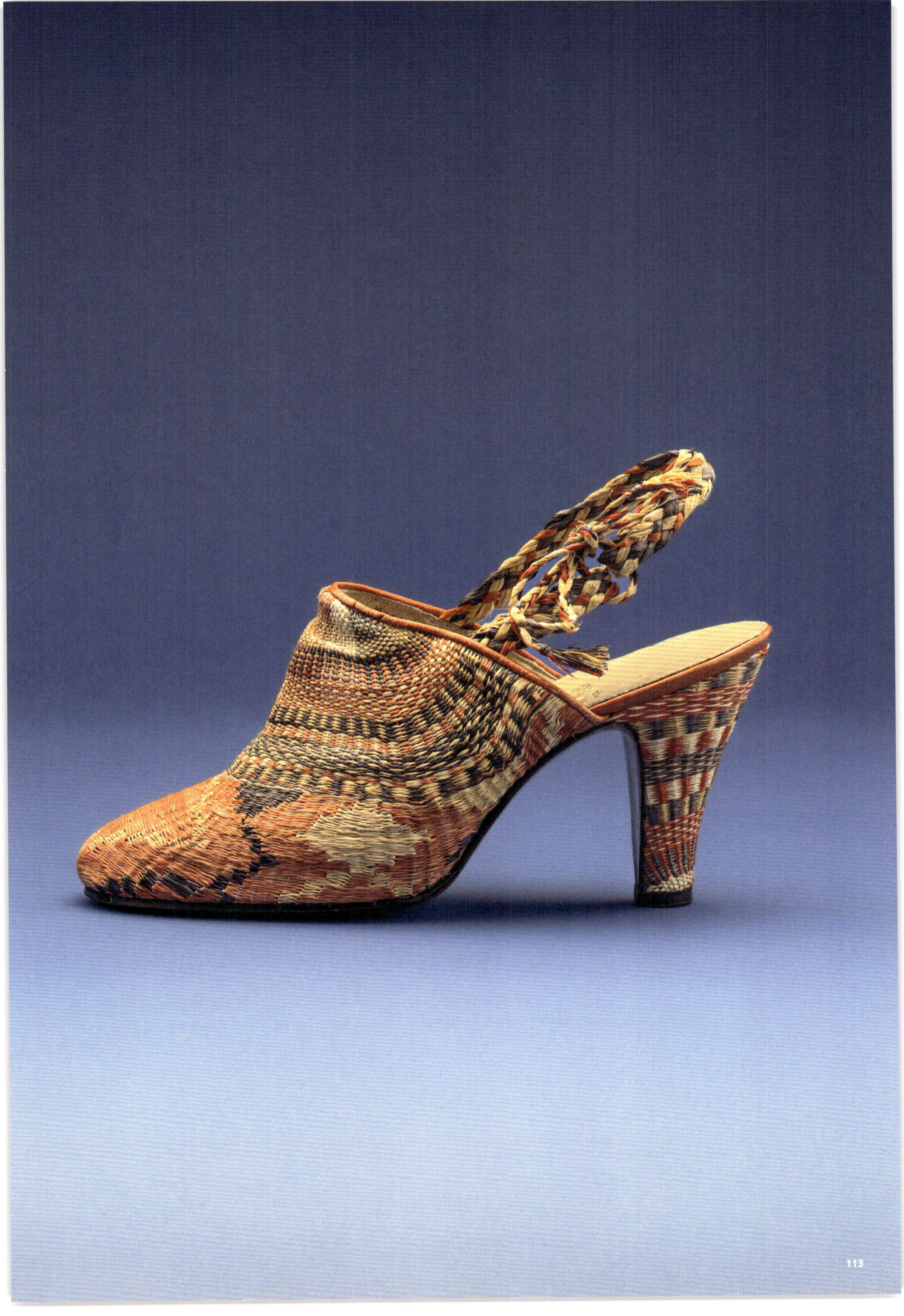

POPLAR BARK
(*RASCELLO*) AND
KIDSKIN SANDAL, 1930

WOVEN POPLAR BARK
(*RASCELLO*) LACED SHOE,
1936–38

DOCUMENTO-MODA, SUMMER 1942. MUSEO FERRAGAMO, FLORENCE

TOP TO BOTTOM: CELLOPHANE SANDAL WITH LAYERED CORK WEDGE HEEL COVERED WITH PATENT KIDSKIN, 1941–42; CELLOPHANE AND KIDSKIN LACED SHOE, 1941; CELLOPHANE SANDAL WITH LAYERED CORK WEDGE HEEL COVERED WITH REPTILE SKIN AND SOLE IN RUBBER DERIVATIVE, 1942–44; *MOLLY*, CELLOPHANE WITH LAYERED CORK WEDGE HEEL COVERED WITH KIDSKIN, 1941–42; CELLOPHANE SANDAL WITH LAYERED CORK WEDGE HEEL COVERED WITH COTTON CANVAS AND SOLE IN RUBBER DERIVATIVE, 1941–42

Salvatore Ferragamo

FIRENZE, VIA TOR
Telegrammi: Ferraga
Casella Postale

Firenze, 16 Ma

Gent.ma Signora
Cecchele
S.Martino Lupari
(Padova)

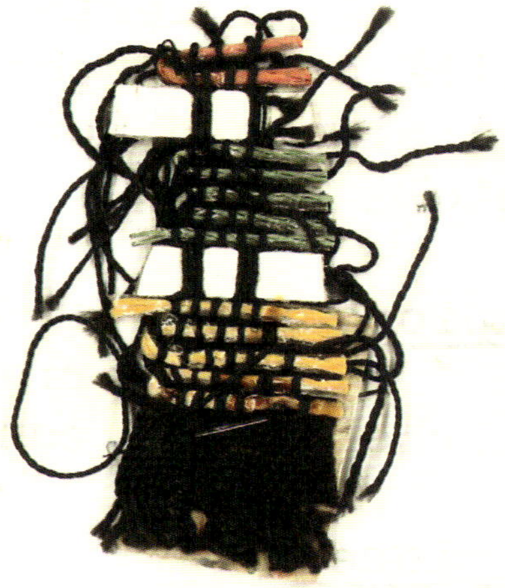

Gentile Signora,

ho ricevuto in questo momento i Suoi campioni e non posso fare a meno di congratularmi con Lei per la squisita interpetrazione che ha dato alle mie idee.

Per quanto sia un po' in ritardo, ugualmente desidererei fare un lavoro immediato per la presentazione in questa stagione, quindi se Lei è in condizioni di potermi assistere dandomi rapide consegne, da parte mia sarà messa tutta la buona volontà.

Non avendo alcuna referenza, Le accludo dei campioni.

<u>Campione n. I</u>

Può senz'altro farmene cinque o sei metri subito, uguale al campione ma con filo bianco. La prego di inviarmi altro campione tessendolo con filo giallo e grezzo chiaro. (1)

<u>Campione n. 2</u>

Anche di questo può farmene subito cinque o sei metri, mettendo invece del listino opaco, un listino di vernice.

LETTER SENT BY SALVATORE FERRAGAMO TO CRAFTSWOMAN ELDA CECCHELE REGARDING AN ORDER FOR SOME FABRIC, MARCH 16, 1956

INTERIA, JACQUARD COTTON FABRIC AND CELLOPHANE, 1956. FABRIC HANDMADE ON A LOOM BY ELDA CECCHELE

VITREA, KIDSKIN AND VINYLITE DECORATED WITH GLASS SEED BEADS AND BEADS, 1955

AZALEA, KIDSKIN AND VINYLITE DECORATED WITH GLASS SEED BEADS AND RHINESTONES, 1955

FILIA, CELLOPHANE AND KIDSKIN, 1954; CELLOPHANE AND KIDSKIN SANDAL, 1957

HAT, FIRST HALF OF THE TWENTIETH CENTURY, STRAW. ASSOCIAZIONE MUSEO DELLA PAGLIA E DELL'INTRECCIO "DOMENICO MICHELACCI," SIGNA (FLORENCE)

RAFFIA AND KIDSKIN SANDAL, 1955

FERRAGAMO

RAFFIA SANDAL WITH
HEEL MADE OF CORK
STOPPERS, 1936–38

COLORED STRAW AND
"PUNTA" STRAW, FIRST
HALF OF THE TWENTIETH
CENTURY. MUSEO CIVICO
DELLA PAGLIA, SIGNA
(FLORENCE)

RAFFIA PLAIT, C. 1960.
ASSOCIAZIONE MUSEO
DELLA PAGLIA E
DELL'INTRECCIO
"DOMENICO
MICHELACCI", SIGNA
(FLORENCE)

RAFFIA SANDAL
WITH PAINTED WOOD
WEDGE AND CUOITAL
SOLE, 1942–44

RAFFIA LACED SHOE
WITH WEDGE HEEL IN
COVERED CORK, 1942

Y 101
MULTI BROWN
MADE IN ITALY
Y 101
MULTI MEXICAN
MADE IN ITALY
Y 101

GIULIANO CORTI COMPANY, *SAMPLE BOOK CONTAINING RAFFIA, STRAW, AND ARTIFICIAL FIBER UPPERS*, THIRD QUARTER OF THE TWENTIETH CENTURY. MUSEO DELLA PAGLIA, SIGNA (FLORENCE)

RAFFIA SANDAL WITH CORK WEDGE HEEL AND SOLE IN LEATHER SUBSTITUTE, 1938–40; RAFFIA AND CALFSKIN LACED SHOE WITH CORK WEDGE HEEL COVERED WITH CALFSKIN, 1942–44

RAFFIA-EMBROIDERED HEMP LACED SHOE WITH WEDGE HEEL IN COVERED CORK AND SOLE IN LEATHER SUBSTITUTE, 1940

RAFFIA SANDAL WITH
CORK WEDGE HEEL, 1942;
RAFFIA SANDAL WITH
CORK WEDGE HEEL,
1942–44

RAFFIA SANDAL WITH
ROPE WEDGE HEEL,
1937–38

VOGUE USA,
JUNE 1, 1940. MUSEO
FERRAGAMO, FLORENCE

SYNTHETIC RAFFIA (*PONTOVA*) AND KIDSKIN SANDAL, 1954

SYNTHETIC RAFFIA (*PONTOVA*) AND KIDSKIN SANDAL, 1958; *CHIOMA*, SYNTHETIC RAFFIA (*PONTOVA*) AND KIDSKIN, 1955

POMPEIA

KIDSKIN SANDAL
WITH CORK PLATFORM
COVERED WITH HAND-
PAINTED SILK SATIN, 1938

CHINESE
CRAFTSMANSHIP,
QING DYNASTY,
WOMEN'S JACKET,
NINETEENTH CENTURY,
EMBROIDERED SILK.
MUSEO STIBBERT,
FLORENCE

LIÙ, EMBROIDERED SILK SATIN WITH INTERNAL CORK WEDGE HEEL, 1950

INDIAN CRAFTSMANSHIP, *FIGURE OF A MAHARATA BRIDE*, EIGHTEENTH CENTURY, EMBROIDERED SILK AND EMBROIDERED TULLE, NINETEENTH-CENTURY WOODEN MANNEQUIN. MUSEO STIBBERT, FLORENCE

EQUILIBRIUM AND ANATOMY

P. 144
TWO PLUMB LINES USED IN CONSTRUCTION. SALVATORE FERRAGAMO AVAILED HIMSELF OF PLUMB LINES, OR PENDULUMS, TO WORK OUT THE BODY'S MEDIAN LINE

FERRAGAMO'S SHOES WERE ALSO FAMOUS FOR THEIR EXTRAORDINARY LIGHTNESS

“I DISCOVERED THE
INTERESTING FACT
THAT THE WEIGHT
OF OUR BODIES WHEN
WE ARE STANDING
ERECT DROPS STRAIGHT
DOWN ON THE ARCH
OF THE FOOT”
(FROM *SHOEMAKER
OF DREAMS*, MILAN:
ELECTA, 2002)

PLASTER CASTS USED BY SALVATORE FERRAGAMO AND HIS NEPHEW JERRY TO RESEARCH "THE SHOE THAT FITS," 1950s

HENRI MATISSE, *ETUDE DE PIED*, C. 1909, BRONZE. THE STATE HERMITAGE MUSEUM, ST. PETERSBURG

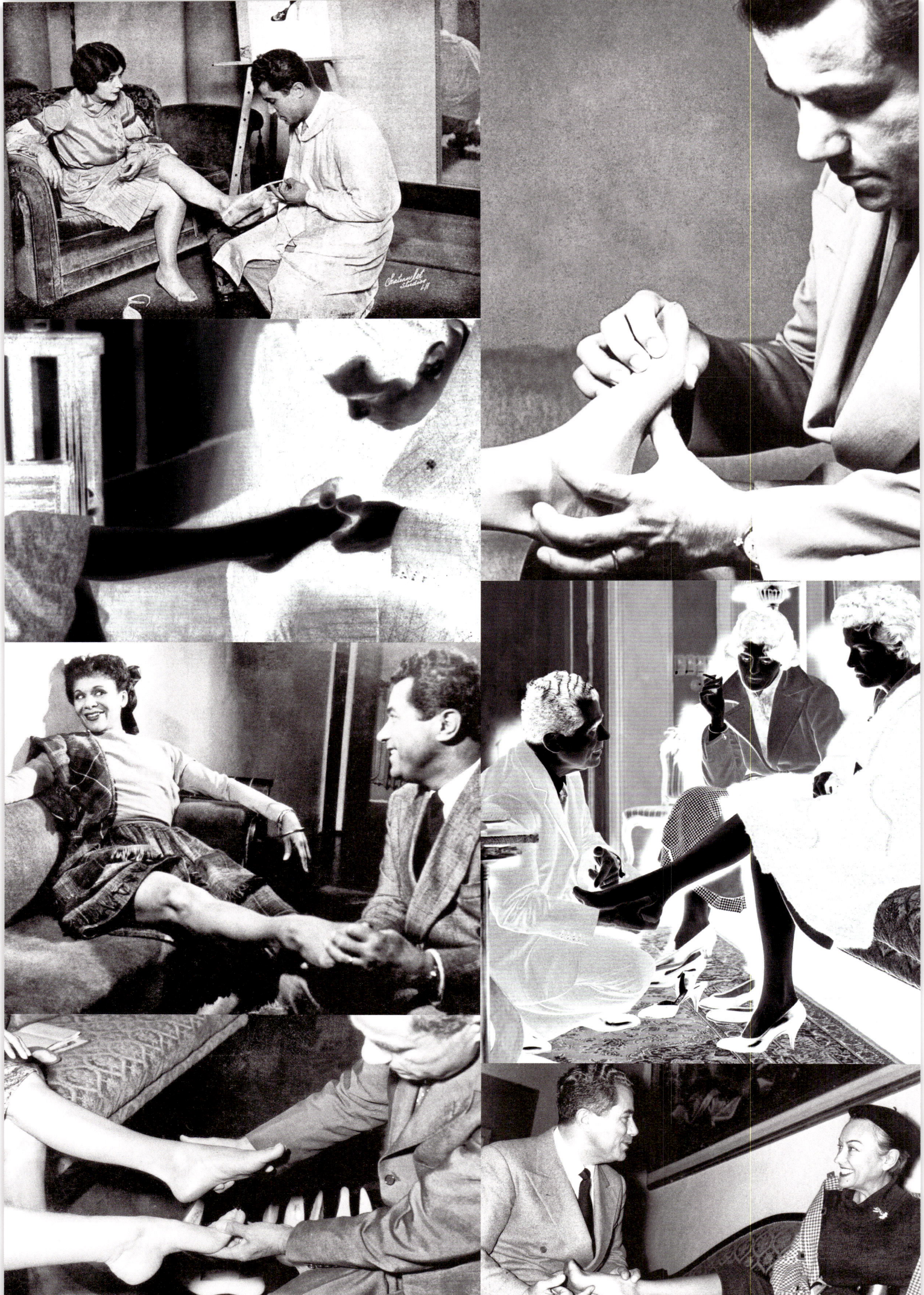

SALVATORE TOUCHING
THE FEET OF HIS CLIENTS,
INCLUDING DANCER KATHERINE
DUNHAM, ACTRESS JANE
RUSSELL, PRINCESSES MARIA
PIA AND MARIA GABRIELLA
OF SAVOY, AND ACTRESS
GLORIA SWANSON, 1928–60

FERRAGAMO'S ARCHIVE
OF THE LASTS FOR HIS
CUSTOMERS' FEET, 1956

LAST FOR SOPHIA
LOREN'S FOOT, 1955

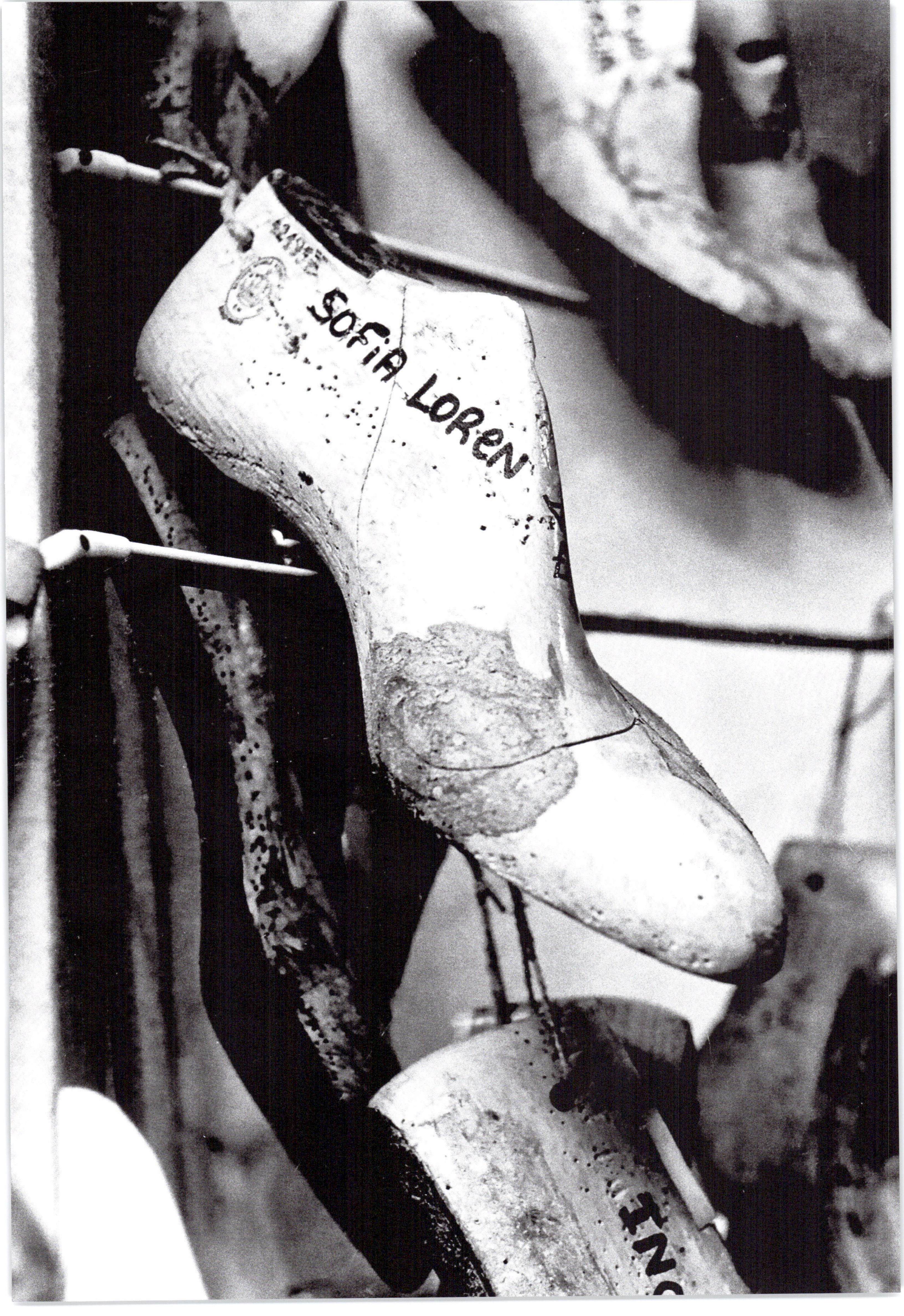
Sofia Loren

SOME OF THE FAMOUS WOODEN LASTS MADE BY SALVATORE FERRAGAMO FOR HIS CLIENTS

SORAYA OF PERSIA
MARLENE DIETRICH
RITA HAYWORTH
148 MARY PICKFORD
MARY PICKFORD
ANNA MAGNANI
Marilyn

MODELS WEARING
FERRAGAMO FOOTWEAR
IN 1953 AND IN 1941

ARCHITECTURAL FORMS

P. 158
IRVING PENN,
GLOVE AND SHOE,
JULY 7, 1947. THE SHOE IN THE SHOT IS A FERRAGAMO MODEL SUEDE CLOSED SHOE, 1935

DETAIL OF PALAZZO DELL'ARTE IN MILAN, BUILT IN 1933 TO A DESIGN BY GIOVANNI MUZIO, IN *LA RIVISTA ILLUSTRATA DEL POPOLO D'ITALIA*, AUGUST 1933. MUSEO FERRAGAMO, FLORENCE

ORNAMENTAL ARCHES IN THE SQUARE OUTSIDE THE PALAZZO DELL'ARTE IN MILAN, DESIGNED BY MARIO SIRONI FOR THE V TRIENNIAL OF DECORATIVE ARTS, IN *LA RIVISTA ILLUSTRATA DEL POPOLO D'ITALIA*, AUGUST 1933. MUSEO FERRAGAMO, FLORENCE

SUEDE CLOSED SHOE, 1930–35; SUEDE LACED SHOE, 1938; SUEDE LACED SHOE WITH FOLDED LAPELS, 1939; SUEDE AND SILK SATIN ANKLE BOOT, 1938–39

HAT FASHIONS FOR THE FALL OF 1940, COMPARED TO THE ARCHITECTURE OF THE MANHATTAN SKYLINE, IN *VOGUE* USA, JULY 5, 1940

PATENT KIDSKIN
TWO-PIECE SHOE WITH
LAYERED WEDGE HEEL
AND PLATFORM IN
COVERED CORK, 1938–39

TWO WOMEN ADMIRE
A MODEL OF THE IDEAL
CITY DESIGNED FOR THE
NEW YORK WORLD'S
FAIR, IN *VOGUE* USA,
MAY 1, 1939. MUSEO
FERRAGAMO, FLORENCE

ORIANA, SUEDE, 1947

MODEL WEARING
THE *ORIANA* SHOE,
LATE 1940s

NICCHIA, SUEDE,
1952–54

COFFEE TABLE
DESIGNED BY
ISAMU NOGUCHI
IN 1944 FOR
HERMAN MILLER

Domande N.
PRIV. IND.
35
Ufficio de...
L'Ufficiale Delegato
NAZIONALE
307
Domande N.
PRIV. IND. N. 6938
a
b
a
c
b2
b1
a
a
b
b

PATENTS

P. 172
SOME SALVATORE
FERRAGAMO PATENTS
CONSERVED BY
ARCHIVIO CENTRALE
DELLO STATO, ROME

PATENT NO. 7815:
LADIES' ELEGANT SHOE
WITH LABYRINTH MOTIF,
JANUARY 28, 1931

LABIRINTO, KIDSKIN WITH
SILK THREAD CHAIN
STITCH EMBROIDERY, 1930

PATENT NO. 6940: LADIES' SHOE WITH LEATHER BOTTOM AND EMBROIDERIES IN DIFFERENT COLOR TONES, NOVEMBER 27, 1929

PUMP IN PATENT CALFSKIN WITH SHADING SILK THREAD CHAIN STITCH EMBROIDERY, 1929

Fig. 1
b
a
d
c
Fig. 2
PER PROCURA

PATENT NO. 354889:
SHOES WITH LIFTED HEEL
BUT WITHOUT STILETTO
HEEL, DECEMBER 13, 1937

GHILLIE, SUEDE AND
CALFSKIN WITH WEDGE
HEEL IN COVERED CORK,
1937

VOGUE USA,
JANUARY 15, 1938

SUEDE SANDAL, 1940

PATENT NO. 15112:
LADIES' SANDAL WITH
FASTENING FIXED AT THE
SIDE, DECEMBER 4, 1938

Domanda N. 1119 1937

PRIV. IND. N. 15112

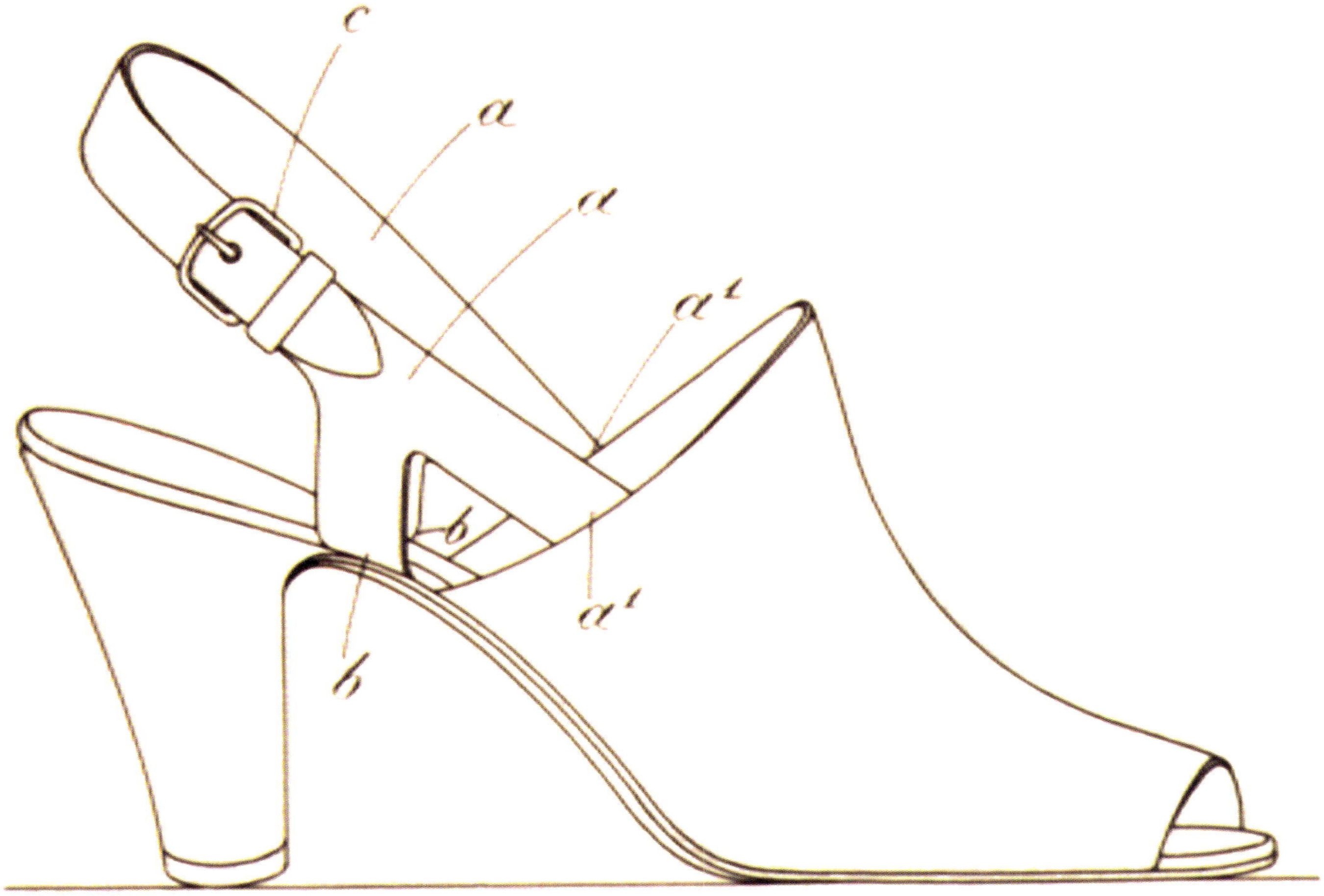

Il Direttore
Zengarini

L'Ufficiale Delegato

MODEL WEARING THE
CORTINA SHOE, 1940s

VOGUE USA, MARCH 15, 1947

PATENT NO. 15113: LADIES' SHOE WITH SPECIAL FASTENING, APRIL 12, 1938

PATENT NO. 15890: LADIES' SHOE WITH A STRAP FORMING ON THE INSTEP AND FASTENED TO THE ANKLE, JANUARY 17, 1939

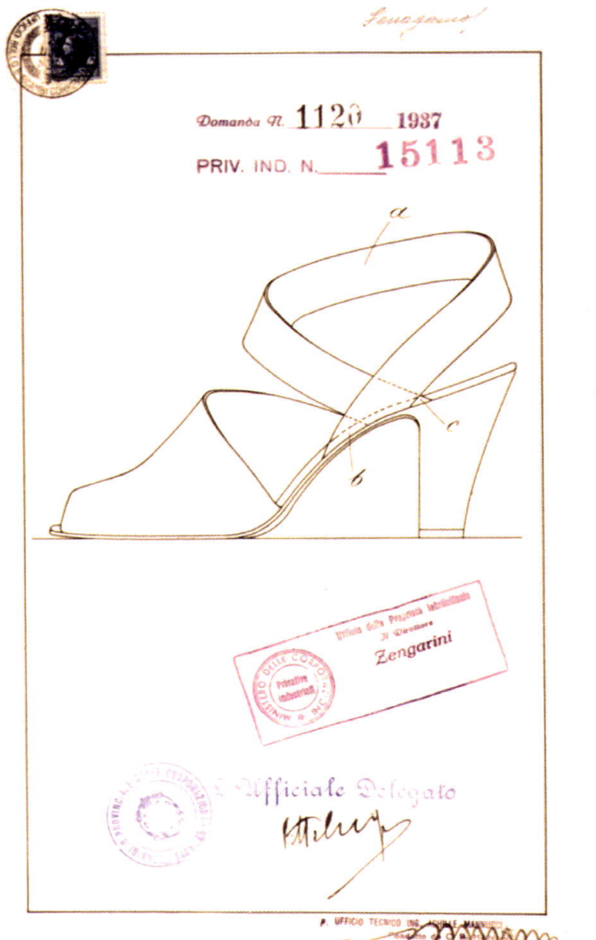

NINFEA, ANTELOPE, 1937;
CORTINA, SUEDE, 1938

SUEDE LACED SHOE AND CLOSED SHOE WITH APPLIQUÉ, 1938

PATENT NO. 15950: LADIES' SHOE WITH UPPER DECORATED WITH SEED-SHAPED APPLIQUÉ, MARCH 10, 1939

Domanda N. [illegible] 1938

PRIV. IND. N. 15950

L'Ufficiale Delegato

UFFICIO TECNICO ING. ACHILLE MANNUCCI

PER PROCURA

FERRAGAMO H

Domanda N. 659 1938

PRIV. IND. N. 16072

L'Ufficiale Delegato

PATENT NO. 16072:
LADIES' SHOE WITH
PATCHWORK UPPER,
MARCH 27, 1939

SUEDE LACED
SHOE, 1938

IRVING PENN, *OPTICIAN'S SHOP WINDOW*, C. 1939

PATENT NO. 16071: FANCY LADIES' SHOE, ITS FRONT PARTLY STITCHED AND PARTLY FREE, WITH OPENINGS INCREASING THEIR WIDTH, MARCH 27, 1939

SUEDE LACED SHOE WITH EYELET DECORATION, 1938

SUEDE AND CALFSKIN
LACED SHOE, 1938

PATENT NO. 15889:
LADIES' SHOE WITH
LEATHER EYELETS
FOR THE FASTENING,
JANUARY 17, 1939

573
Domanda N.
PRIV. IND. N. 15889
Il Direttore
Zengarini
Ufficiale Delegato

Domanda N. 666 1938

PRIV. IND. N. 15952

Ufficio della Proprietà Intellettuale
Il Direttore
Zengarini

L'Ufficiale Delegato

PATENT NO. 15952:
SHOE MADE UP OF TWO
OVERLAPPING FORE
PARTS AND A FASTENING
LACE, MARCH 10, 1939

SUEDE CLOSED
SHOE, 1938

SUEDE AND CALFSKIN CLOSED SHOES WITH WEDGE HEEL IN COVERED CORK, 1938

PATENT NO. 16077: LADIES' SHOE WITH WIDE OPENINGS FOR LACES AND PATCHED STRIPS, MARCH 27, 1939

Domanda N. 663 1938

PRIV. IND. N. 16077

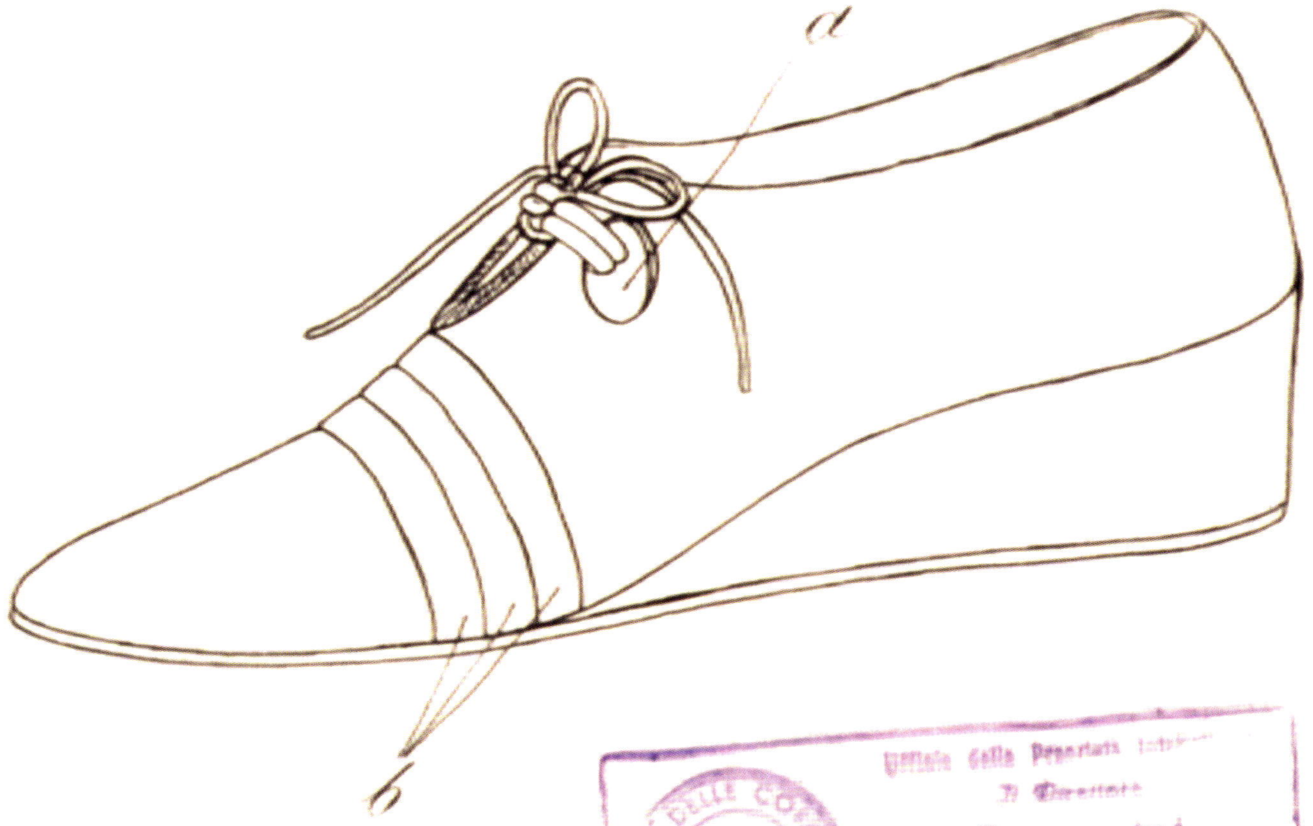

Il Direttore

Zengarini

L'Ufficiale Delegato

UFF.CIO TECNICO ING. ACHILLE MANNUCCI

PER PROCURA

Domanda N. 601 1938

PRIV. IND. N. 16074

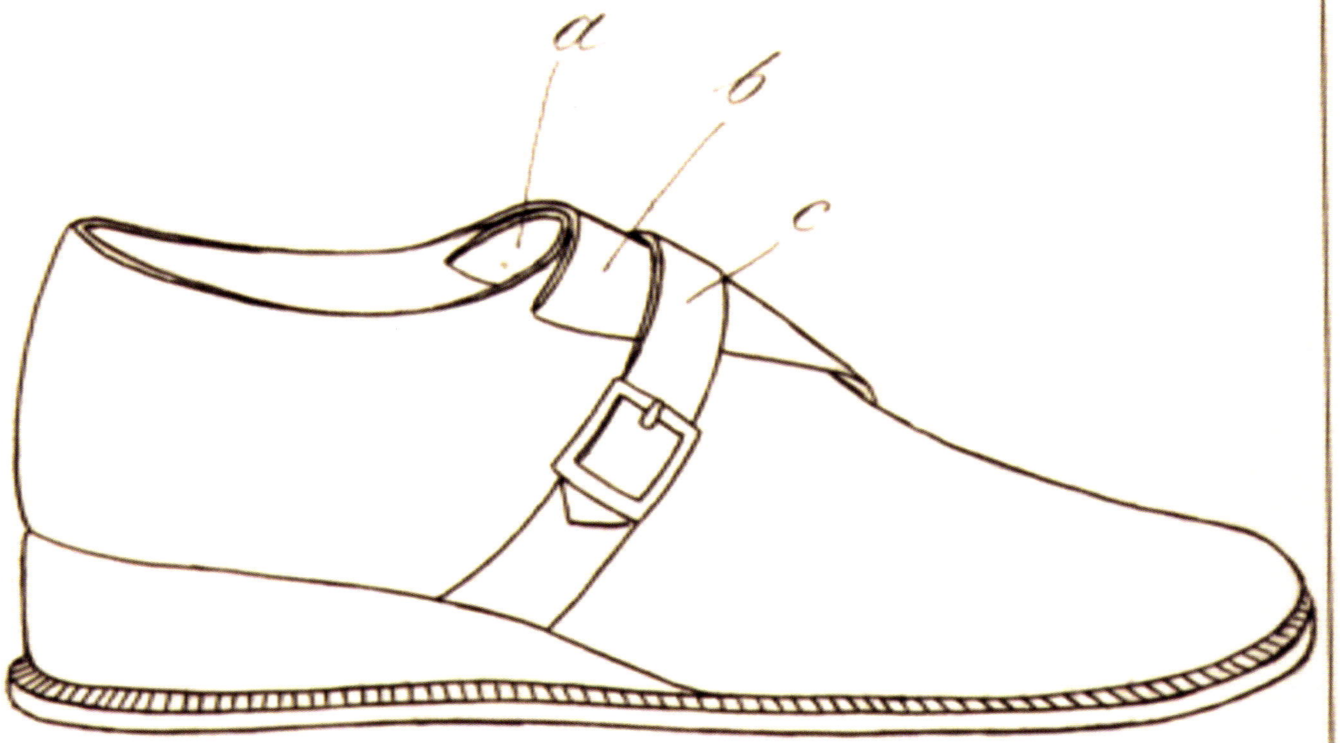

Ufficio della Proprietà Intell...

Il Direttore

Zengarini

Privative industriali

L'Ufficiale Delegato

Ufficio Tecnico Ing. Achille Mannucci

PATENT NO. 16074: SHOE MADE UP OF TWO OVERLAPPING FORE PARTS AND A FASTENING LACE, MARCH 27, 1939

ATTICA, SUEDE AND CALFSKIN WITH WEDGE HEEL IN COVERED CORK, 1942

SILK SATIN SANDAL
WITH VERTICAL
FLUTED CORK
PLATFORM COVERED
WITH KIDSKIN, 1940

PATENT NO. 15953:
SOLE FOR SHOES,
SANDALS, AND THE
LIKE, MADE UP OF
SEVERAL LAYERS
OF CORK WRAPPED
WITH FABRIC,
MARCH 10, 1939

SILK SATIN SANDAL
WITH SHAPED CORK
PLATFORM AND
LAYERED WEDGE
HEEL COVERED WITH
KIDSKIN, 1938

FERRAGAMO
Domanda N. 671 193
PRIV. IND. N. 15953

Domanda N. 797 /1939
BREV. MOD. N. 17188
a
a
a
a

PATENT NO. 17188:
HIGH-HEELED SHOE,
UPPER DECORATED WITH
LEATHER TONGUES OF
DIFFERENT LENGTHS,
FEBRUARY 10, 1940

FIAMMA, SUEDE AND
CALFSKIN, 1939

CALFSKIN, SUEDE, AND
CROCODILE PUMP,
1930–35

PATENT NO. 17187:
SHOE WITH UPPER
DESIGNED IN
GEOMETRICAL PATTERNS,
FEBRUARY 10, 1940

MINISTERO DELLE CORPORAZIONI
Ufficio della Proprietà Intellettuale
Domanda N. 796/1939
BREV. MOD. N. 17187
a
a
a
a
a
a
Ufficiale Delegato

MODEL WEARING
SANDALS WITH
PLATFORM AND HEEL
COVERED WITH
MOSAIC-PATTERNED
MIRRORS, 1940s

PATENT NO. 17137:
FANCY HEEL AND
SOLE FOR LADIES'
SHOES WITH METAL
FRAMEWORK AND
GOLDEN MIRRORS IN
VERTICAL STRIPES,
FEBRUARY 10, 1940

PATENT NO. 17083:
HEEL AND SOLE
FOR LADIES' SHOES
WHOSE SURFACE
IS DECORATED
WITH LITTLE PIECES
OF QUADRANGULAR
MIRRORS, FEBRUARY 1,
1940

CORK PLATFORM AND
HEEL DECORATED WITH
MOSAIC-PATTERNED
MIRRORS, 1939

565
/1939
17083

PATENT NO. 17182:
LACE-UP SANDAL
WITH HEEL DECORATED
WITH MIRRORS,
FEBRUARY 10, 1940

KIDSKIN SANDAL WITH
HEEL COVERED WITH
MOSAIC-PATTERNED
MIRRORS, 1939

17182

Fig. 1
Fig. 2

PATENT NO. 17084: HEEL FOR LADIES' SHOE, SHAPED LIKE A REVERSED FRUSTUM OF A CONE, DECORATED WITH DEEP COLUMN-LIKE GROOVES, FEBRUARY 9, 1940

PATENT NO. 17085: HEEL FOR LADIES' SHOE, MADE OF FOUR COLUMNS IN THE SHAPE OF A CROSS, FEBRUARY 9, 1940

SANDAL IN CANVAS WITH COTTON THREAD HALF STITCH EMBROIDERY AND KIDSKIN, HEEL MADE OF COVERED CORK STOPPERS, 1936

LEFT:
DETAIL OF THE PRESS PAVILION DESIGNED BY LUCIANO BALDESSARI, 5TH TRIENNIAL EXHIBITION OF DECORATIVE ARTS (PALAZZO DELL'ARTE, MILAN, 1933), IN *LA RIVISTA ILLUSTRATA DEL POPOLO D'ITALIA*, AUGUST 1933. MUSEO FERRAGAMO, FLORENCE

PATENT NO. 17173:
SLIPPER-LIKE SHOE WITH
THREE-WEDGED HEEL,
THREE ROUNDED BANDS
ON THE UPPER, AND TOE
CURVED UPWARD,
FEBRUARY 10, 1940

SUEDE AND KIDSKIN
MULE WITH LAYERED WEDGE
HEEL IN COVERED CORK, 1939

PATENT NO. 17258:
SLIPPER-LIKE SHOE WITH
TRIANGULAR WEDGE HEEL,
ROUNDED BANDS ON THE
UPPER, AND TOE CURVED
UPWARD, FEBRUARY 14, 1940

MOORISM, SUEDE AND
KIDSKIN WITH WEDGE HEEL
IN COVERED CORK, 1939

PATENT NO. 17172:
SLIPPER-LIKE SHOE WITH
TRIANGULAR WEDGE HEEL
AND TOE CURVED UPWARD,
FEBRUARY 10, 1940

SIRIANO, SUEDE AND
KIDSKIN WITH WEDGE HEEL
IN COVERED CORK, 1939

777 /1939
MOD. N. 17
g
g
a
c
b
1939
d
e
f
c
a
f
b

FIRENZE - FERRAGAMO

NOVUS, SUMMER 1940.
MUSEO FERRAGAMO,
FLORENCE

PATENT NO. 17174:
LADIES' SHOE WITH
FOUR-COLUMNED HEEL,
FEBRUARY 10, 1940

SUEDE AND KIDSKIN
SANDAL WITH HEEL
MADE OF COVERED
CORK STOPPERS, 1939

BOARSKIN AND
CALFSKIN LACED SHOE
WITH WEDGE HEEL IN
COVERED CORK, 1939

PATENT NO. 17175:
LADIES' SPORTS SHOES
WITH LOW-WEDGED
HEEL, SQUARE TOE
AND BACK, WITH A
FULLY FRONT-CUT AND
PARTIALLY LACED UPPER,
FEBRUARY 10, 1940

FERRAGAMO 72

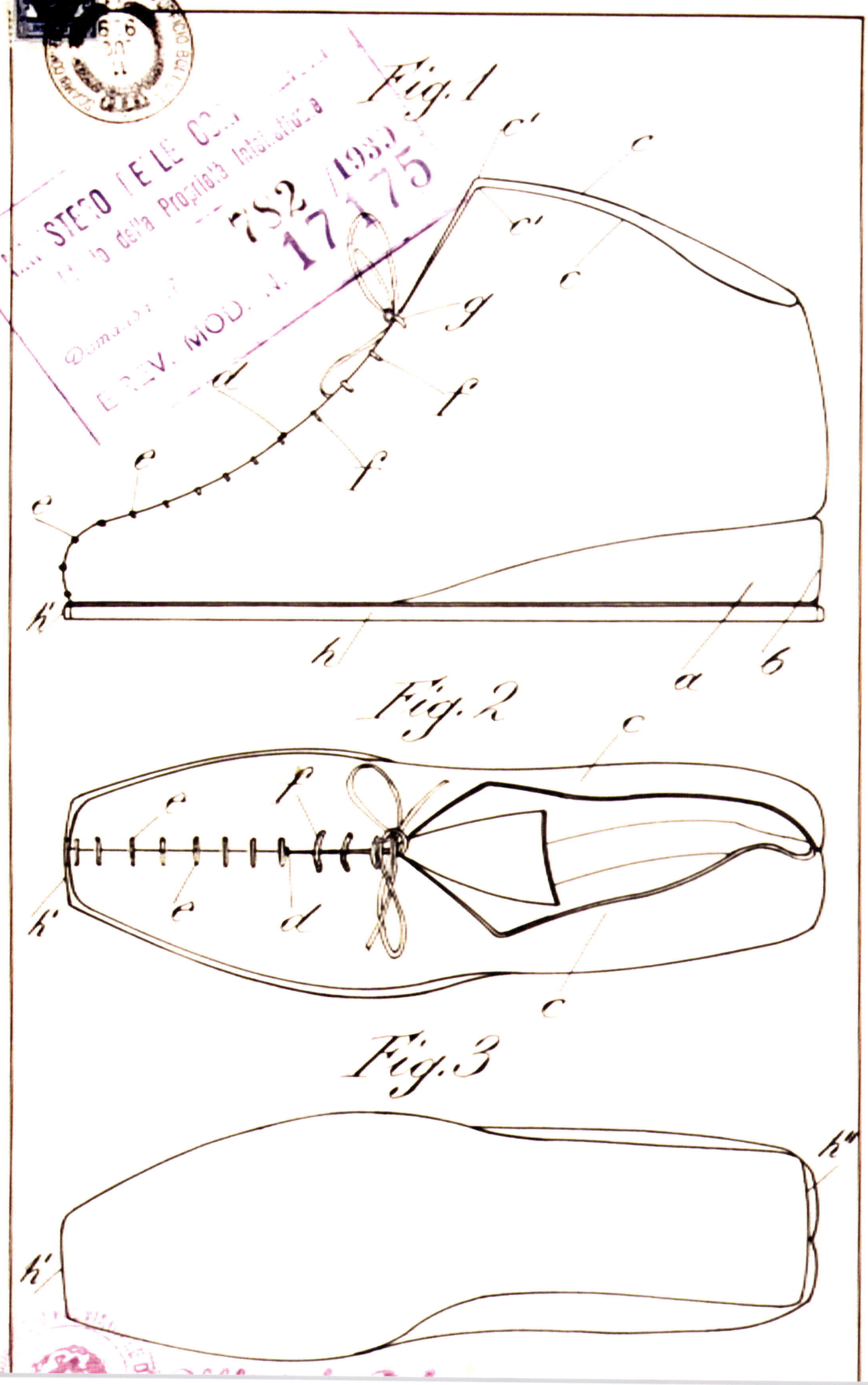

FERRAGAMO
14
789 /1939
MOD. N. 17180
b
a
Ufficiale Delegato

PATENT NO. 17180:
MULE WITH WEDGED
HEEL AND INSIDE-
OUT LATERAL EDGES,
FEBRUARY 10, 1940

SUEDE AND SILK SATIN
ANKLE BOOT WITH
WEDGE HEEL IN
COVERED CORK, 1939

788 /1989
17179
OFFICIO TECNICO

PATENT NO. 17179:
ANKLE BOOT WITH
HIGH-WEDGE HEEL AND
UPPER EXTENDING UPWARD
ON THE INSTEP WITH
PARTIAL LACING,
FEBRUARY 10, 1940

VELA, SUEDE WITH WEDGE
HEEL IN COVERED CORK,
1939

PATENT NO. 17181:
HIGH-WEDGE-HEELED
MULE WITH UPPER AND
COUNTER COVERED BY
A CHALICE OF LEAVES,
FEBRUARY 10, 1940

NINFEA, SUEDE AND SILK
SATIN WITH WEDGE HEEL
IN COVERED CORK, 1938

KIDSKIN SANDAL, 1939

PATENT NO. 17183:
SANDAL WITH DOUBLE-
CHAINED FRAMEWORK
AND FRONT LACING,
FEBRUARY 10, 1940

MINISTERO DELLE CORPORAZIONI
Ufficio della Proprietà Intellettuale
Domanda N. 792 /1939
BREV. MOD. N. 17183

Ufficiale Delegato

UFFICIO TECNICO ING. ACHILLE MANNUCCI
PER PROCURA

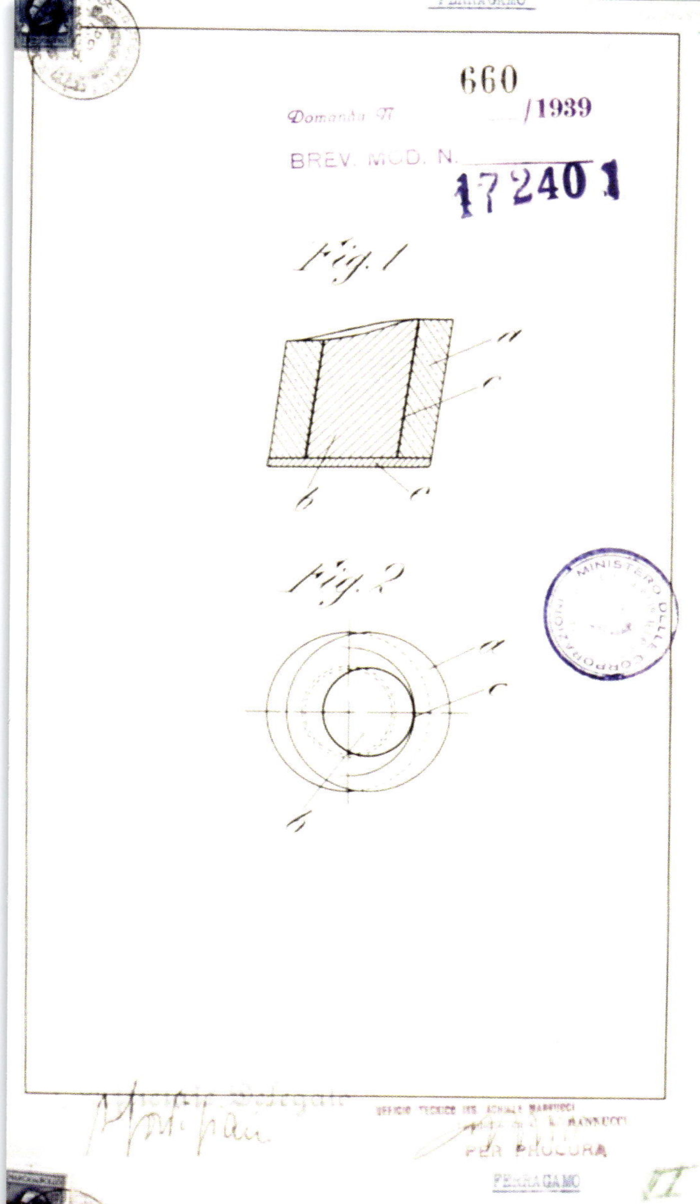

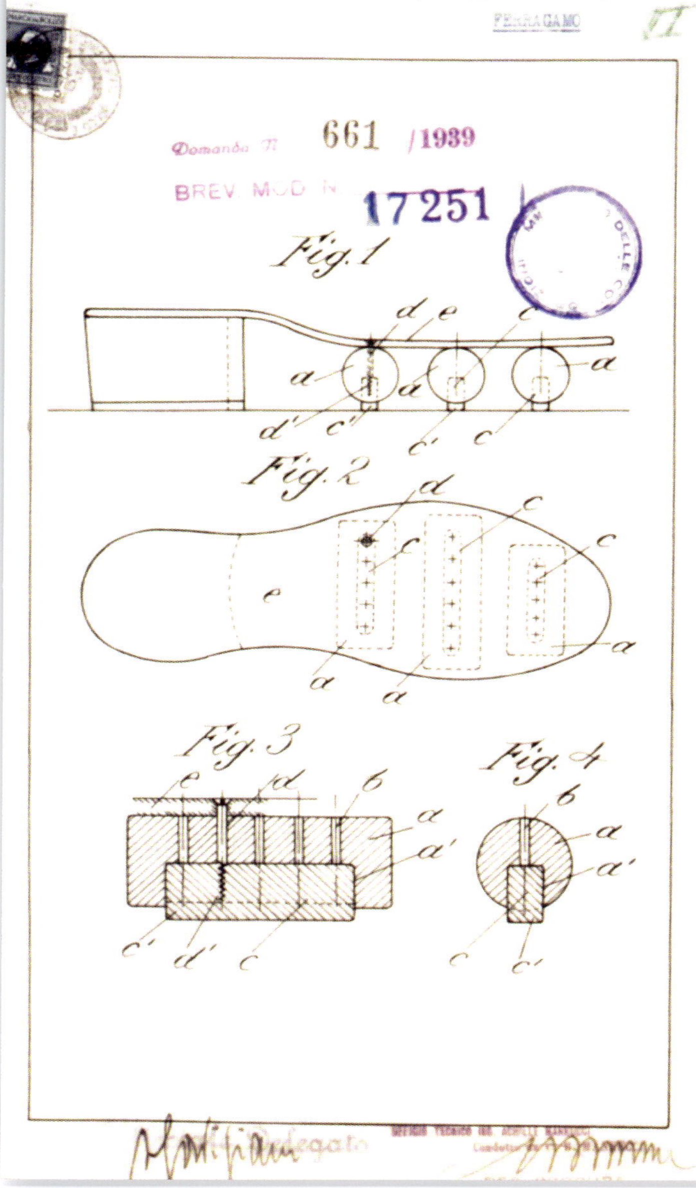

KIDSKIN SANDAL WITH BAKELITE HEEL, LAYERED BAKELITE AND COVERED CORK PLATFORM, 1939

PATENT NO. 17240: CYLINDRICAL GLASS HEEL FILLED WITH CORK OR OTHER ELASTIC MATERIAL, DESIGNED ESPECIALLY FOR LADIES' SHOES, FEBRUARY 14, 1940

PATENT NO. 17251: LOWER SUPPORT FOR LADIES' SHOE WHICH REPLACES THE SOLE, MADE UP OF THREE CYLINDERS OF GALATITE, GLASS, OR SIMILAR MATERIAL, FEBRUARY 14, 1940

MODEL WEARING A SANDAL WITH A GALATITE SOLE, 1940s

CALFSKIN CLOSED SHOE, 1939

MODEL WEARING A SHOE WITH HORN-SHAPED DECORATION, 1940s

PATENT NO. 17260: LADIES' SHOE WITH LACE AND BUCKLE, WEDGE HEEL AND A HORN-SHAPED PROJECTION ABOVE THE UPPER, FEBRUARY 14, 1940

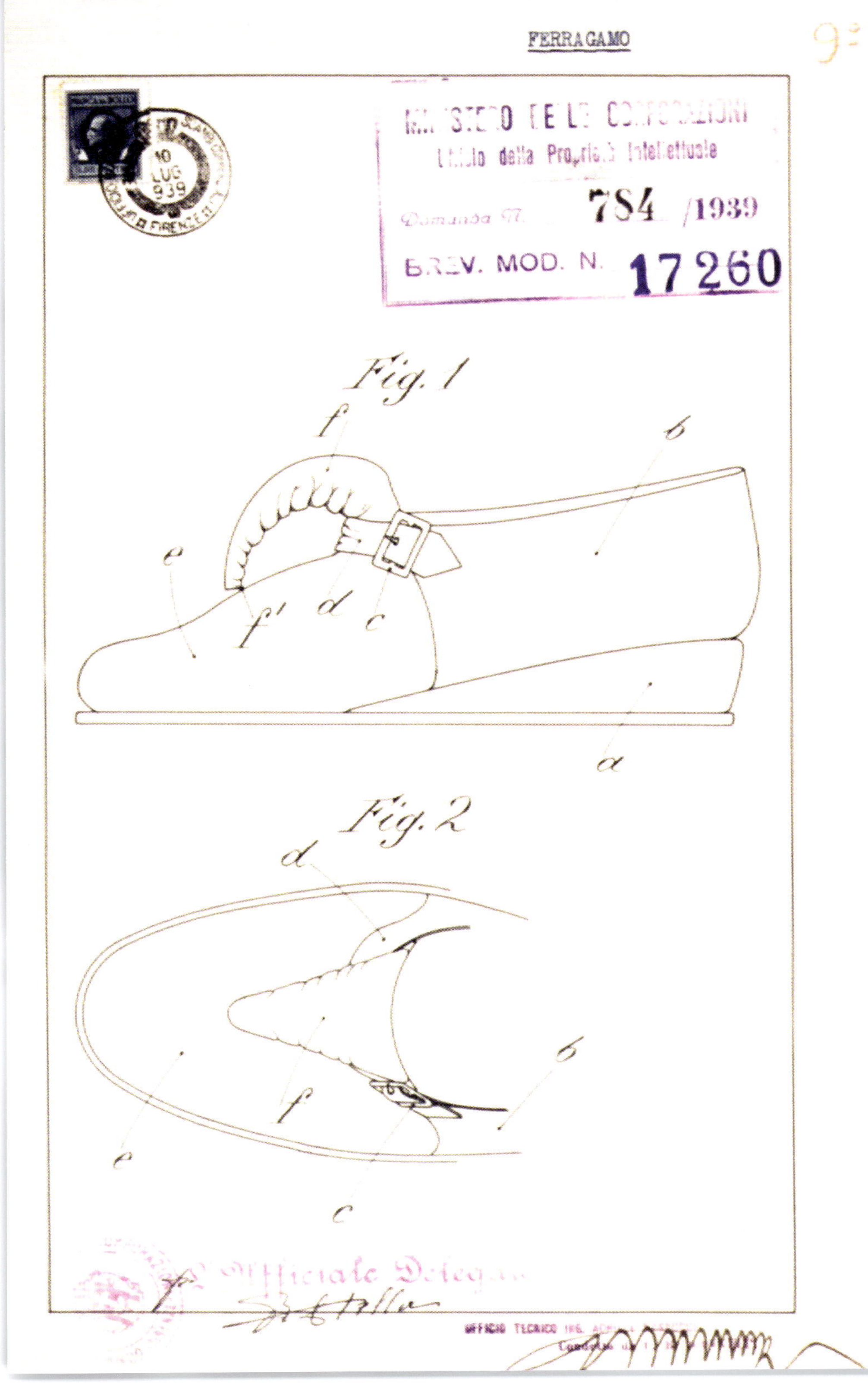

MODELS DESIGNED BY
SALVATORE FERRAGAMO
IN 1939

PATENT NO. 17259:
HIGH-SOLED LIGHT
SHOE WITH HEEL MADE
OF TWO MODELED
ROUNDED WEDGES,
FEBRUARY 14, 1940

FERRAGAMO

Ufficio della Proprietà Intellettuale

Domanda N. 778 /1939

BREV. MOD. N. 17259

L'Ufficiale Delegato

PATENT NO. 17366:
LADIES' SHOE WITH
WEDGE SUPPORT
OF THE HEEL, CURVING
IN THE REAR PART,
FEBRUARY 21, 1940

SUEDE AND KIDSKIN
SANDAL WITH WEDGE
HEEL IN COVERED
CORK, 1939

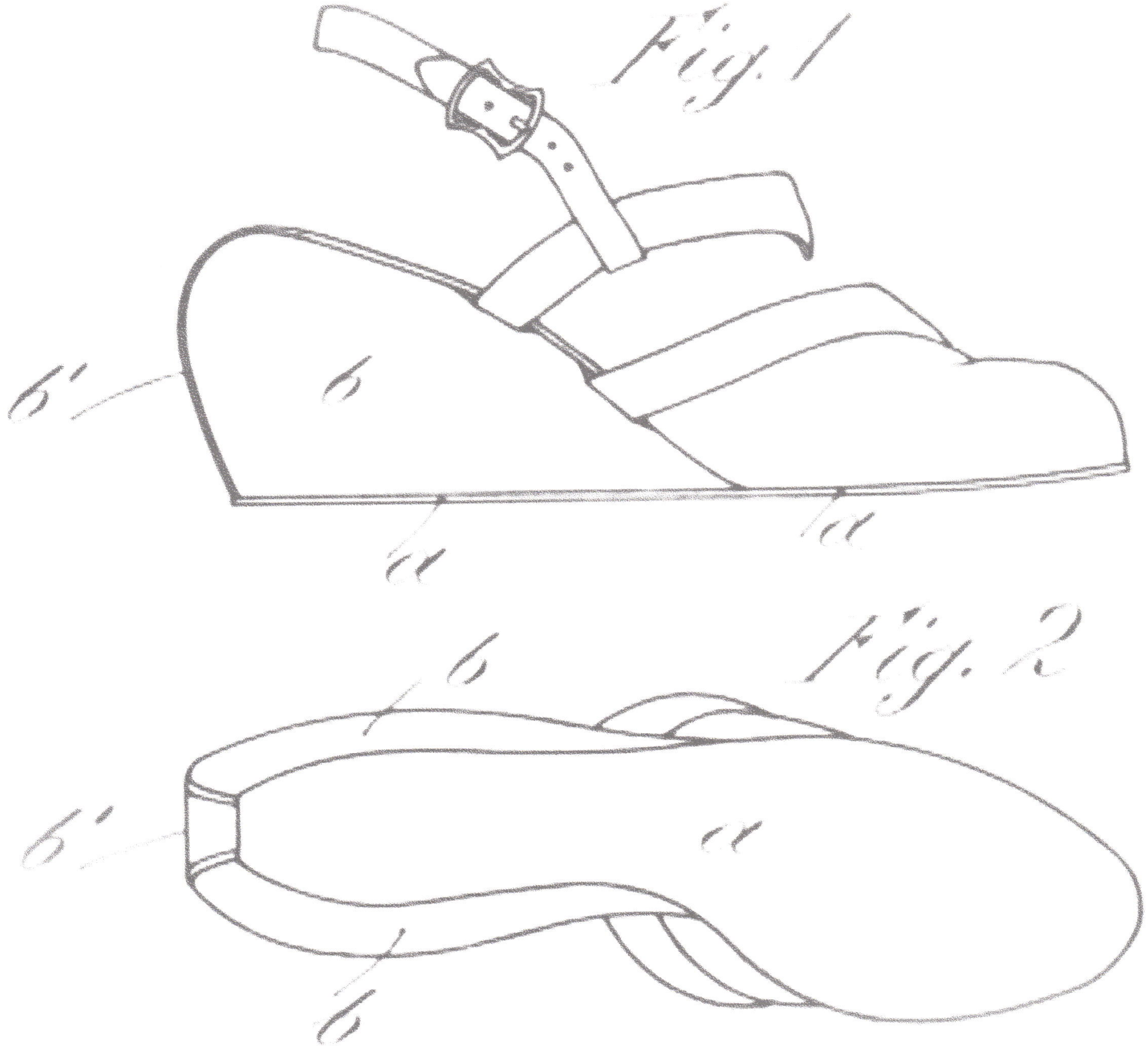

Fig. 3

MODEL WEARING SANDALS
WITH BRASS AND STONE
DECORATED PLATFORM, 1940s

PATENT NO. 17607:
ORNAMENTAL DECORATIONS
WITH SCROLLS, LINES, AND
FLOWERS IN WHITE, GREEN,
RED, AND BLUE STONES FOR THE
HEEL AND SOLE OF WOMEN'S
FOOTWEAR, SEPTEMBER 3, 1940

CUT AND ENGRAVED
BRASS FRAMEWORK WITH
INSET STONES, 1938

Domanda N.
BREV. MOD. N.

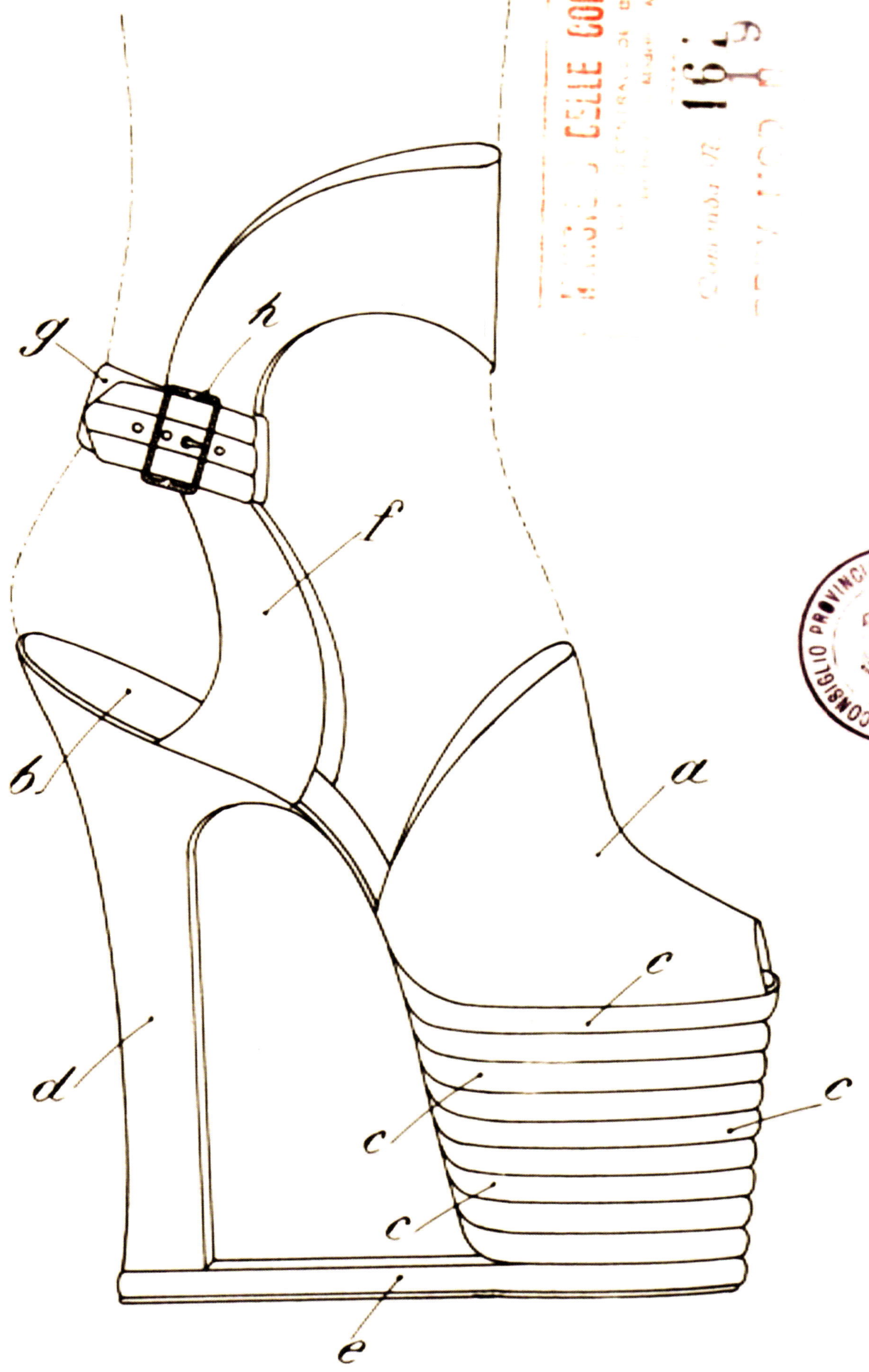
g
h
f
b
a
c
c
c
c
c
d
e

PATENT NO. 19736:
LADIES' SANDAL WITH
MULTI-LAYER RAISED
SOLE AND CONNECTION
BETWEEN SOLE AND
HEEL, JULY 23, 1941

VELVET AND KIDSKIN
SANDAL WITH FRONT
PLATFORM IN COATED
CORK LAYERS AND HEEL
AND CONNECTION
BETWEEN THE TWO PARTS
IN COVERED WOOD, 1940

SUEDE AND FUR
ANKLE BOOT, 1940

PATENT NO. 18672:
LADIES' ANKLE BOOT
WITH A BROAD CUFF
IN FUR OR SIMILAR,
NORMAL HIGH HEEL
AND PARTIAL LACING
ON THE FRONT,
OCTOBER 31, 1940

MINISTERO DELLE CORPORAZIONI

936

V MOD N 18672 -

L'Ufficiale Delegato

UFFICIO PROVINCIALE DELLE CORPORAZIONI DI FIRENZE

PATENT NO. 393784:
PROCEDURE
TO PRODUCE A
MATERIAL SUITABLE
FOR MAKING SHOE
UPPERS, APRIL 10, 1942

DOCUMENTO-MODA,
SUMMER 1942. MUSEO
FERRAGAMO, FLORENCE

CALFSKIN SANDAL WITH
FELT SOLE, 1942–44

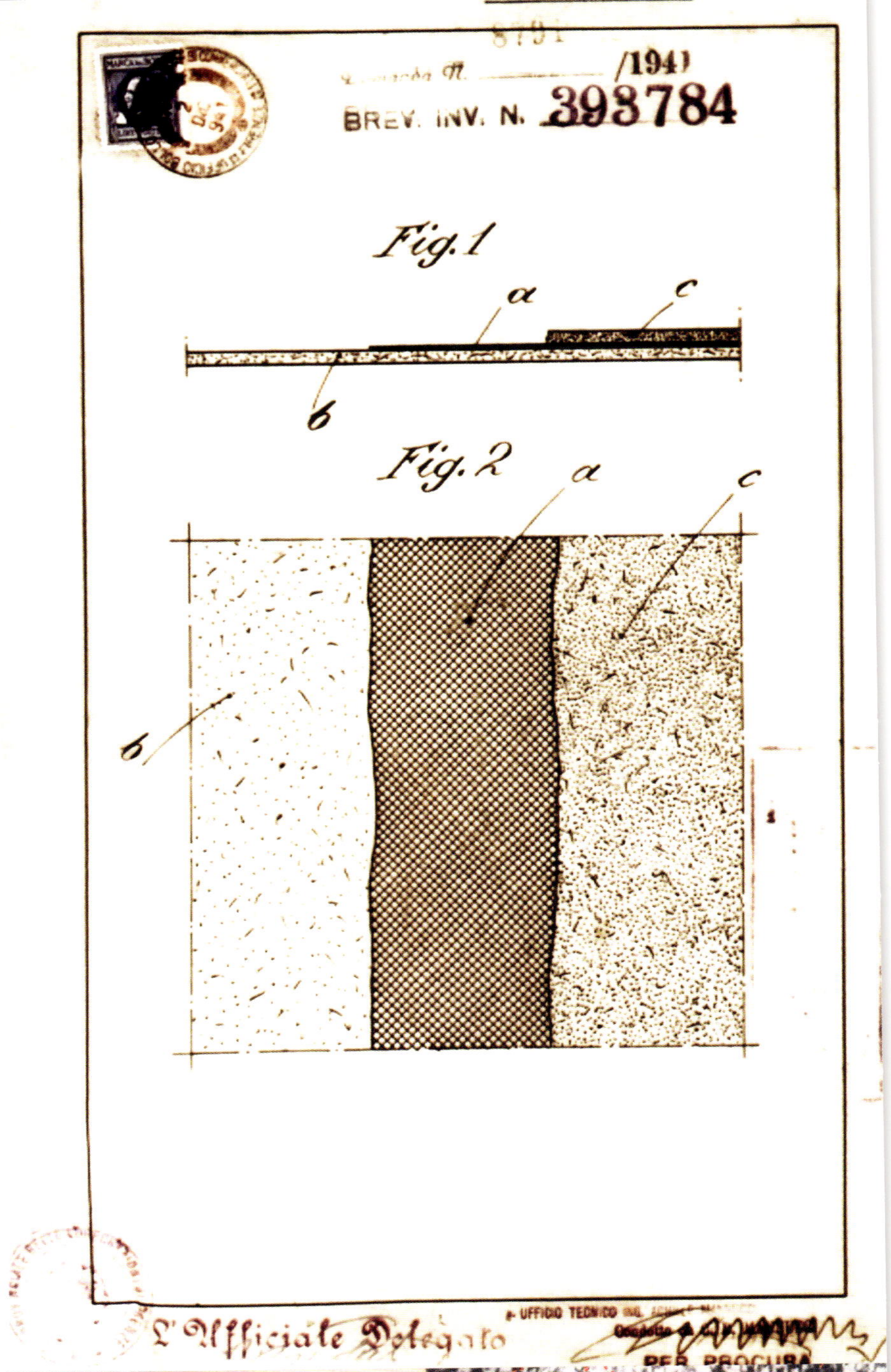

Fig. 1

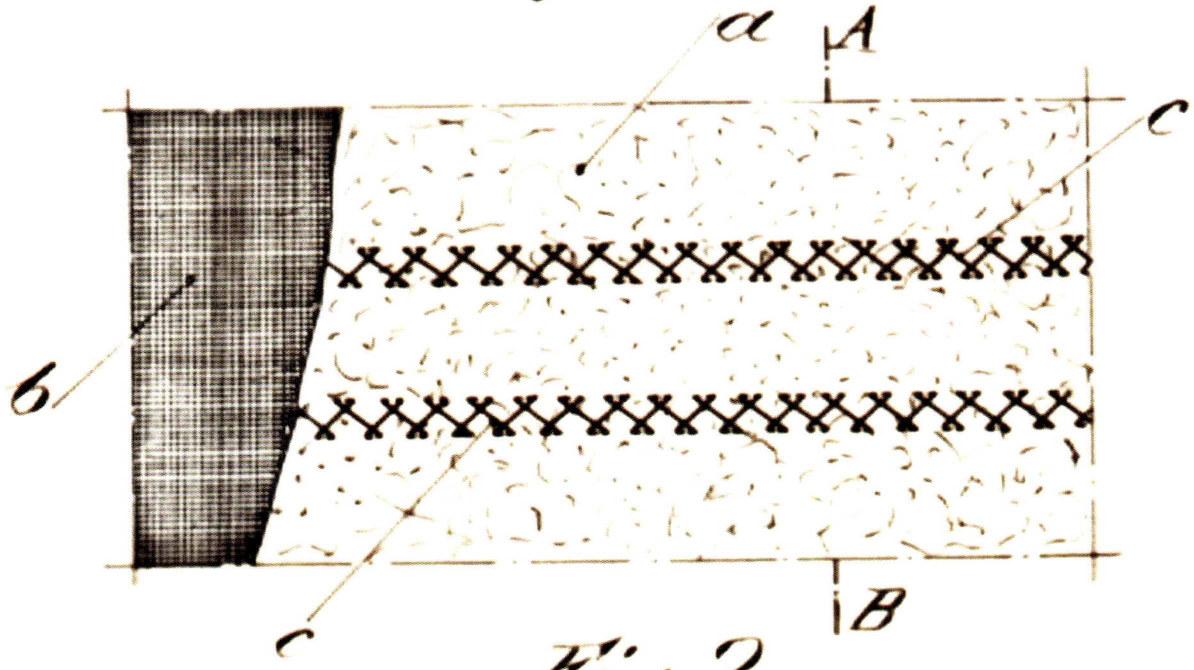

Fig. 2

Fig. 3

Fig. 4

PATENT NO. 21458:
FELT REINFORCEMENT
TO MAKE IT SPECIALLY
SUITED TO CRAFTING
SHOE UPPERS OR
SIMILAR, MARCH 30, 1942

SUEDE AND KIDSKIN
FLIP-FLOPS WITH
FELT SOLE, 1944

MODEL WEARING THE SANDALS WITH PAINTED WOODEN PLATFORM AND WEDGE, 1940s

PATENT NO. 22887: SABOT DIVIDED IN TWO PARTS WITH NOOSES AND STRING TO FASTEN IT TO THE FOOT, APRIL 20, 1943

SUEDE SANDALS WITH PAINTED WOOD PLATFORM AND WEDGE, 1943

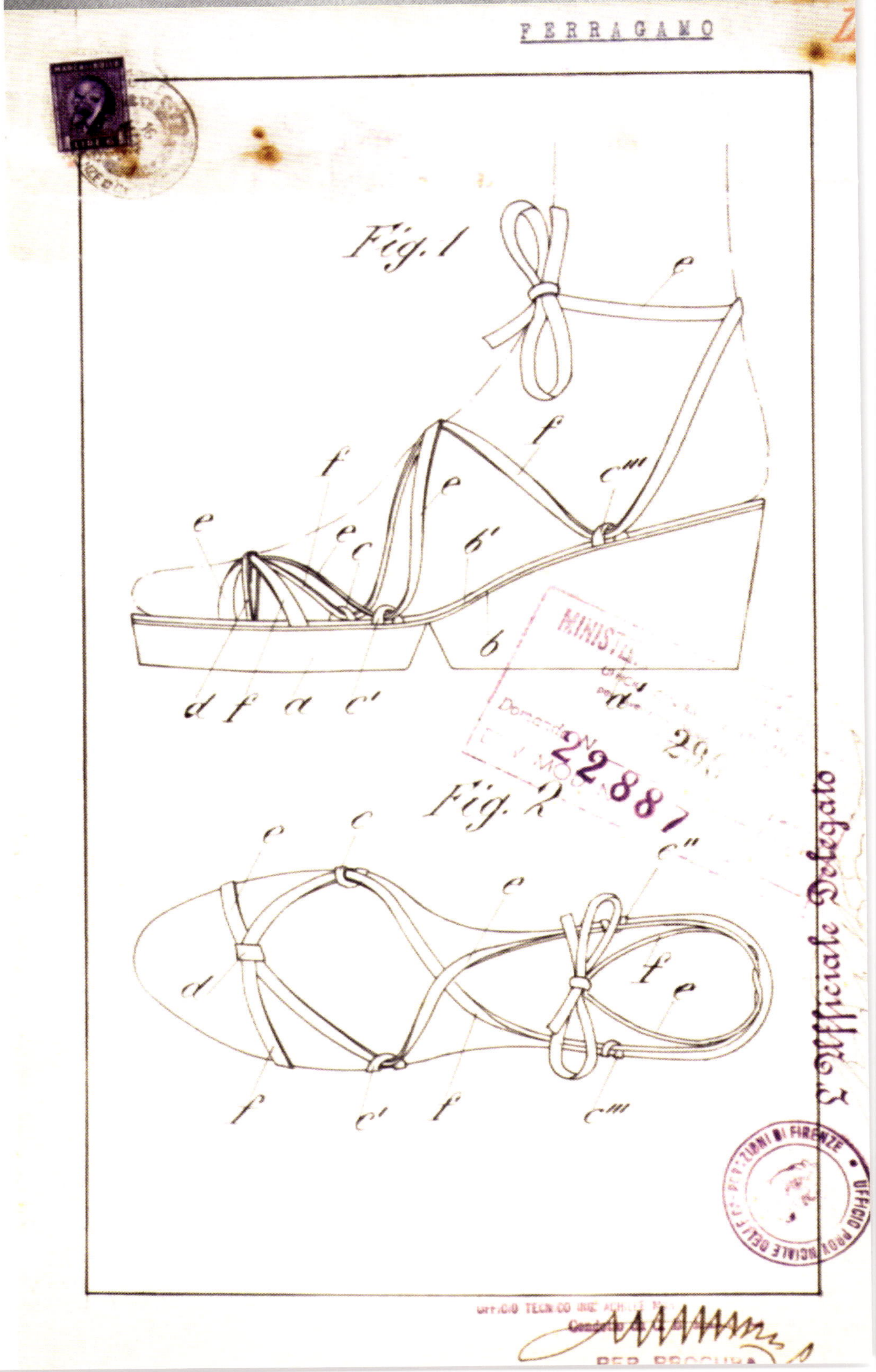

PATENT NO. 26233:
LADIES' SHOE WITH
FRONT DECORATION
MADE OUT OF A
STRAP STARTING
BETWEEN SOLE AND
UPPER, MARCH 1, 1947

SUEDE AND KANGAROO
LACED SHOE, 1946

PATENT NO. 26141:
LADIES' CLOSED SHOE
WITH "MUSKETEER"
DECORATION
AND METAL BUCKLE,
FEBRUARY 15, 1947

SUEDE CLOSED
SHOE WITH BRASS
BUCKLE, 1946

Fig. 1
3
1
6
5
Fig. 2
5
A
1
A
6
Fig. 6
IL DIRETTORE

PATENT NO. 25506: LADIES' SHOE WITH UPPER IN ONE PIECE TIED AND STITCHED AT THE TOE, NOVEMBER 16, 1946

CALFSKIN LACED SHOE WITH WEDGE HEEL IN COVERED CORK, 1946

PATENT NO. 353152: LACING SYSTEM FOR FOOTWEAR OR SIMILAR WITHOUT LACE PASSING THROUGH THE INSIDE OF THE SHOE, OCTOBER 6, 1937

VENE, CALFSKIN AND SUEDE WITH WEDGE HEEL IN COVERED CORK, 1937

SERGIO CONTI, LUCIANO GRASSI, AND MARISA FORLANI, *CUBO ARMCHAIR*, 1978, IRON AND NYLON THREAD WEAVE. FROM THE *MONOFILO* SERIES, DESIGNED BETWEEN 1954 AND 1966

PATENT NO. 426001: PROCEDURE FOR MANUFACTURING A SHOE WITH THE UPPER MADE OUT OF SEAMLESS THREAD, TWINE, RIBBON AND THE LIKE, OCTOBER 17, 1947

INVISIBILE, NYLON THREAD AND SUEDE WITH SHAPED WEDGE HEEL IN COVERED WOOD, 1947

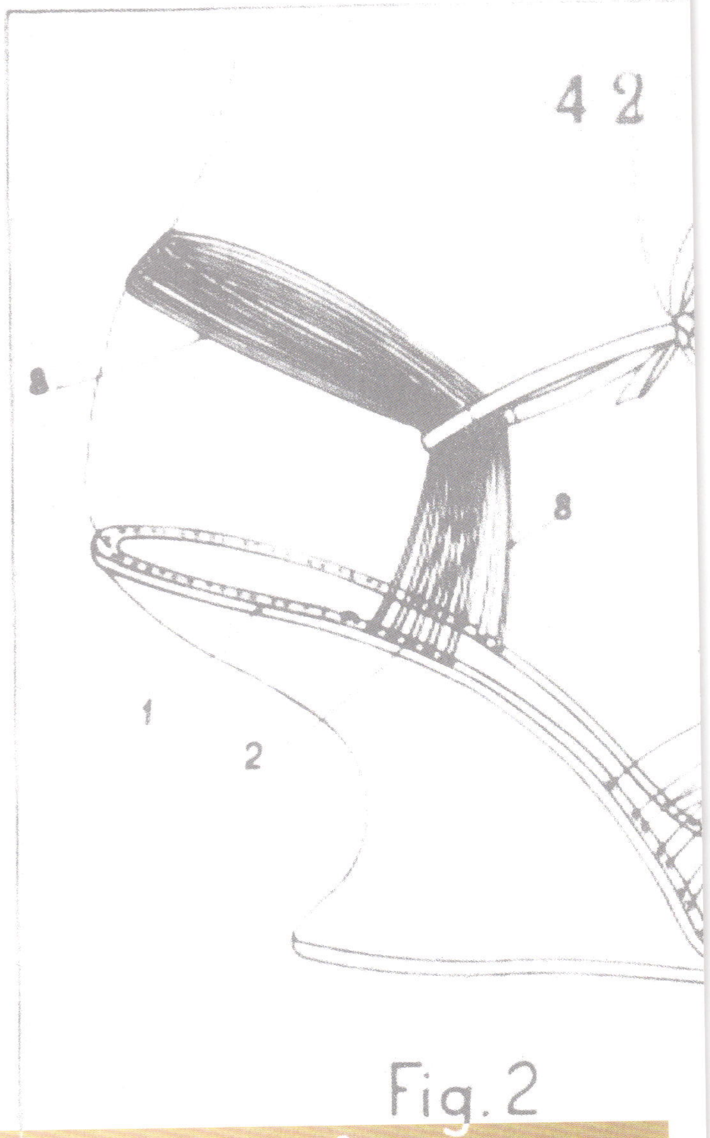

Fig.1

INVISIBILE, NYLON THREAD AND KIDSKIN, 1947

PATENT NO. 426001: PROCEDURE FOR MANUFACTURING A SHOE WITH THE UPPER MADE OUT OF SEAMLESS THREAD, TWINE, RIBBON AND THE LIKE, OCTOBER 17, 1947

MODEL WEARING A VARIANT OF THE *INVISIBILE* SANDAL, LATE 1940s

FERRAGAMO
426001
Fig. 5
Fig.10
Fig.11
Fig 12
Fig. 6
Fig.7
Fig.8
Fig.9

SUEDE SANDAL WITH
SHAPED WEDGE HEEL IN
COVERED WOOD, 1947

PATENT NO. 26673:
SUPPORT SHAPE FOR
LADIES' SHOE SOLE, WITH
CENTRAL SPUR AND
SUPPORT FOR THE HEEL,
MAY 10, 1947

Fig. 2

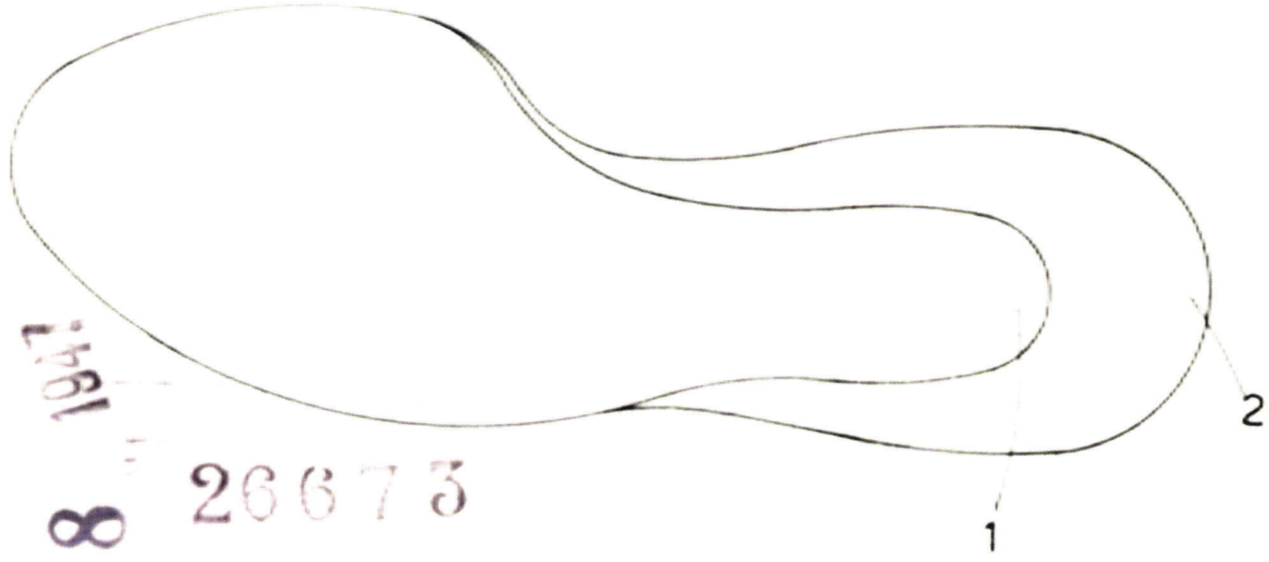

Fig. 1

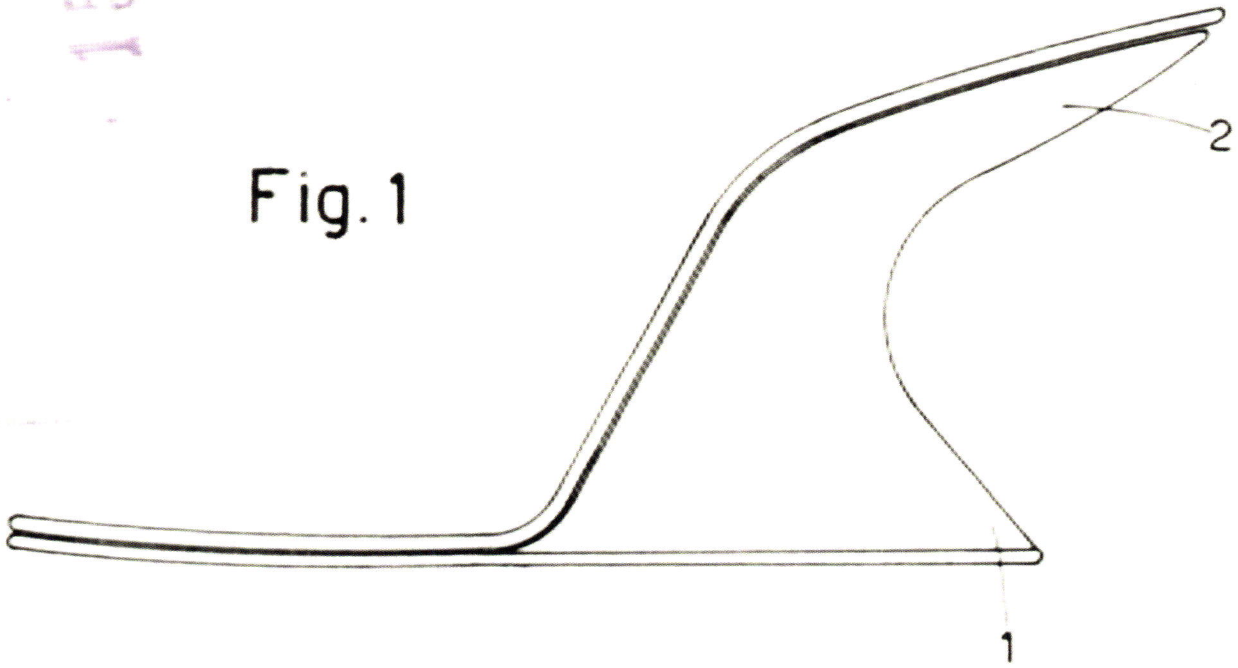

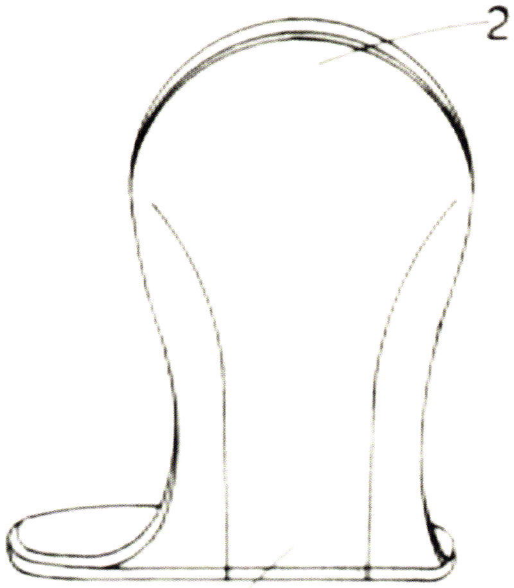

Fig. 3

MODEL WEARING A
SANDAL DECORATED
WITH SMALL BOWS, 1947

PATENT NO. 26334:
OPEN LADIES' SHOE
WITH DECORATIVE SMALL
BOWS ON THE UPPER,
MARCH 15, 1947

SUEDE AND KIDSKIN
SANDAL WITH LAYERED
WEDGE HEEL IN COVERED
CORK, 1946

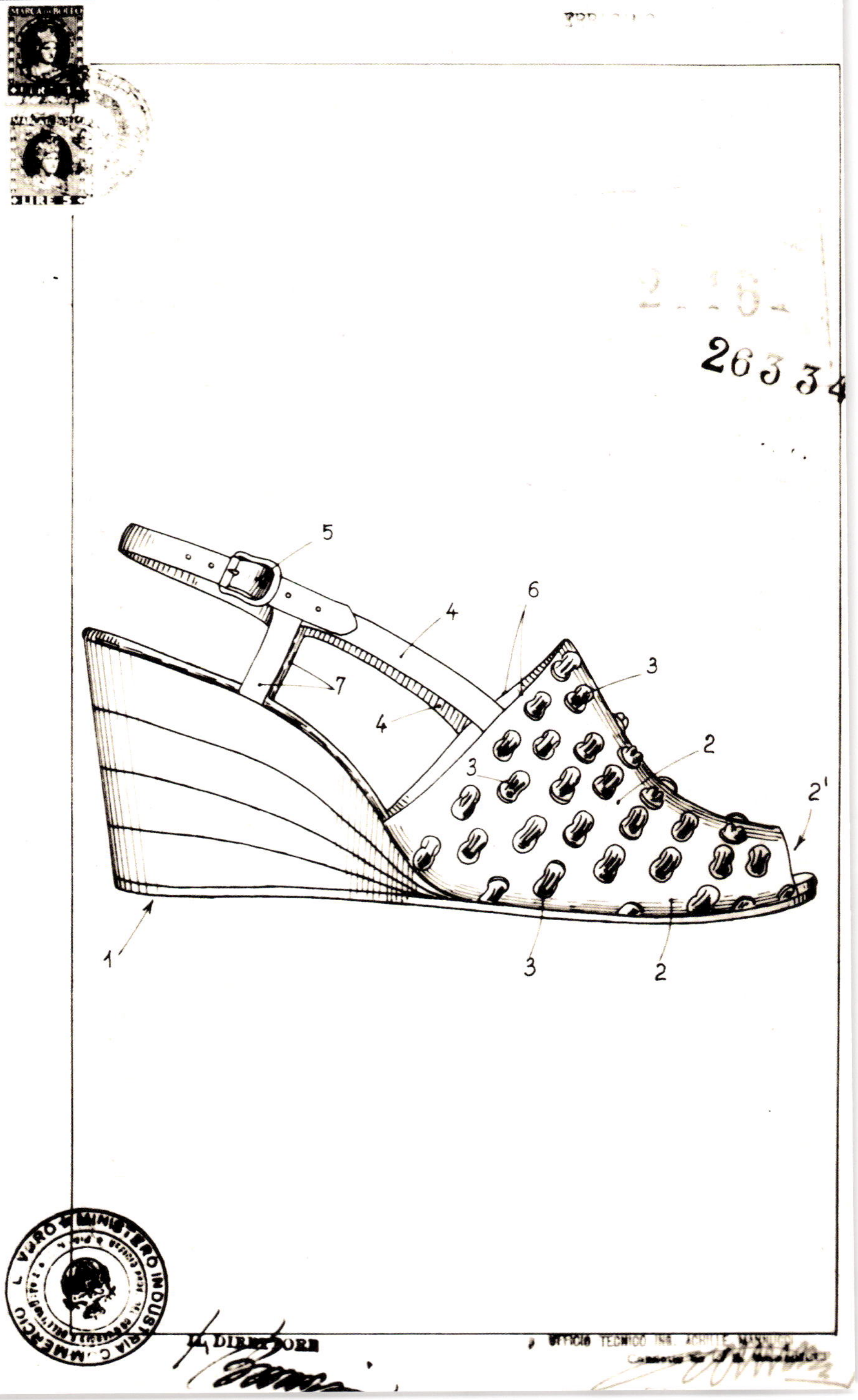

CENTIPEDE, CALFSKIN WITH SHAPED WEDGE HEEL IN COVERED WOOD, 1947

PATENT NO. 26330: LADIES' SANDAL WITH ORTHOPEDIC HEEL AND KNOTTED LACES, MARCH 15, 1947

MODEL WEARING A SANDAL WITH KNOTTED LACES, 1947

Fig.1
Fig. 2
Fig. 3

PATENT NO. 28537: LADIES' SANDAL WITH UPPER IN TWO LATERAL PARTS TIED BY CROSSED STRAPS, MAY 31, 1948

ARFOA, SUEDE AND KIDSKIN, 1948

PATENT NO. 28787: LADIES' OPEN SHOE WITH A TRANSVERSAL BRAID ON THE UPPER, JULY 5, 1948

SUEDE AND KIDSKIN SANDAL, 1948

PATENT NO. 28500:
LOW-HEELED LADIES'
SHOE WITH TRIPLE
FRONT FLAP,
MAY 20, 1948

TWO-PIECE SUEDE
SHOE, 1948

PATENT NO. 28698:
OPEN LADIES' SHOE
WITH HOLLOWED HEEL,
UPPER MADE OF LACED-UP
STRIPES ENCOMPASSING
THE INSTEP, JUNE 22, 1948

RODI, SUEDE, 1948

KIDSKIN LACED SHOE WITH
LAYERED WEDGE HEEL IN
COVERED CORK, 1949–50

PATENT NO. 31126:
LADIES' SHOE WITH LOW
WEDGE HEEL SEAMLESSLY
COVERED BY THE UPPER,
WITH CROSSING LACES,
APRIL 14, 1949

3 1 1949

3 1 1 2 6

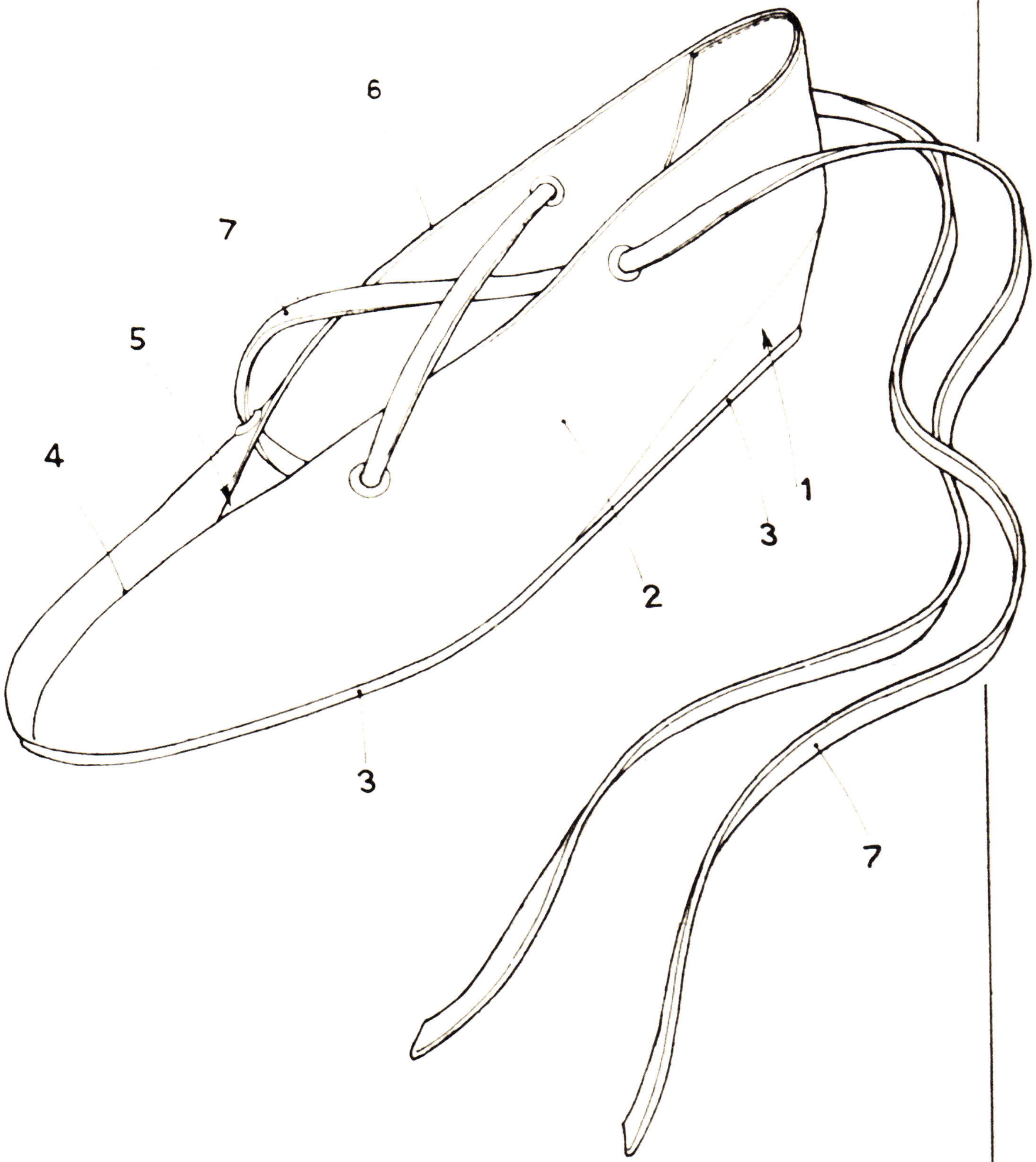

IL DIRETTORE

UFFICIO TECNICO ING. ACHILLE ...

PATENT NO. 25494:
LADIES' SHOE WITH UPPER
IN TWO PIECES, TIED BY
A RING, SEPTEMBER 7, 1946

CALFSKIN SANDAL, 1946

TIBETIA, SUEDE AND TWINE WITH WEDGE HEEL IN COVERED CORK, 1950

PATENT NO. 36686: PATTERNED LADIES' SHOE WITH UPPER IN LEATHER (OR OTHER MATERIAL) AND THREAD, JANUARY 22, 1951

FERRAGAMO
30086
1950
c
e
e
d
g
a
f
e
e
b
b
L'UFFICIALE DELEGATO

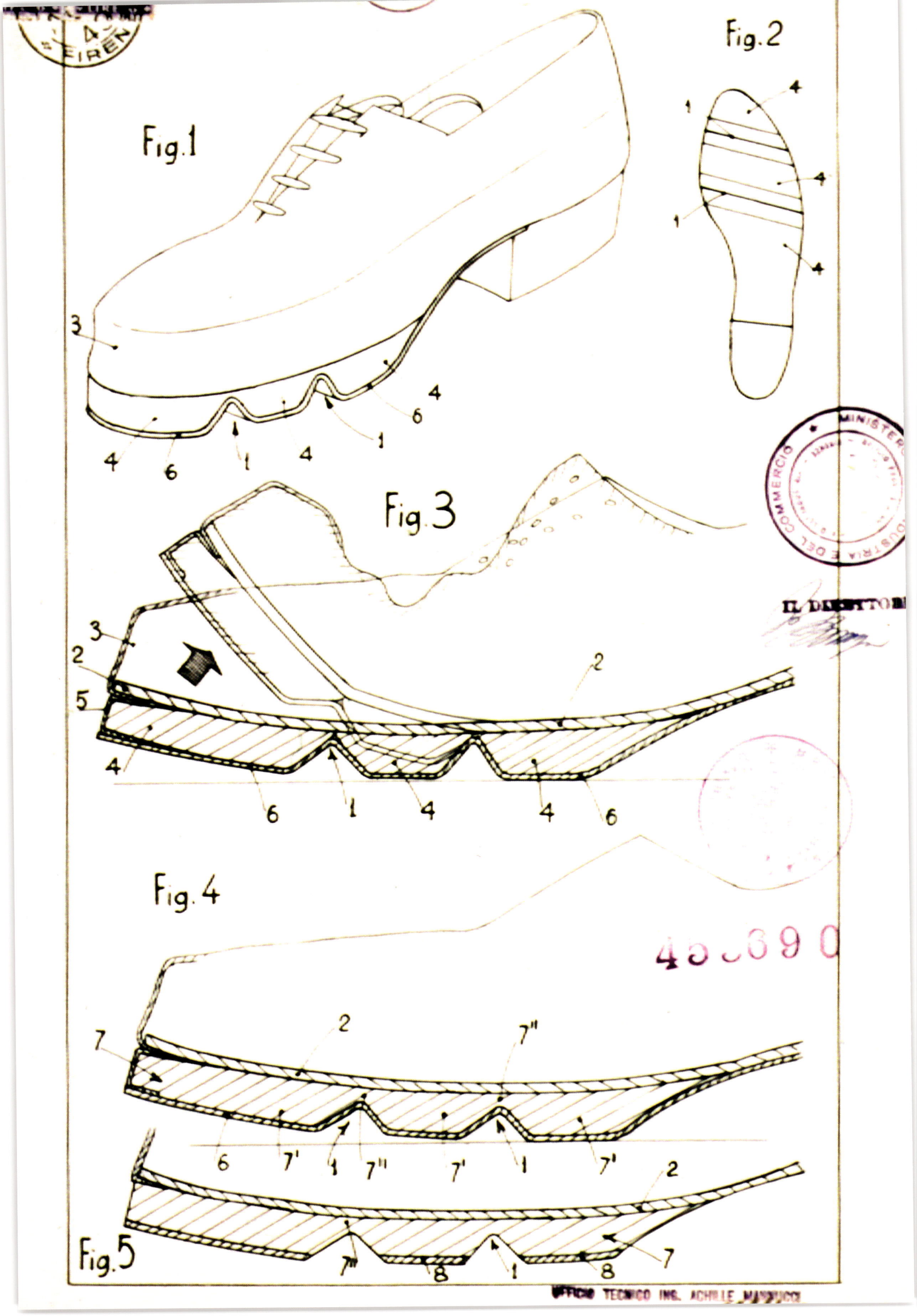
Fig.1
Fig.2
Fig.3
Fig.4
Fig.5
MINISTERO INDUSTRIA E DEL COMMERCIO
IL DIRETTORE
UFFICIO TECNICO ING. ACHILLE MANNUCCI

PATENT NO. 455690:
HIGH-THICKNESS
SEGMENTED SOLES FOR
SHOES, MARCH 9, 1950

PODCA, SUEDE AND
CALFSKIN WITH HEEL AND
PLATFORM IN COVERED
WOOD, 1949

CROCODILE SANDAL, 1950;
PRANIA, CROCODILE, 1950

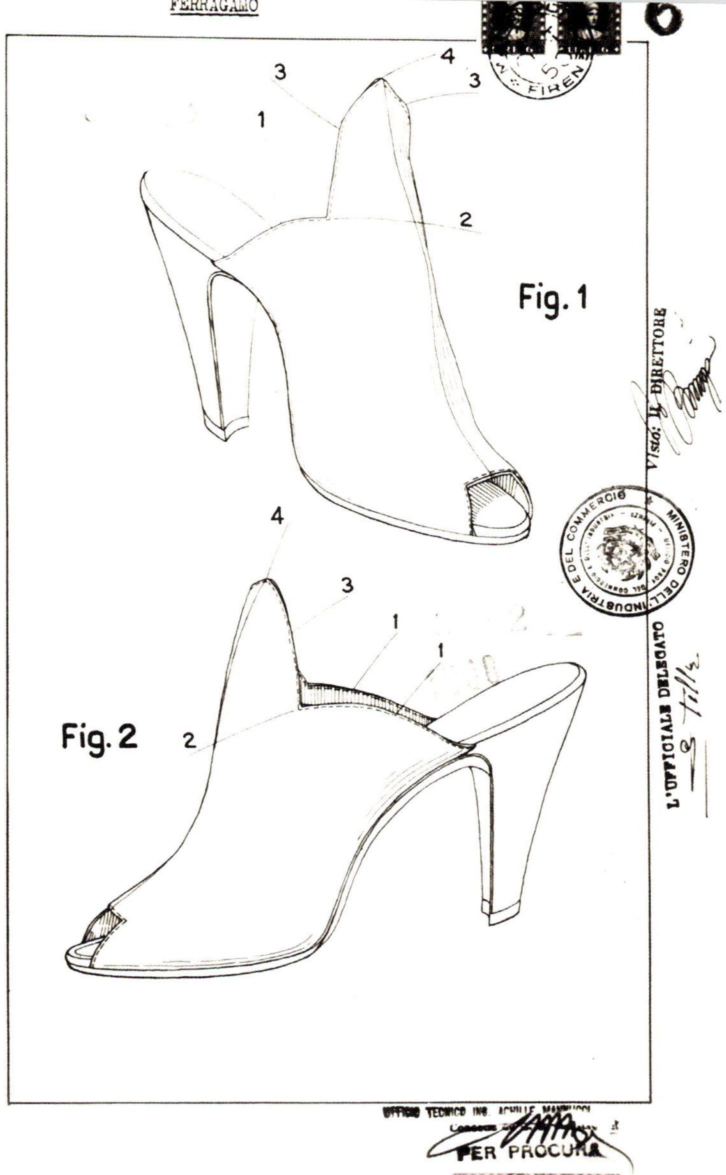

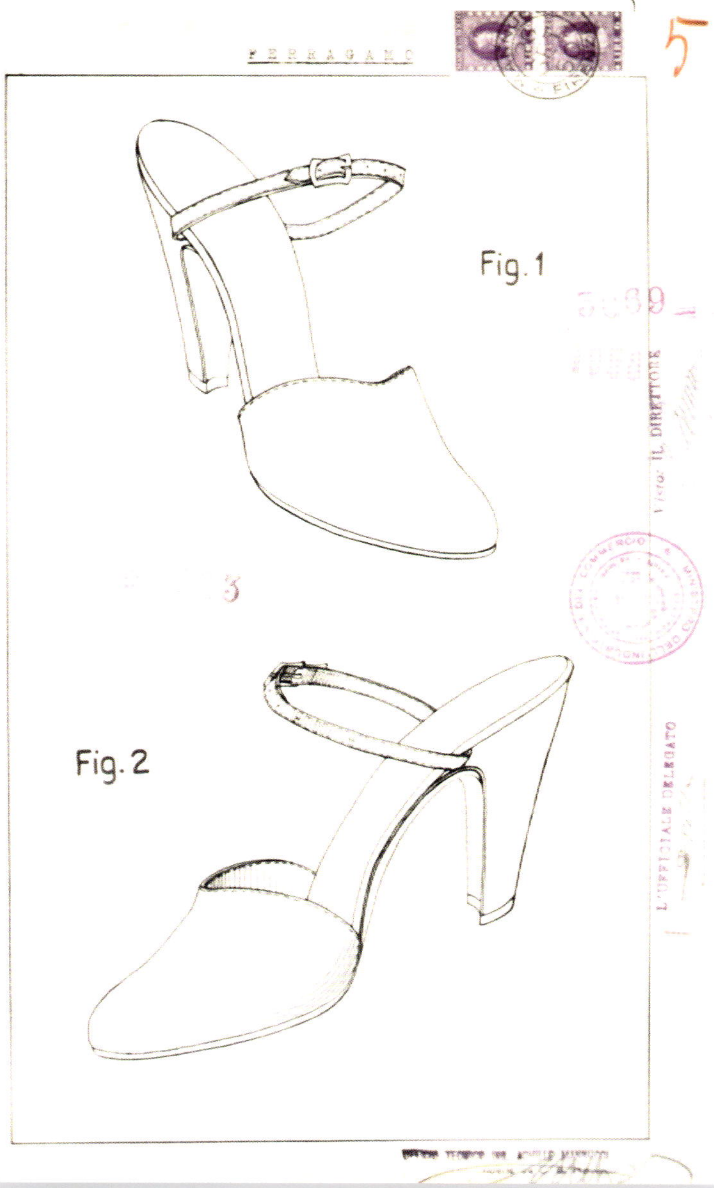

Here is construction news, a triumph in shoe engineering: the sandal held on by a halter strap slanted over the instep only—leaving the heel and ankle in the clear. It clings, stays put. No slipping, no clip-clop. These sandals for late day at resorts, for all summer long with dinner dresses. Lilac-pink sandal, $32.50; purple-lilac, $30. Both, in suède: Lord & Taylor; Wanamaker's, Phila.; J. W. Robinson. Needed with these beauties: smooth heels; sandal-foot nylon stockings. Those with the pink sandal: in "Pink Ribbon," by Munsingwear; at Gimbel's. With the purple: "Suntint" by Hanes; Lord & Taylor. For smoothing heels: "Akimbo" by Charles of the Ritz.

NEWS! FERRAGAMO'S HALTER-STRAP SANDAL

PATENT NO. 36643: LADIES' SHOE WITH THIN, SLENDER HEEL AND BROAD TWO-PART UPPER EXTENDING UPWARD IN A POINT, JANUARY 18, 1951

PATENT NO. 36623: LADIES' HIGH-HEELED SHOE WITH SMALL FRONT UPPER AND LACE ON THE INSTEP, JANUARY 18, 1951

VOGUE USA, FEBRUARY 15, 1951. MUSEO FERRAGAMO, FLORENCE

PATENT NO. 36687:
LADIES' SHOE WITH
HIGH UPPER AND OPEN
TOE, JANUARY 22, 1951

PATENT NO. 36406:
LADIES' SHOE WITH
COLLAR PUSHED UPWARD,
JANUARY 5, 1951

SUEDE MULE WITH
INTERNAL CORK WEDGE,
1950; *PANTIA*, SUEDE AND
KIDSKIN WITH PARTIAL
WEDGE IN COVERED
CORK, 1950–51

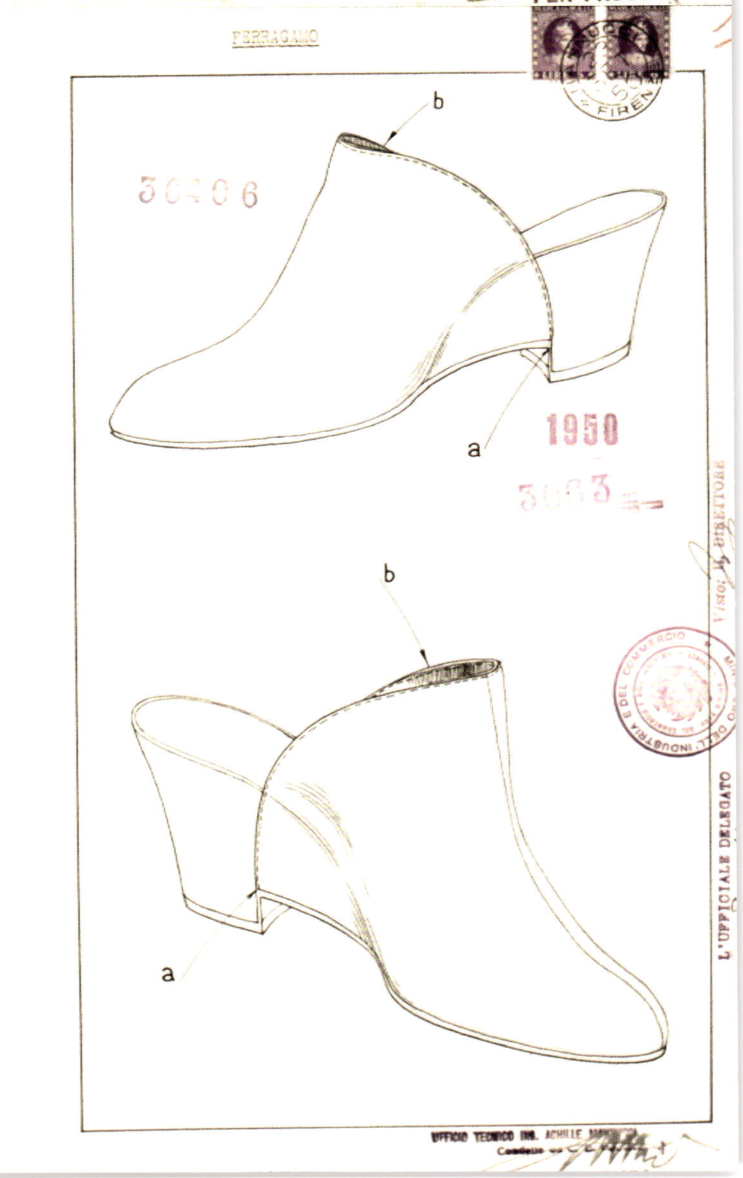

SUEDE MULE, 1950–51

PATENT NO. 36935:
LADIES' SHOE WITH
RAISED TOE AND
FRINGE ON THE INSTEP,
FEBRUARY 15, 1951

3593
1950

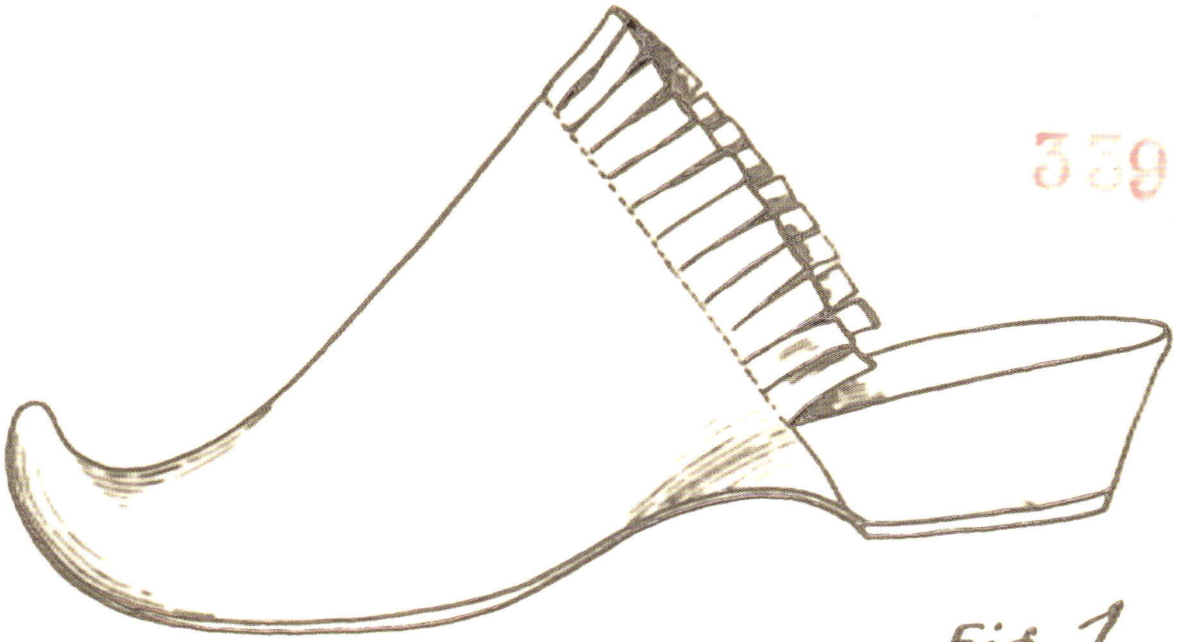

Fig. 1.

36035

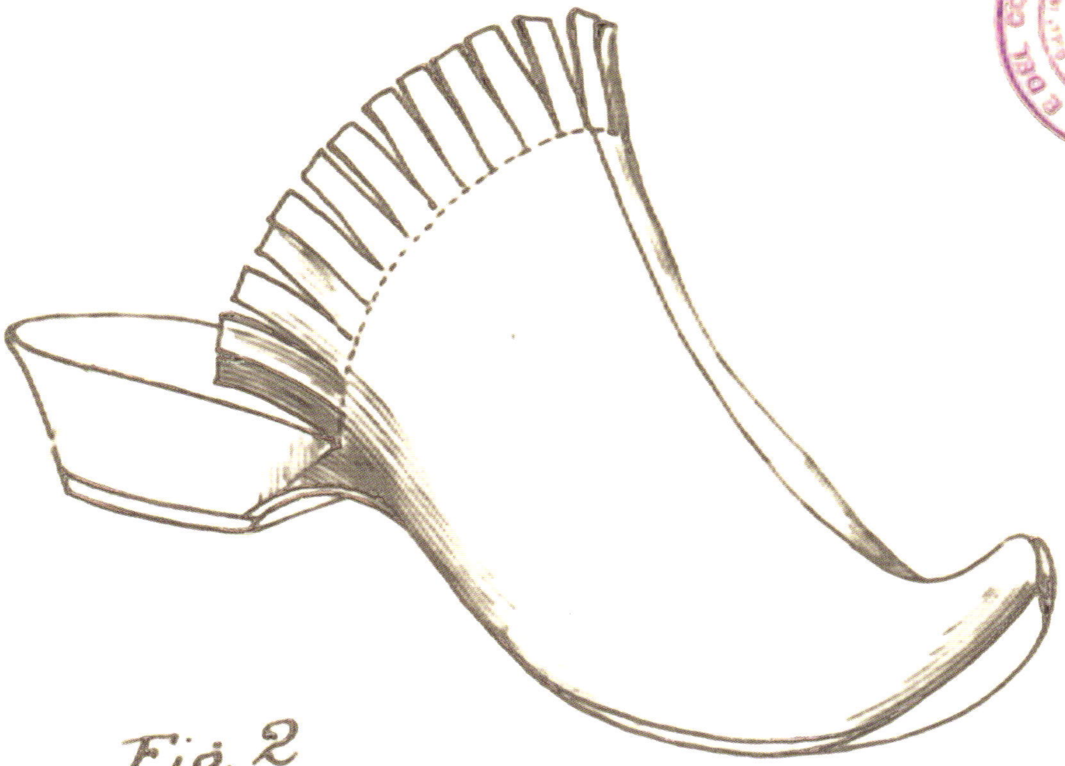

Fig. 2

Visto: IL DIRETTORE

MINISTERO DELL'INDUSTRIA E DEL COMMERCIO

L'UFFICIALE DELEGATO

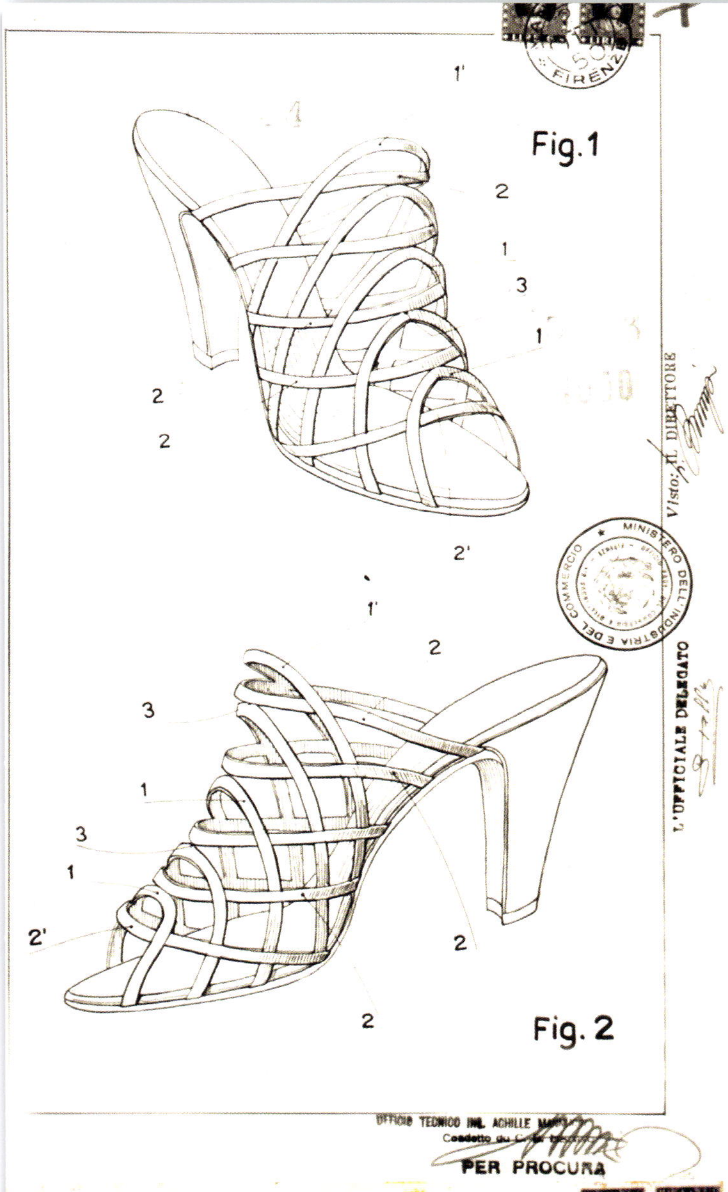

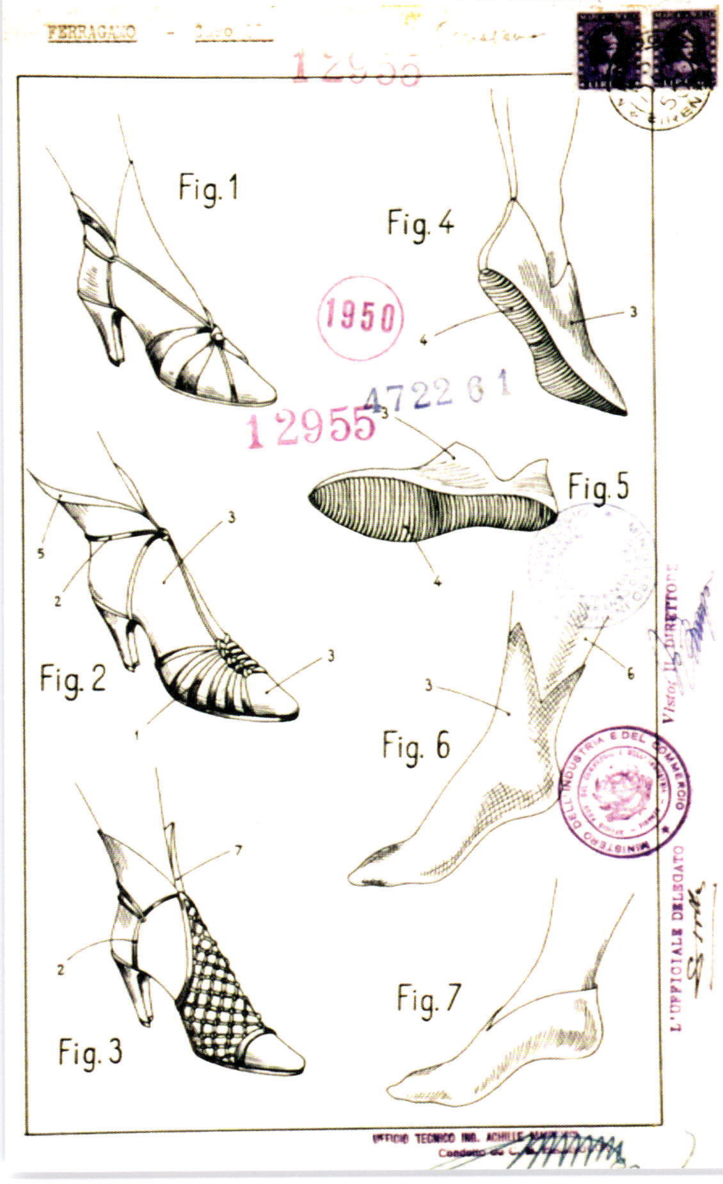

KIMO, SANDAL IN KIDSKIN WITH SILK SATIN AND LEATHER SOCKLETS, 1951

PATENT NO. 36644: LADIES' HIGH-HEELED SHOE WITH UPPER MADE OF SMALL RIBBONS PLACED TO FORM AN ARCH, JANUARY 18, 1951

PATENT NO. 472261: LADIES' SANDAL COMBINED WITH A SOCKLET STICKING TO THE FOOT, JUNE 13, 1952

SALVATORE FERRAGAMO WITH STYLIST EMILIO SCHUBERTH, FEBRUARY 1951. FERRAGAMO PRESENTS THE *KIMO* SANDAL

SANDAL IN FABRIC WORKED IN A NET-LIKE PATTERN AND KIDSKIN, 1951

PATENT NO. 36646: PATTERNED SHOE WITH UPPER MADE OF A NETWORK OF RAFFIA (OR SIMILAR MATERIAL) AND FULLY OPEN TOE, JANUARY 18, 1951

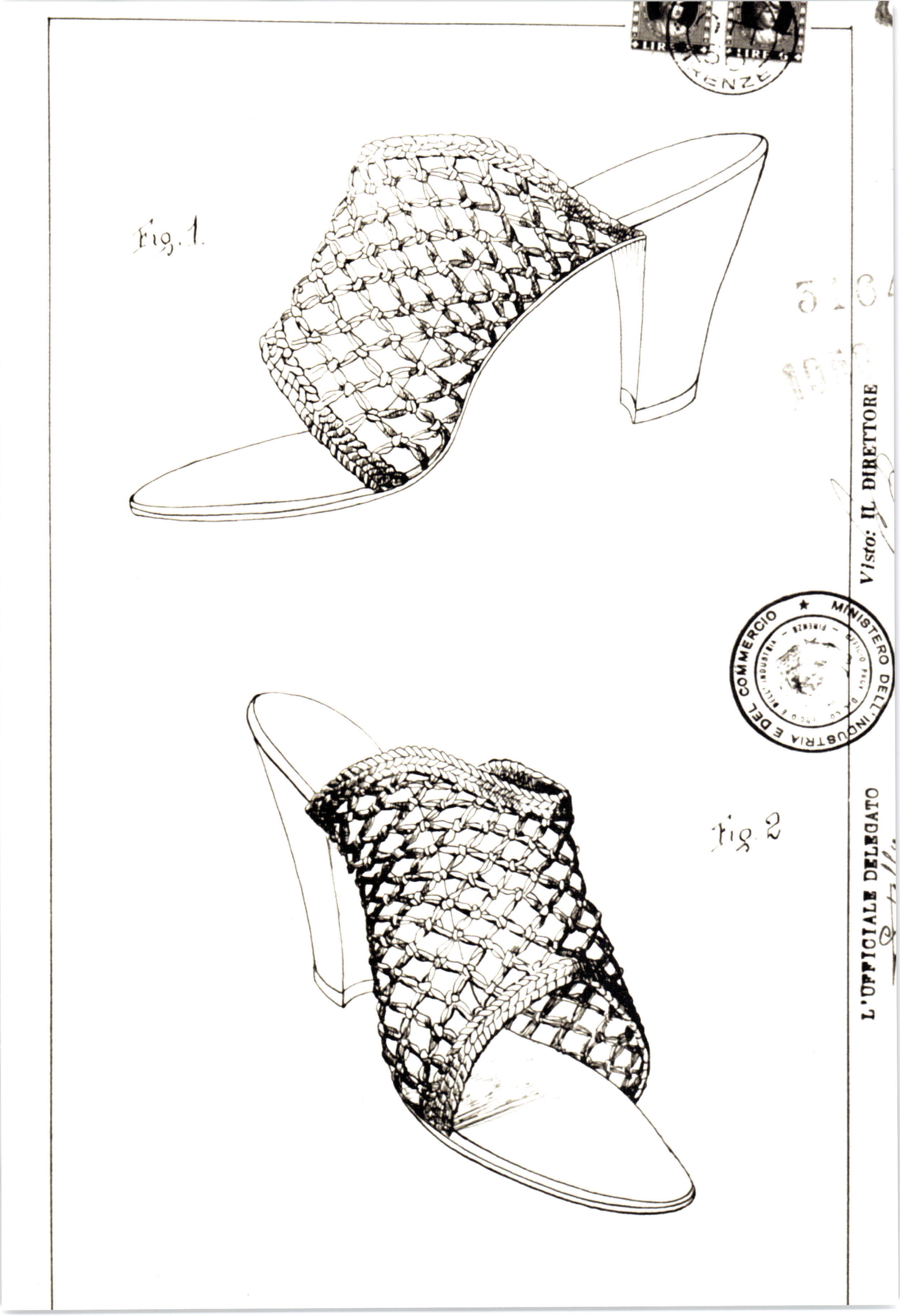
Fig. 1
Fig. 2
Visto: IL DIRETTORE
L'UFFICIALE DELEGATO
MINISTERO DELL'INDUSTRIA E DEL COMMERCIO

BELLEZZA, MAY 1950. MUSEO FERRAGAMO, FLORENCE

PATENT NO. 31023: LADIES' SANDAL WITH UPPER MADE OF ALTERNATING CROSS BANDS IN MESH AND INTERWOVEN FABRIC, MARCH 31, 1949

RAFFIA AND KIDSKIN SANDAL, 1948

1
2
3
4

RAFFIA SANDAL
WITH WEDGE HEEL IN
COVERED CORK, 1950

PATENT NO. 35850:
LADIES' SANDAL IN
VEGETAL FIBER LIKE
RAFFIA, KNOTTED ON
THE UPPER AND
FEATURING A DOUBLE
LACE, NOVEMBER 20,
1950

Fig.1

Fig. 2

Fig. 1

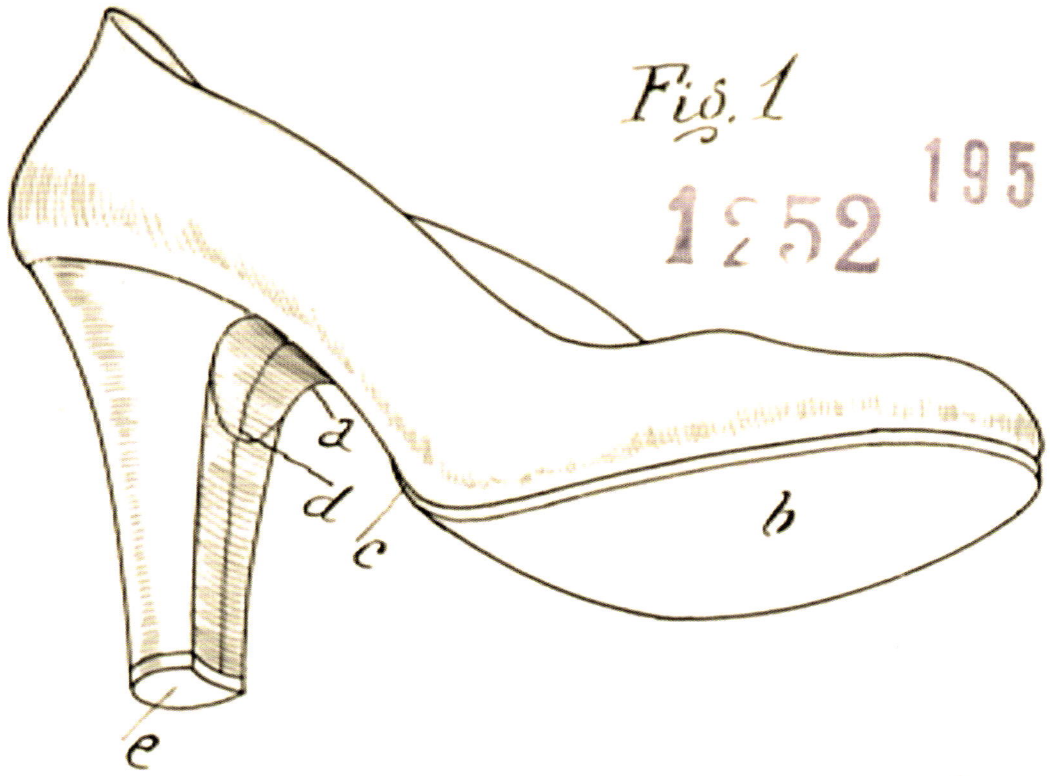

Fig. 2

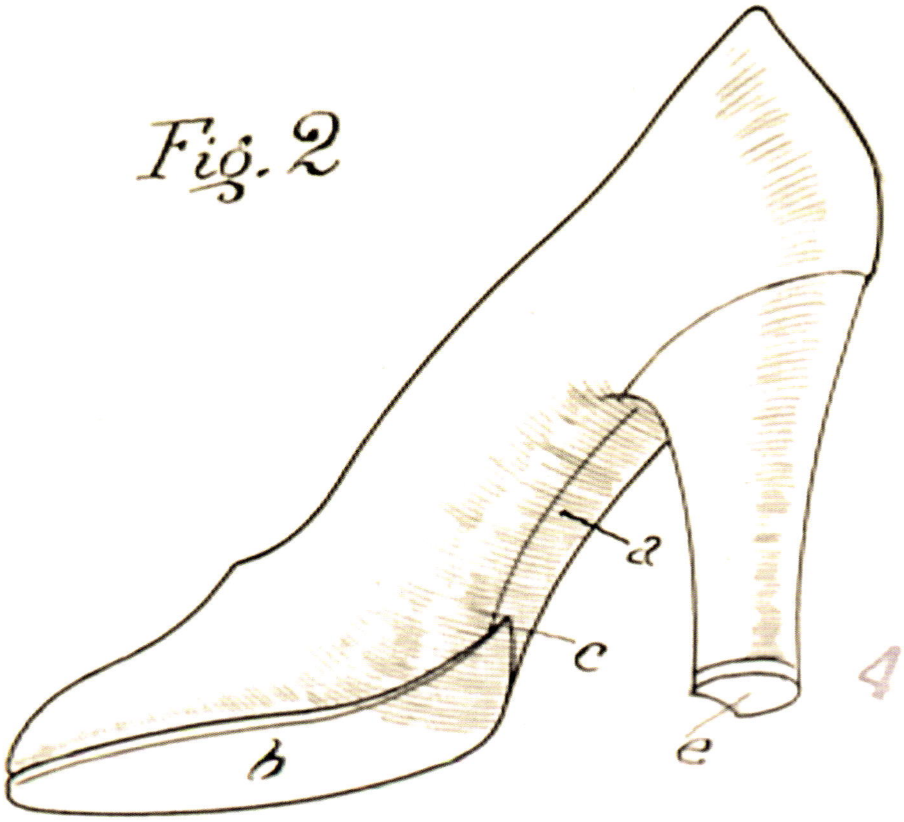

PATENT NO. 41888:
HALF-SOLE SHOE WITH
GLOVED ARCH IN THE
SAME MATERIALS AS THE
UPPER, JULY 7, 1952

CALFSKIN PUMP WITH
GLOVED ARCH, 1952

SUEDE CLOSED
SHOE WITH GLOVED
ARCH, 1952

PATENT NO. 41889:
LADIES' SHOE
WITH OVAL HEEL,
JULY 7, 1952

FERRAGAMO

41839

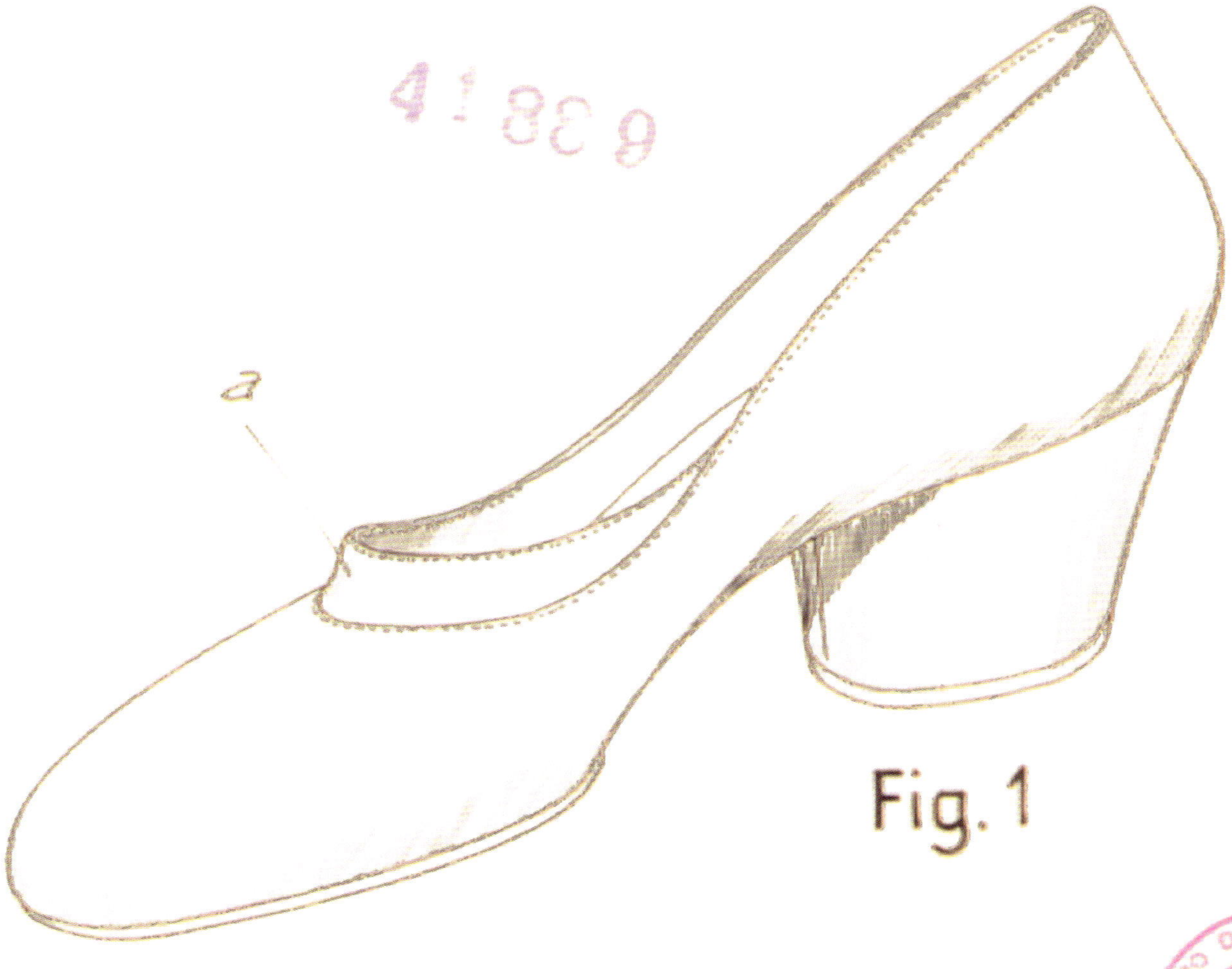

Fig. 1

1957

1952

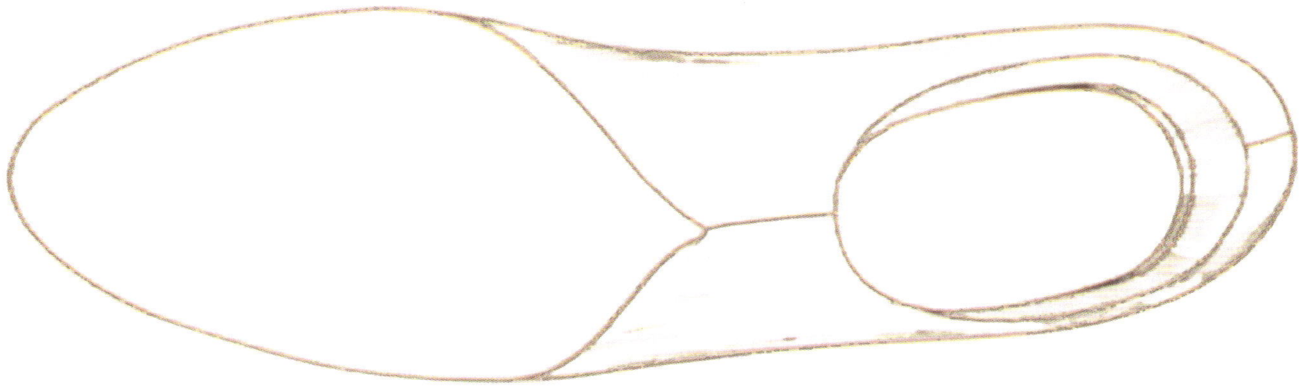

Fig. 2

Visto: IL DIRETTORE

MINISTERO DELL'INDUS…

L'UFFICIALE DELEGATO

CALIPSO, SILK SATIN WITH BRASS CAGE HEEL, 1956

PATENT NO. 482872: METAL HEEL FOR LADIES' SHOES, FORMED OF ELEMENTS ASSEMBLED TOGETHER AS A CAGE, JULY 13, 1953

PATENT NO. 547227: HEEL FOR LADIES' SHOES CONSISTING OF A METAL FRAMEWORK FORMED BY THREADLIKE ELEMENTS, AUGUST 20, 1956

PATENT NO. 549050: SHEATH (ALSO PARTIAL) TO BE USED IN HEELS OF LADIES' SHOES AND HEELS COVERED BY THE SHEATH, AS WELL AS THE PROCESS OF APPLYING THE SHEATH ON THE HEELS, OCTOBER 4, 1956

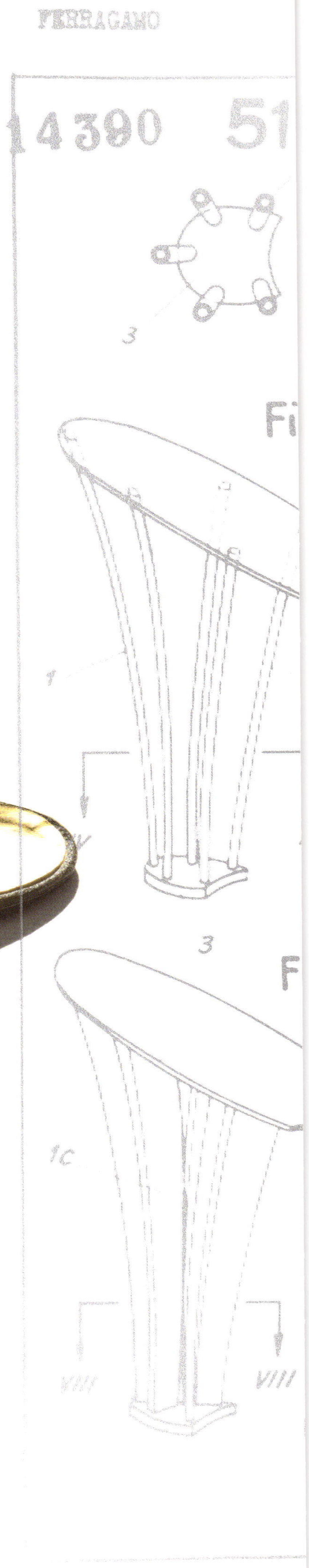

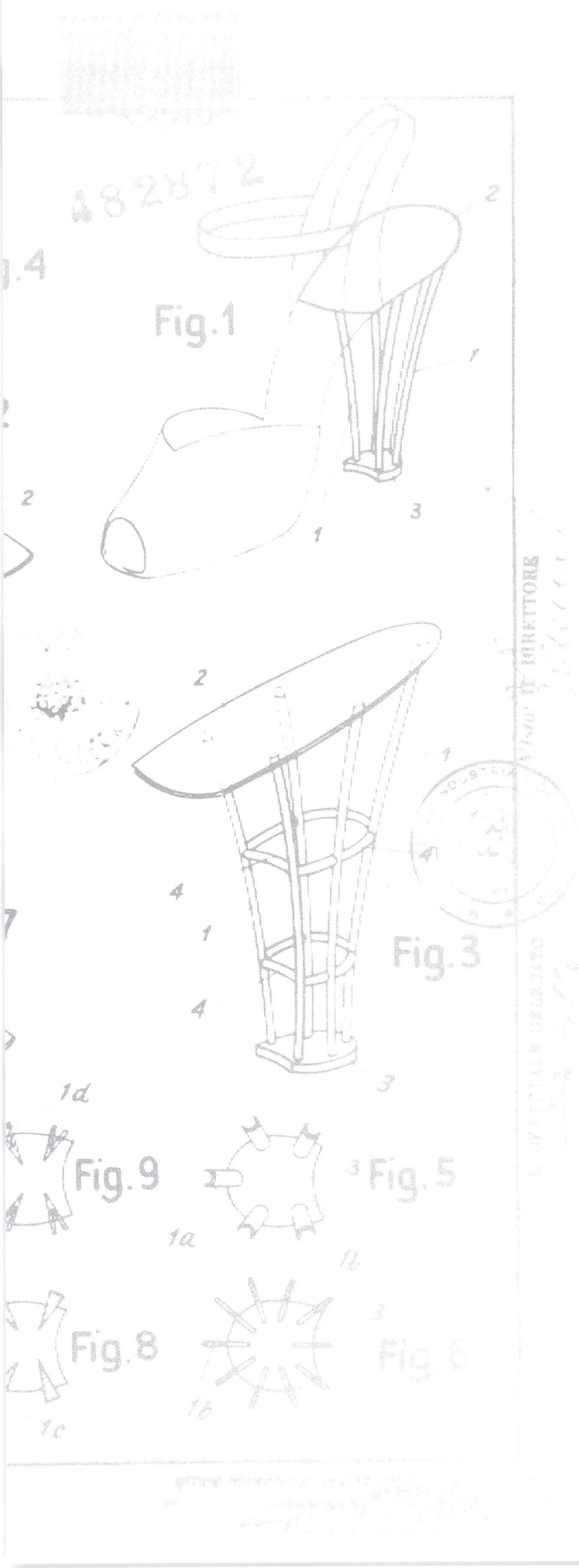
Fig.1
Fig.3
Fig.9
Fig.5
Fig.8

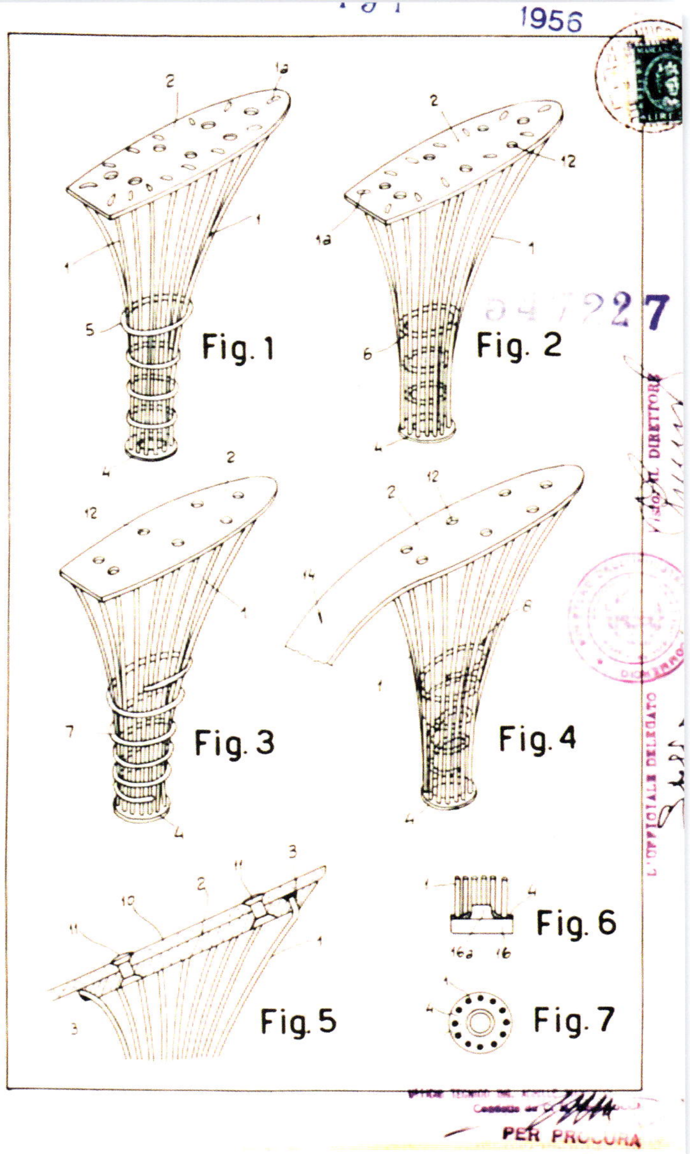
1956
Fig. 1
Fig. 2
Fig. 3
Fig. 4
Fig. 5
Fig. 6
Fig. 7
PER PROCURA

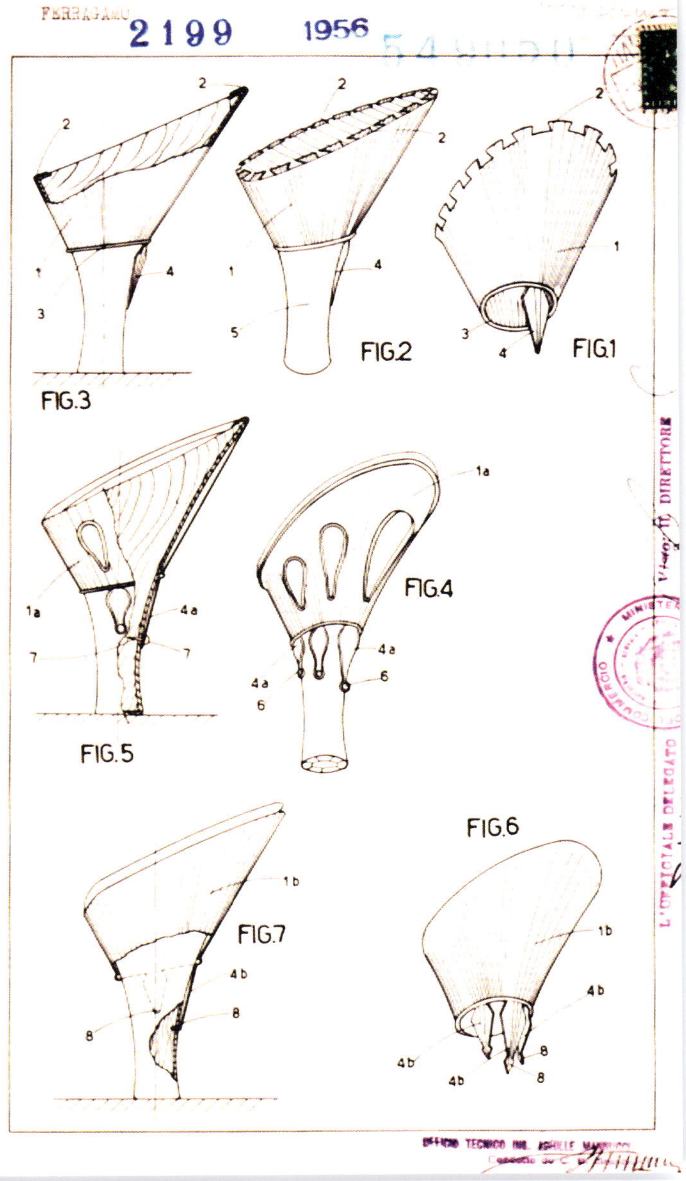
FERRAGAMO
2199
1956
FIG.3
FIG.2
FIG.1
FIG.5
FIG.4
FIG.7
FIG.6

PATENT NO. 55183:
LADIES' SANDAL WITH
LOW-HEELED SOLE
AND A BIG ROUND
BRAIDED CORD
SERVING AS AN UPPER,
AUGUST 13, 1955

RITZ, KIDSKIN, 1955

PATENT NO. 42923:
LADIES' LOW HEEL
WITH AN OUTER
GROOVE,
OCTOBER 24, 1952

KIDSKIN SANDAL,
1952–53

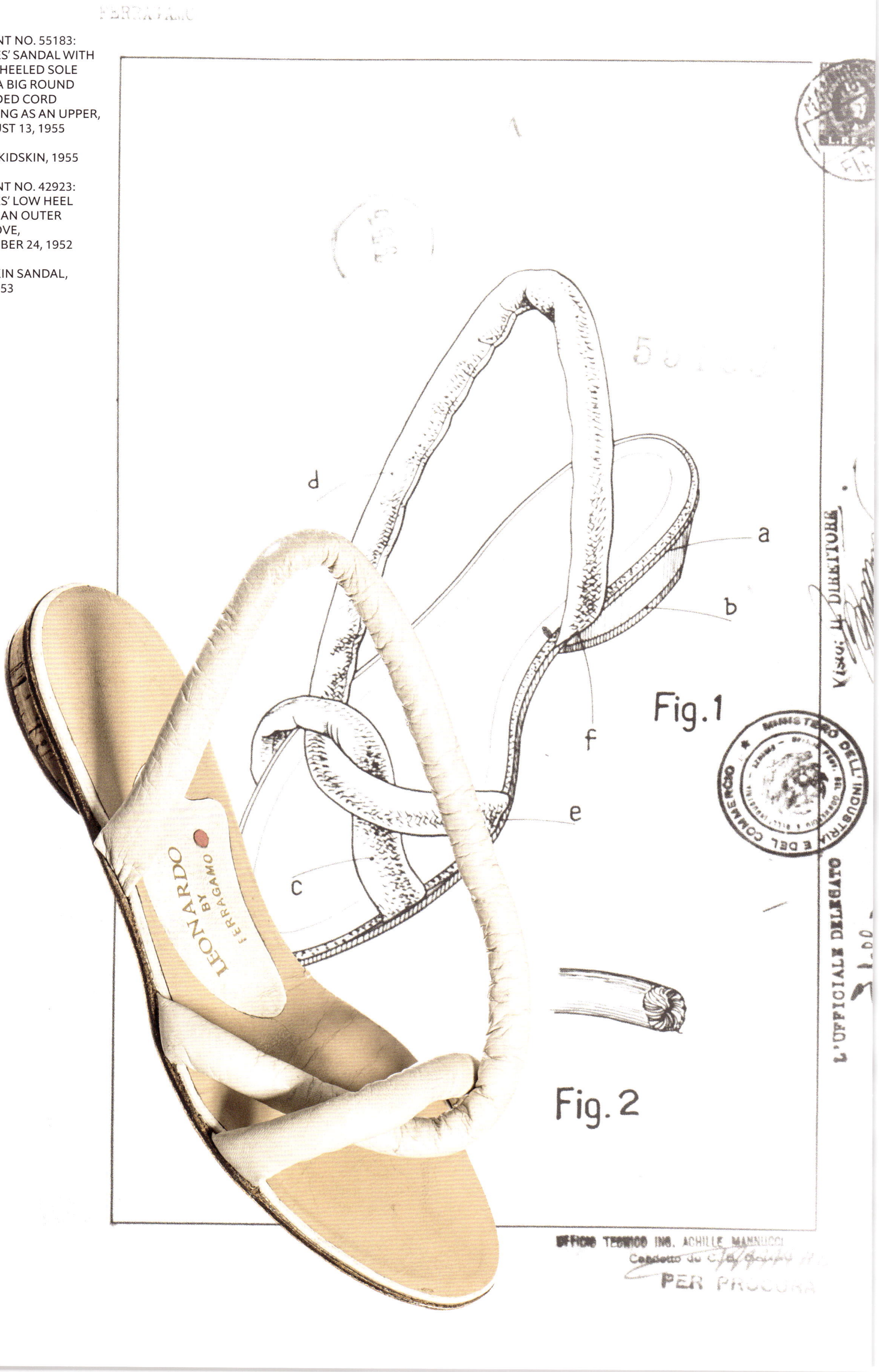

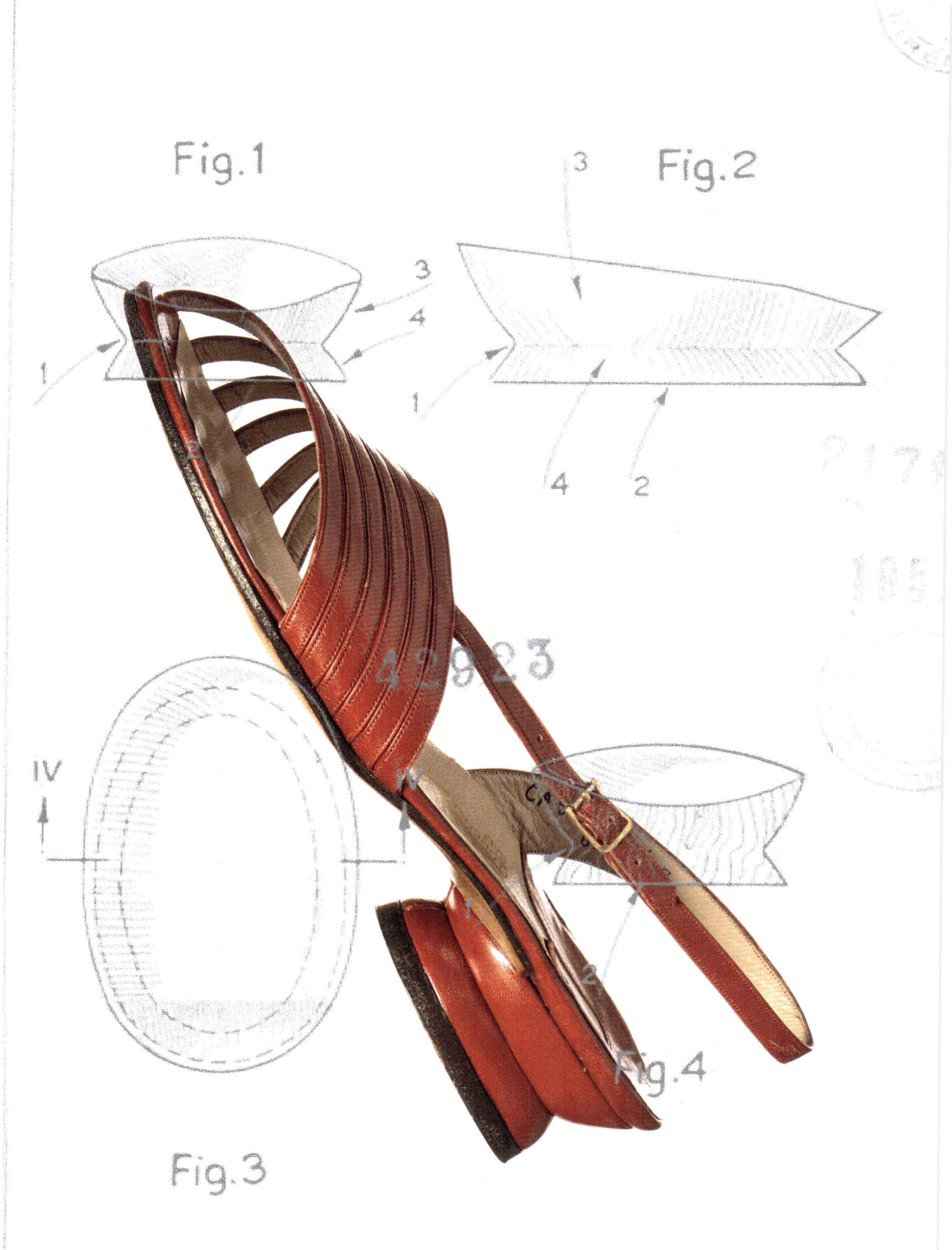
Fig.1
Fig.2
Fig.3
Fig.4
42923
IV
IV
1
2
3
4
1
2
3
4
1
2

559719

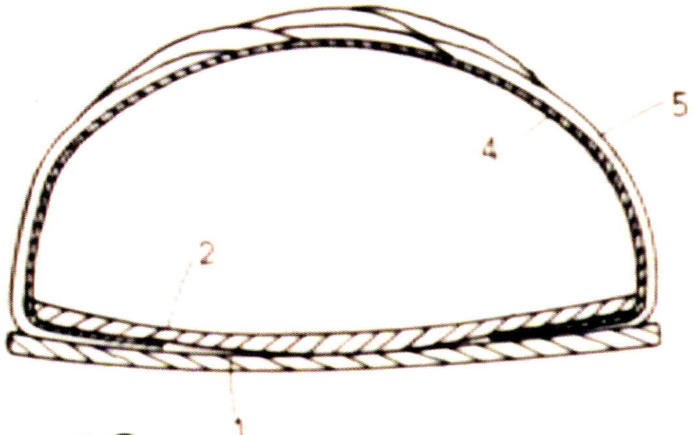

FIG.2

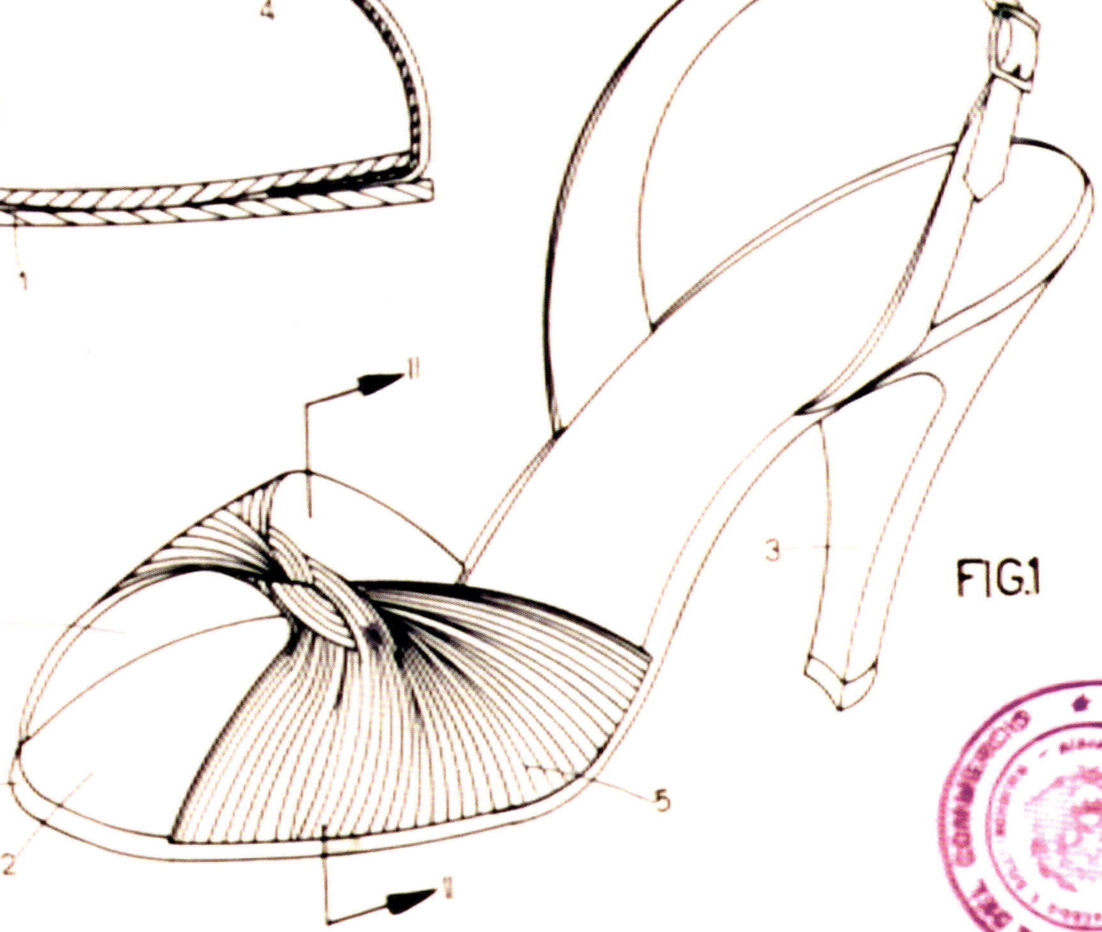

FIG.1

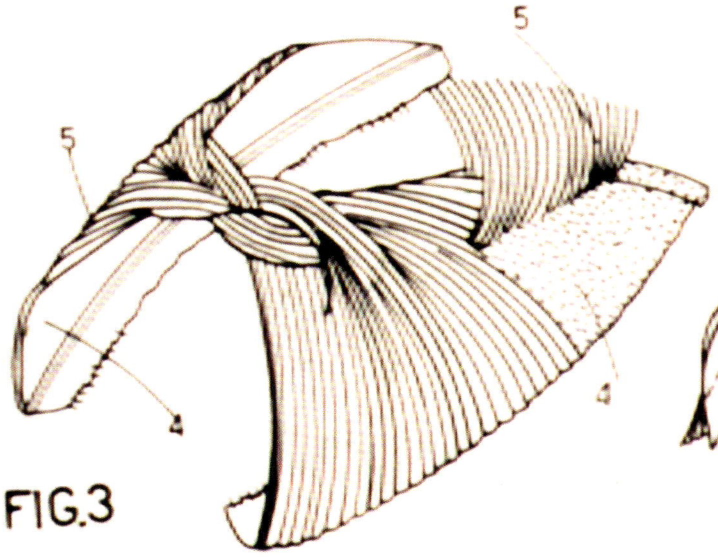

FIG.3

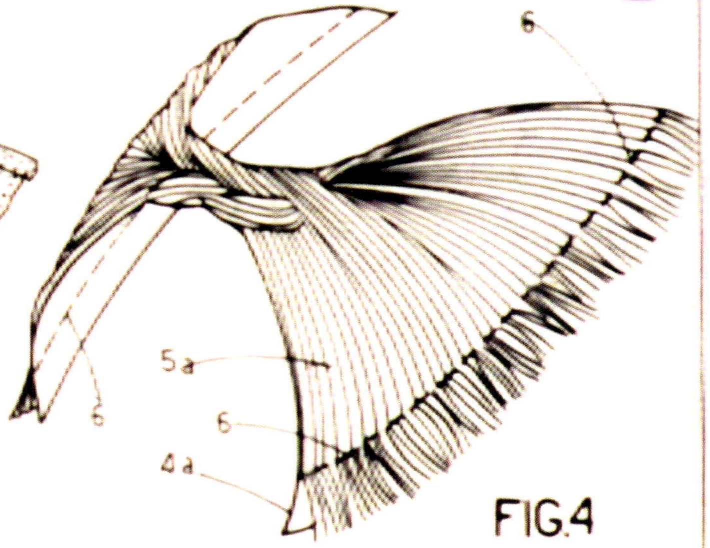

FIG.4

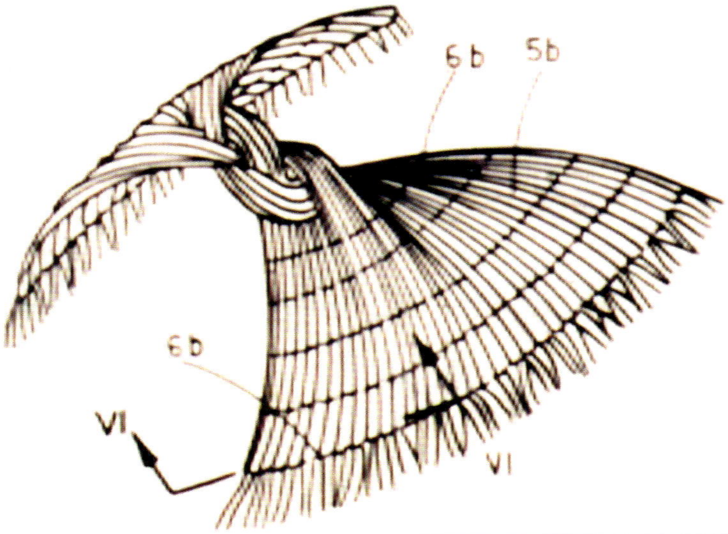

FIG.5

FIG.6

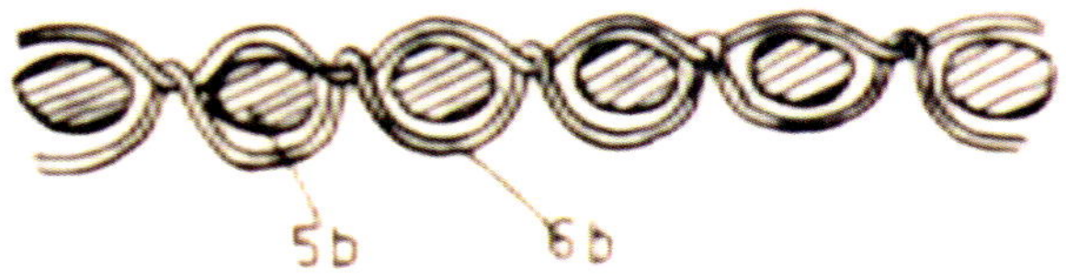

PATENT NO. 559719: PROCEDURE FOR MANUFACTURING SUCH PRODUCTS AS SHOE UPPERS (ESPECIALLY OPEN ONES), BAGS, BELTS, CAPS, AND OTHER ARTICLES USING THREADLIKE ELEMENTS AND PRODUCTS OBTAINED WITH THIS PROCESS, MARCH 27, 1957

SIMONA, SILK SOUTACHE AND CALFSKIN, 1956

EURO, SUEDE, 1957

PATENT NO. 66159:
SHOE WITH CLOSED
UPPER AND AN EDGE
SUITABLE FOR
CLOSING ELASTICALLY
AROUND THE INSTEP,
JANUARY 16, 1958

FIG.1

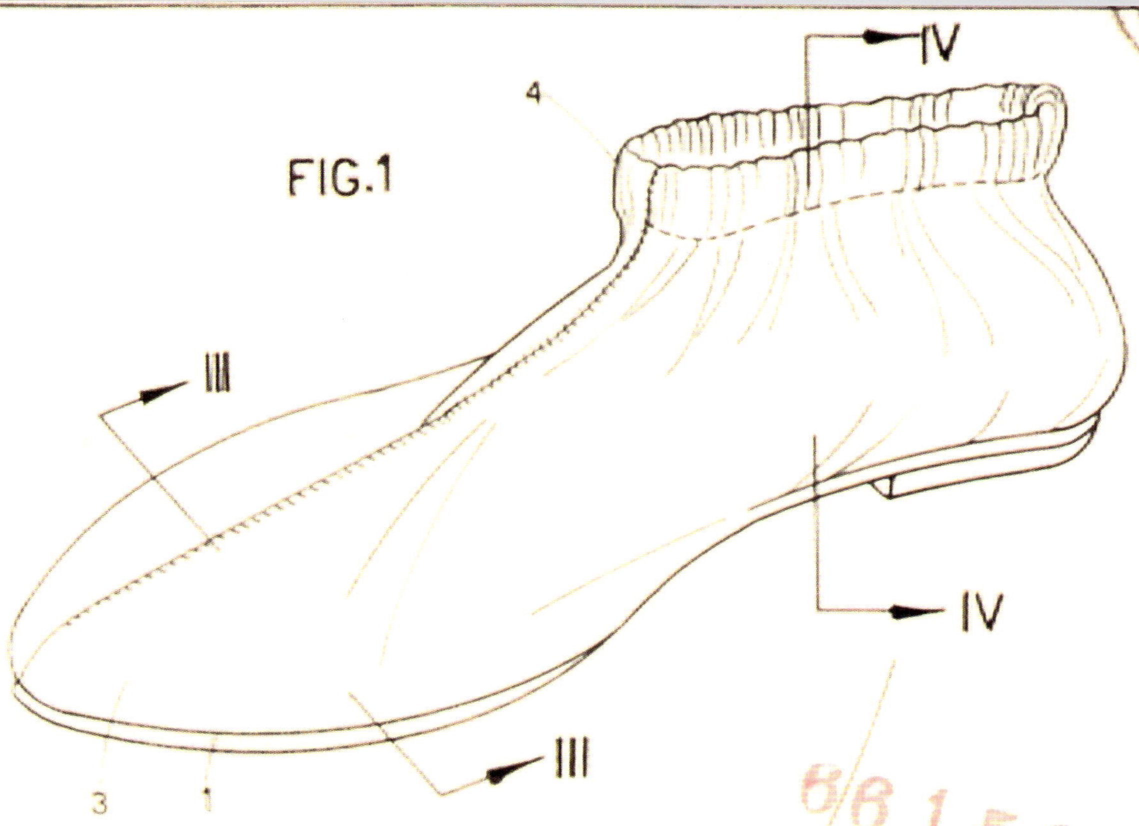

FIG.2

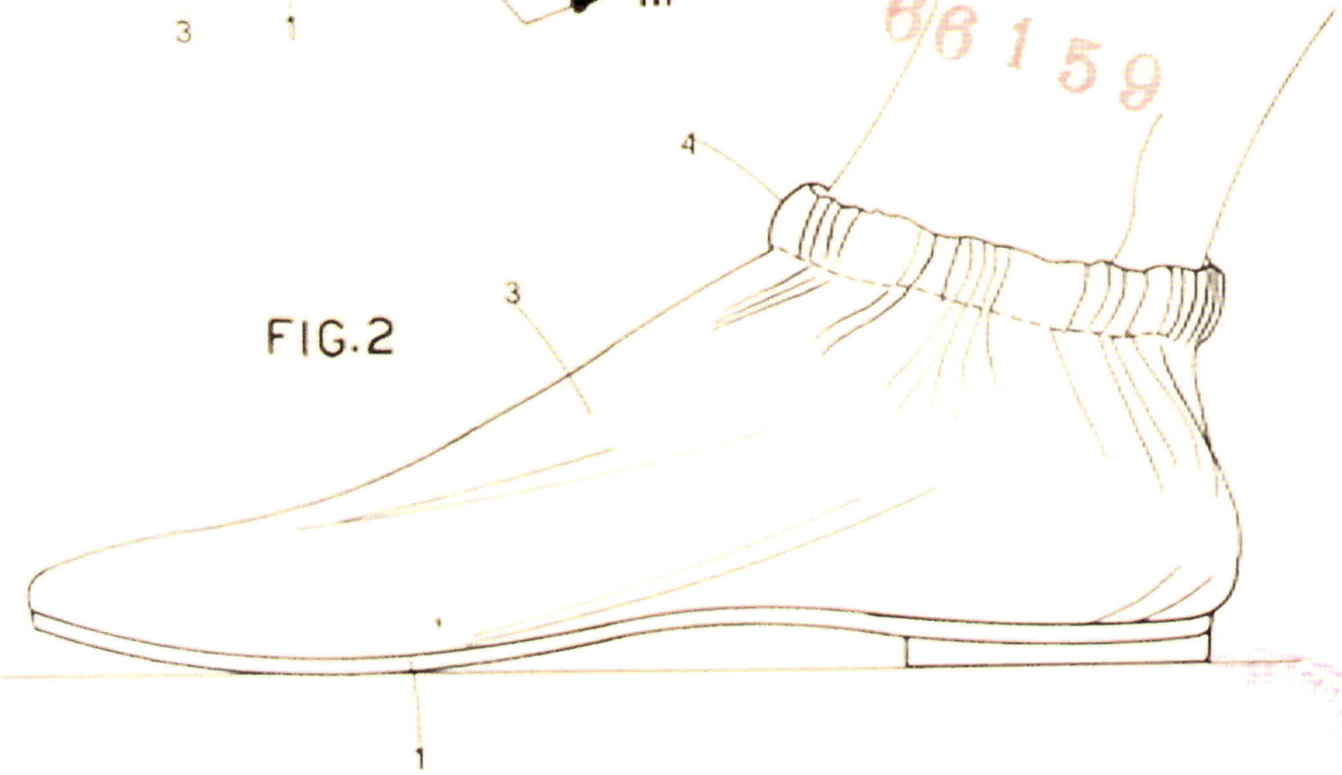

FIG.3

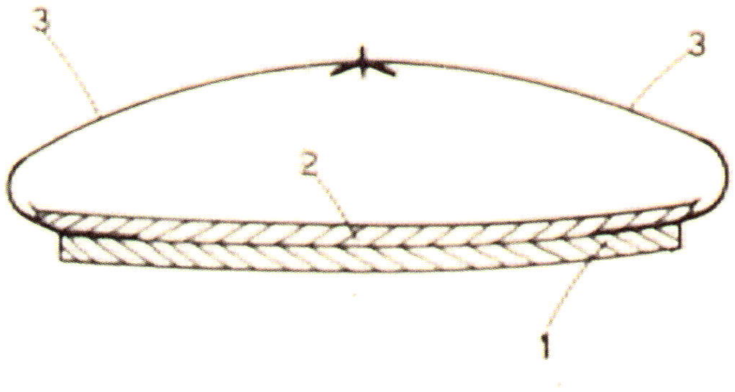

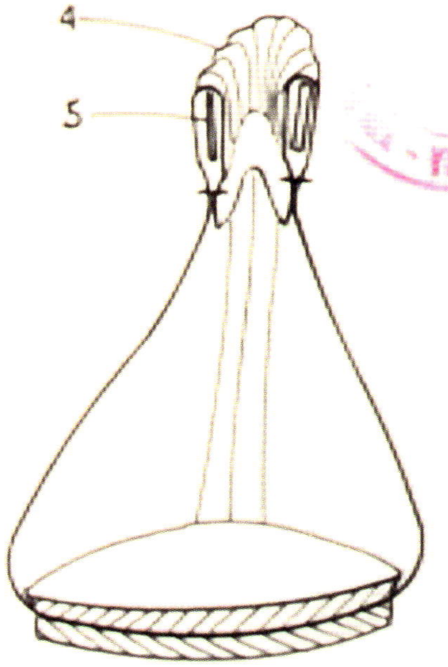

FIG.4

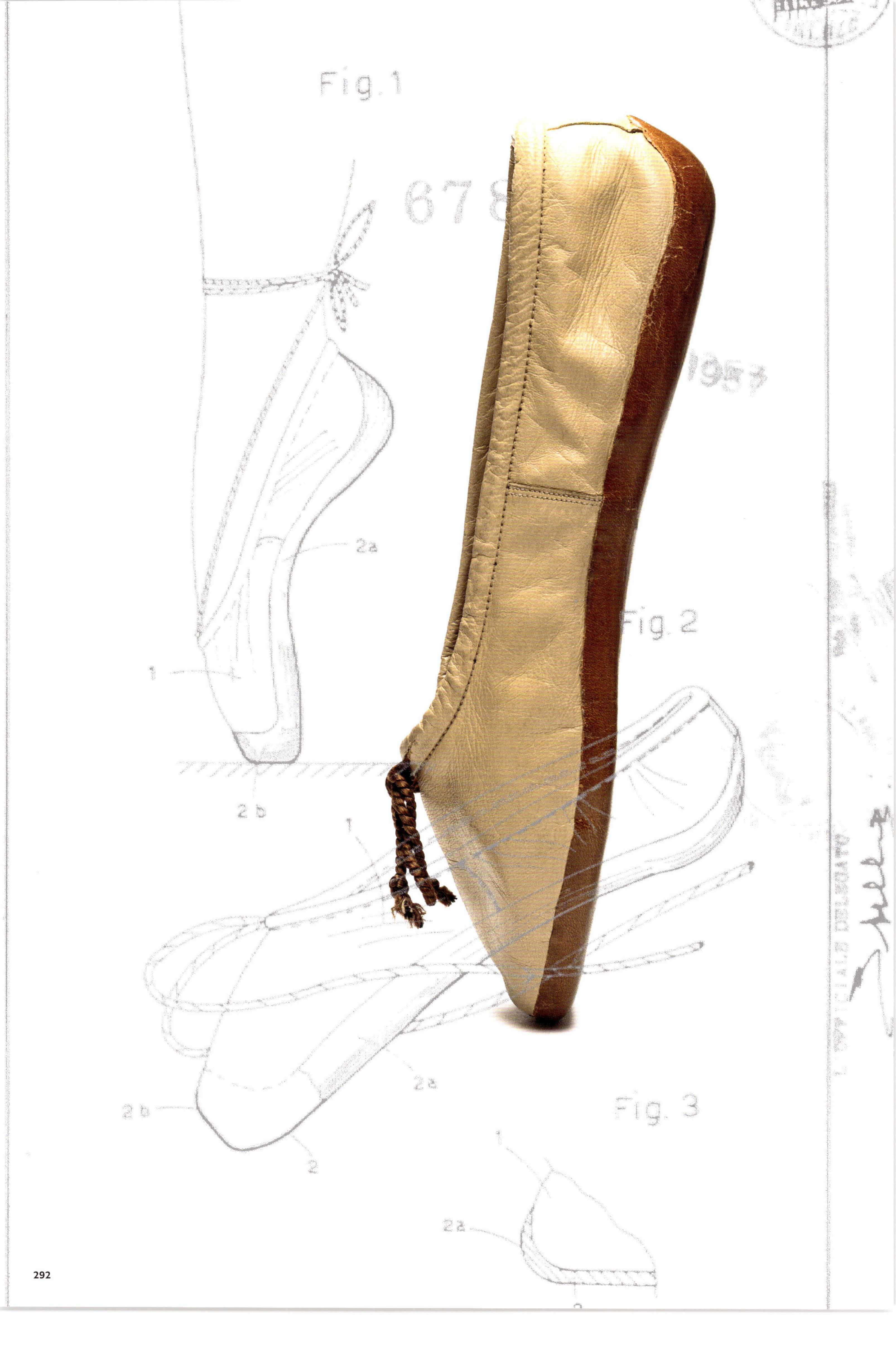
Fig. 1
Fig. 2
Fig. 3
1
2a
2b
2

PATENT NO. 67890:
BALLET COURT SHOE
WITH SOLE FEATURING
A TAPERED EDGE GLUED TO
THE SIDES OF THE UPPER
AND REINFORCING THE TOE,
APRIL 22, 1958

KIDSKIN BALLET SHOE
WITH SHELL SOLE, 1957

PATENT NO. 67106: LADIES' SANDAL FEATURING A SOLE WITH EDGES RAISED ON SIDES AND TIED WITH A BUCKLE STRAP, SLING BACK FASTENED AT SIDES TO ENCOMPASS THE HEEL, MARCH 7, 1958

PATENT NO. 66014: LADIES' SANDAL MADE OF A PIECE OF LEATHER CUT TO SOLE, WITH VARIOUS PROJECTING APPENDAGES THAT HAVE CUTS TO LET A TAPE THROUGH AND CONNECT THE WHOLE WITH THE FOOT, JANUARY 31, 1958

CHICCA, KIDSKIN WITH SHELL SOLE, 1957;
COCCA, LEATHER AND COTTON, 1957

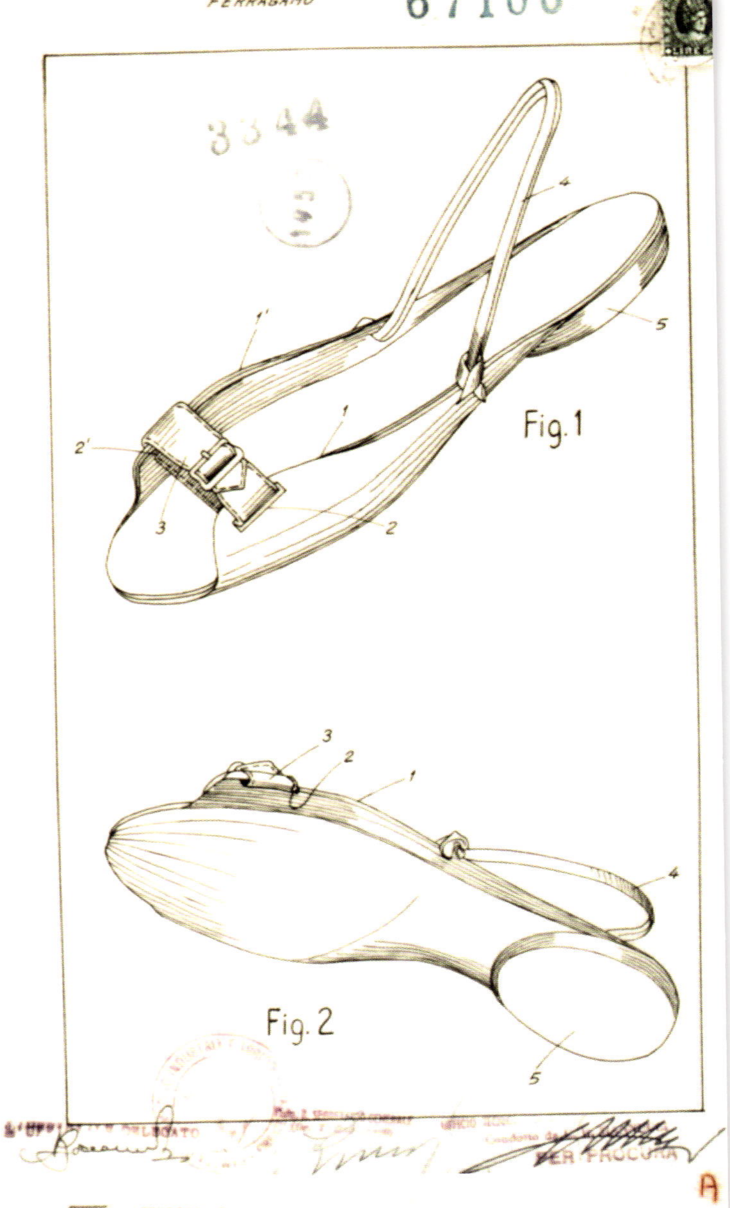

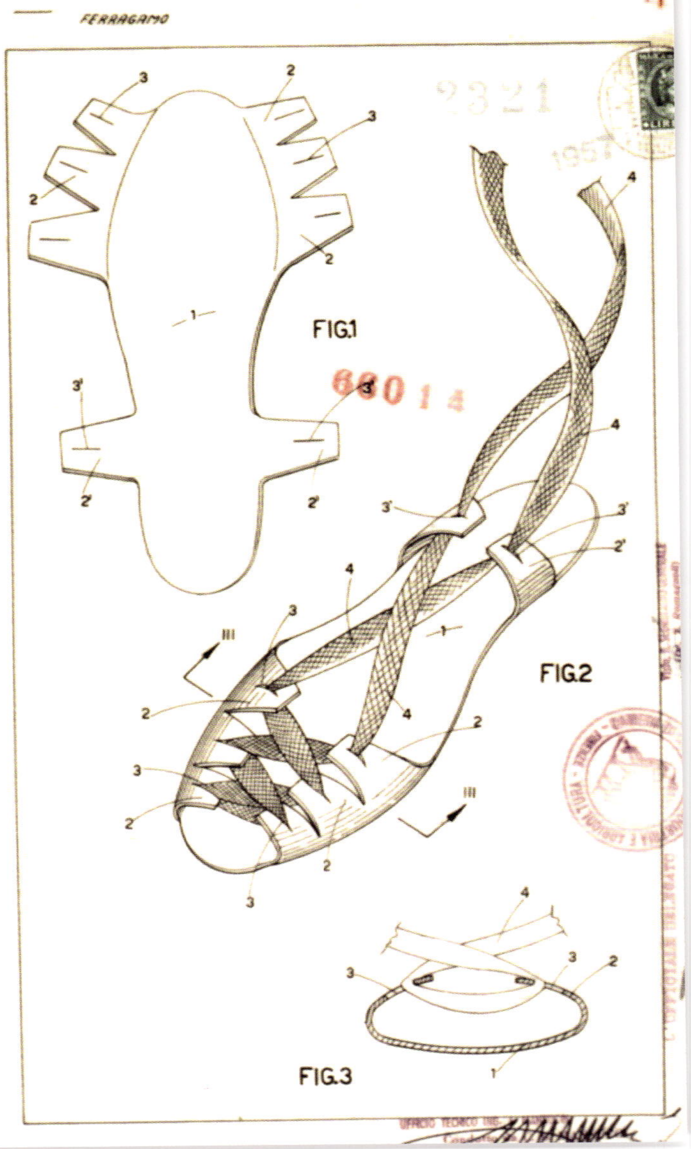

78902

4600 1959

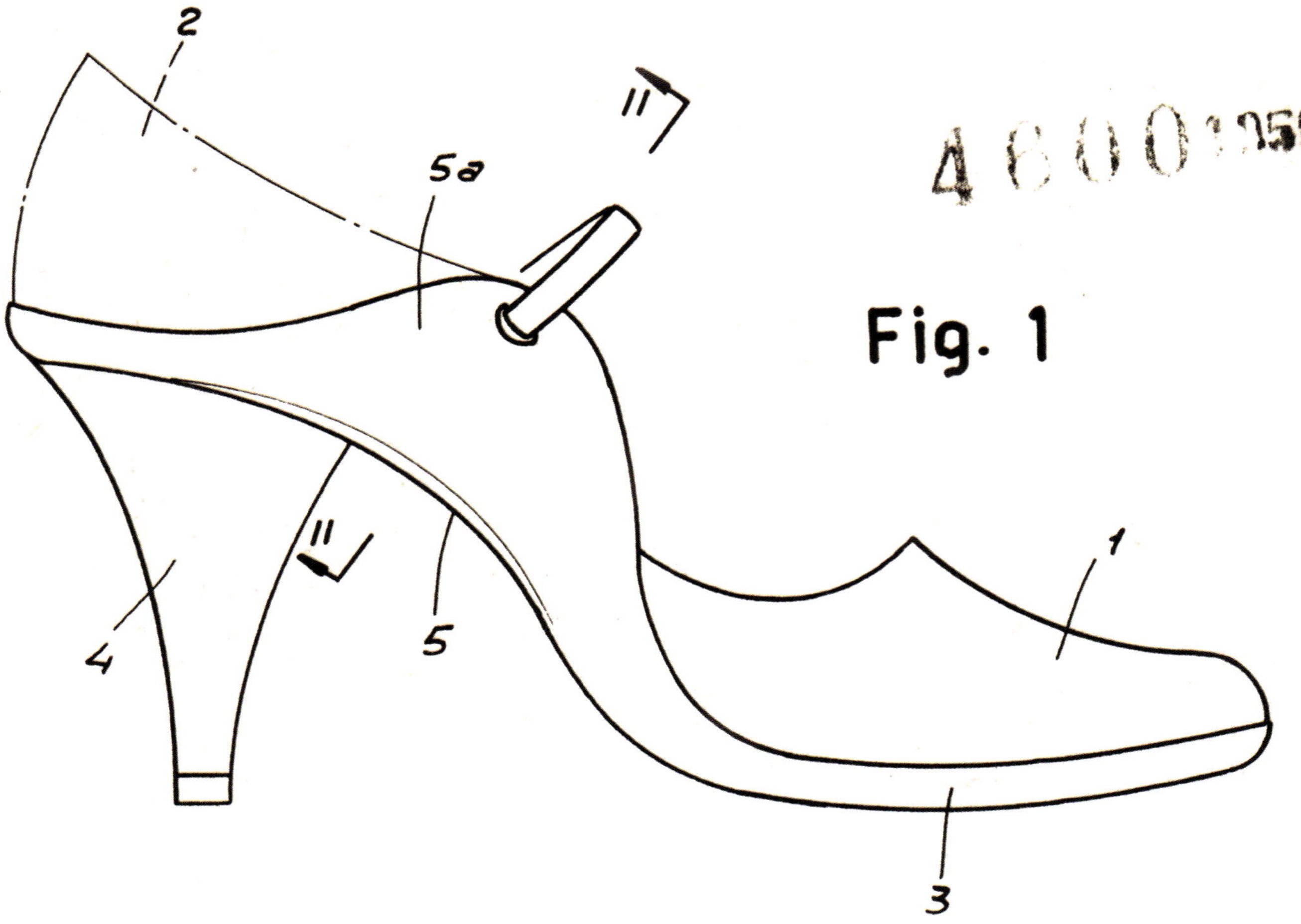

Fig. 1

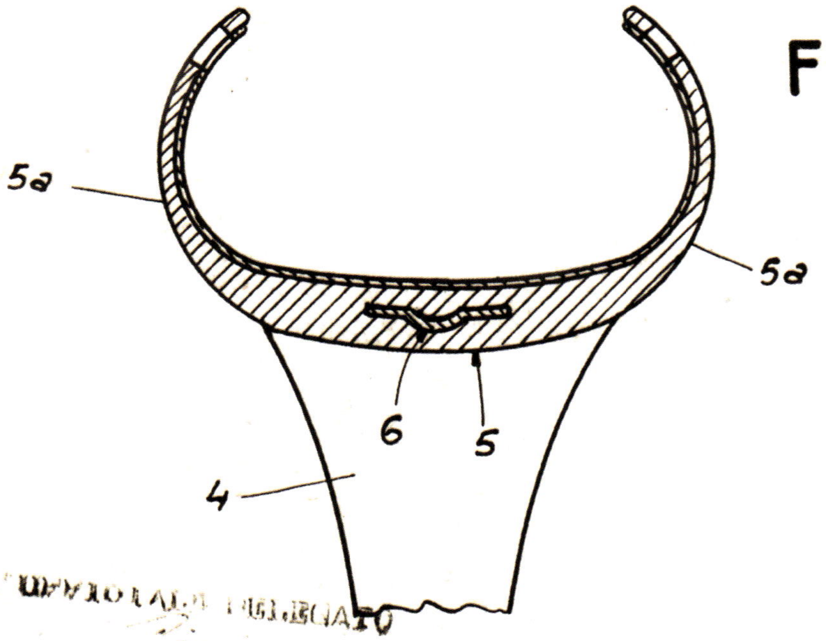

Fig. 2

PATENT NO. 78902:
LADIES' SHOE WITH THE SOLE PROLONGING OVER THE BACK OF THE FOOT BY THE ARCH OF THE WAIST IN ORDER TO IMPROVE STIFFNESS AND FOOT SUPPORT, JUNE 9, 1960

SUEDE PUMP WITH SHELL SOLE, 1959

PIC NIC AND *SPEDITA*,
SUEDE WITH SHELL
SOLE, 1957; *VIVETTE*,
SUEDE WITH SHELL
SOLE, 1960

PATENT NO. 578173:
PROCEDURE FOR
MANUFACTURING SHOES
FEATURING A METHOD
OF BINDING THE SOLE AND
THE UPPER, JUNE 20, 1958

FIG. 6

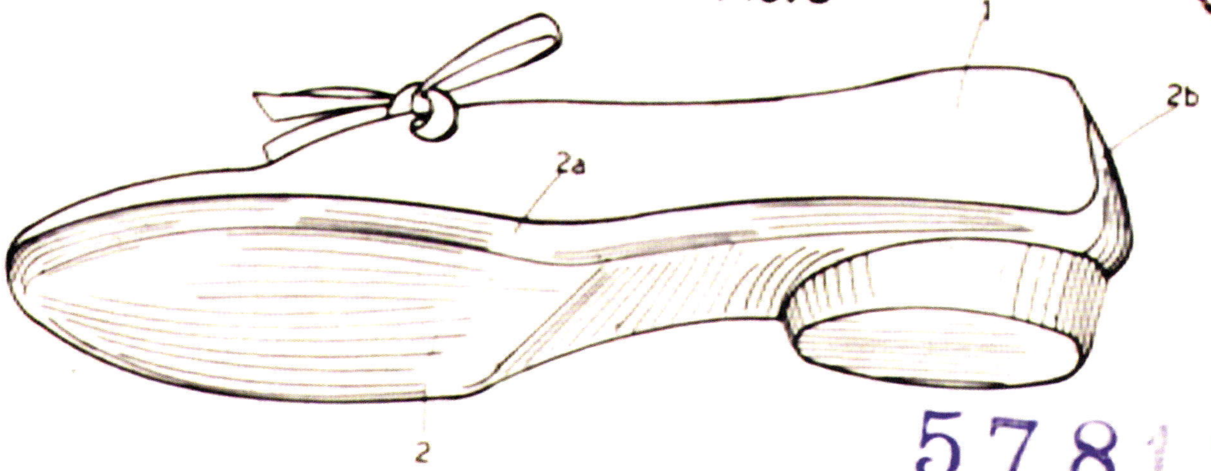

578173

FIG.5

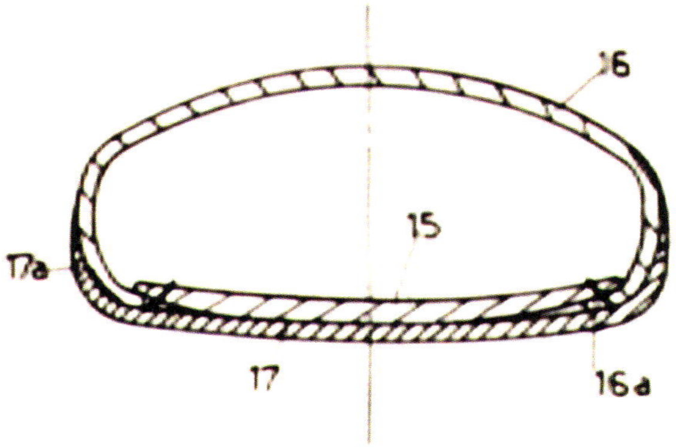

FIG.4

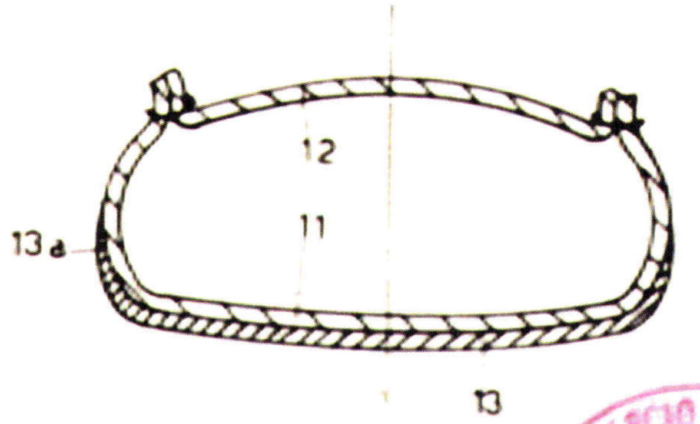

FIG.2

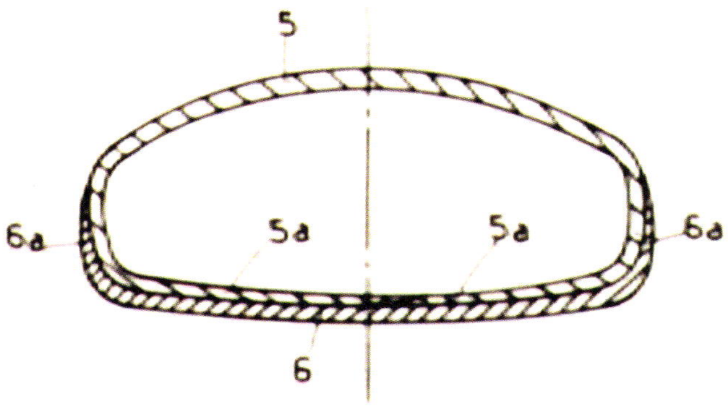

FIG. 3

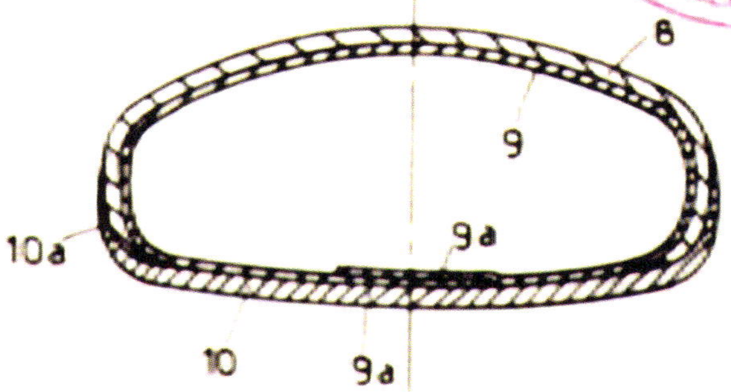

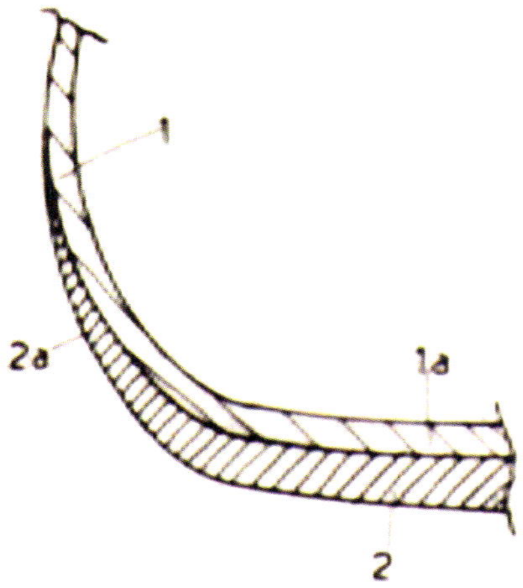

FIG.1

NEW RENAISSANCE

P. 300
SALVATORE FERRAGAMO AMONG CRAFTSMEN IN HIS WORKSHOP AT PALAZZO SPINI FERONI, C. 1939

SALVATORE FERRAGAMO'S TOOLS AND WORKBENCH, LATE 1930s. MUSEO FERRAGAMO, FLORENCE

18-KARAT GOLD SANDAL, 1956. MODEL CREATED IN PARTNERSHIP WITH GOLDSMITHS AT THE PALAZZO DELL'ORO NEAR PONTE VECCHIO IN FLORENCE

DETAIL OF CHISELED FLOWER ON THE GOLDEN SANDAL

ANTONIO DI SALVI, *"PACE" REPRESENTING THE LAMENTATION OVER THE DEAD CHRIST* (DETAIL), LATE FIFTEENTH CENTURY, CHISELED, ENGRAVED, AND GILDED SILVER, TRANSLUCENT ENAMEL, AND NIELLO ON SILVER. MUSEO NAZIONALE DEL BARGELLO, FLORENCE

ISELWORK
ON THE HEEL OF THE
GOLDEN SANDAL

GRAND DUCAL
WORKSHOPS, GIOVAN
BATTISTA CERVI,
SHELL-SHAPED GOBLET
(DETAIL), 1576, LAPIS
LAZULI, CAST, CHISELED,
AND ENAMELED GOLD.
GALLERIE DEGLI UFFIZI,
TESORO DEI GRANDUCHI,
FLORENCE

CREATIVITY IN COLOR

OF *DIVA*,
1941

P. 308

PRUA, SUEDE AND CALFSKIN, 1953–54; *FIAMMA*, SUEDE AND KIDSKIN, 1950; *MONA*, SUEDE AND CALFSKIN, 1955; KIDSKIN AND CALFSKIN LACED SHOE WITH LAYERED WEDGE HEEL IN COVERED CORK, 1947; KIDSKIN SANDAL WITH LAYERED WEDGE HEEL IN COVERED CORK, 1945–47; SUEDE SANDAL WITH LAYERED WEDGE HEEL AND PLATFORM IN COVERED CORK, 1940

KIDSKIN SANDAL WITH LAYERED WEDGE HEEL AND PLATFORM IN COVERED CORK, 1942; KIDSKIN SANDAL WITH LAYERED WEDGE HEEL AND PLATFORM IN COVERED CORK, 1942; KIDSKIN SANDAL WITH LAYERED WEDGE HEEL IN COVERED CORK, 1938; KIDSKIN SANDAL WITH LAYERED WEDGE HEEL IN COVERED CORK, 1947

LEFT TO RIGHT: *INVISIBILE*, NYLON THREAD AND KIDSKIN WITH SHAPED WEDGE HEEL IN COVERED WOOD, 1947; *POPPEA*, KIDSKIN AND PVC WITH SHAPED WEDGE HEEL IN COVERED WOOD, 1959

ESTASI, SUEDE, 1955; SUEDE SANDAL, 1949; SUEDE AND KIDSKIN SANDAL WITH WEDGE HEEL IN COVERED CORK, 1939; SUEDE SANDAL WITH WEDGE HEEL AND PLATFORM IN COVERED CORK LAYERS, DESIGNED IN 1942 FOR CARMEN MIRANDA; SUEDE AND KIDSKIN SANDAL WITH LAYERED WEDGE HEEL IN COVERED CORK, 1946; *MARINA*, SUEDE, 1939

TOP TO BOTTOM: SEA LEOPARD PUMP, 1959; SILK SATIN MULE, 1955–56; *INVISIBILE*, NYLON THREAD AND CALFSKIN WITH SHAPED WEDGE HEEL IN COVERED WOOD, 1947

KIDSKIN LACED SHOE WITH WEDGE HEEL IN COVERED CORK, 1942; CALFSKIN SANDAL WITH LAYERED WEDGE HEEL IN COVERED CORK, 1940; KIDSKIN AND LIZARD BROGUE SHOE, 1929

TOP TO BOTTOM:
TIRASSEGNO, SUEDE AND KIDSKIN, 1957; CALFSKIN SANDAL, 1950; *DRAPIA*, SUEDE AND CALFSKIN, 1950–52

SPAGHETTI, SUEDE, 1938; *DIVA*, SUEDE WITH LAYERED WEDGE HEEL IN COVERED CORK, 1941; SUEDE CLOSED SHOE WITH LAYERED WEDGE HEEL IN COVERED CORK, 1942

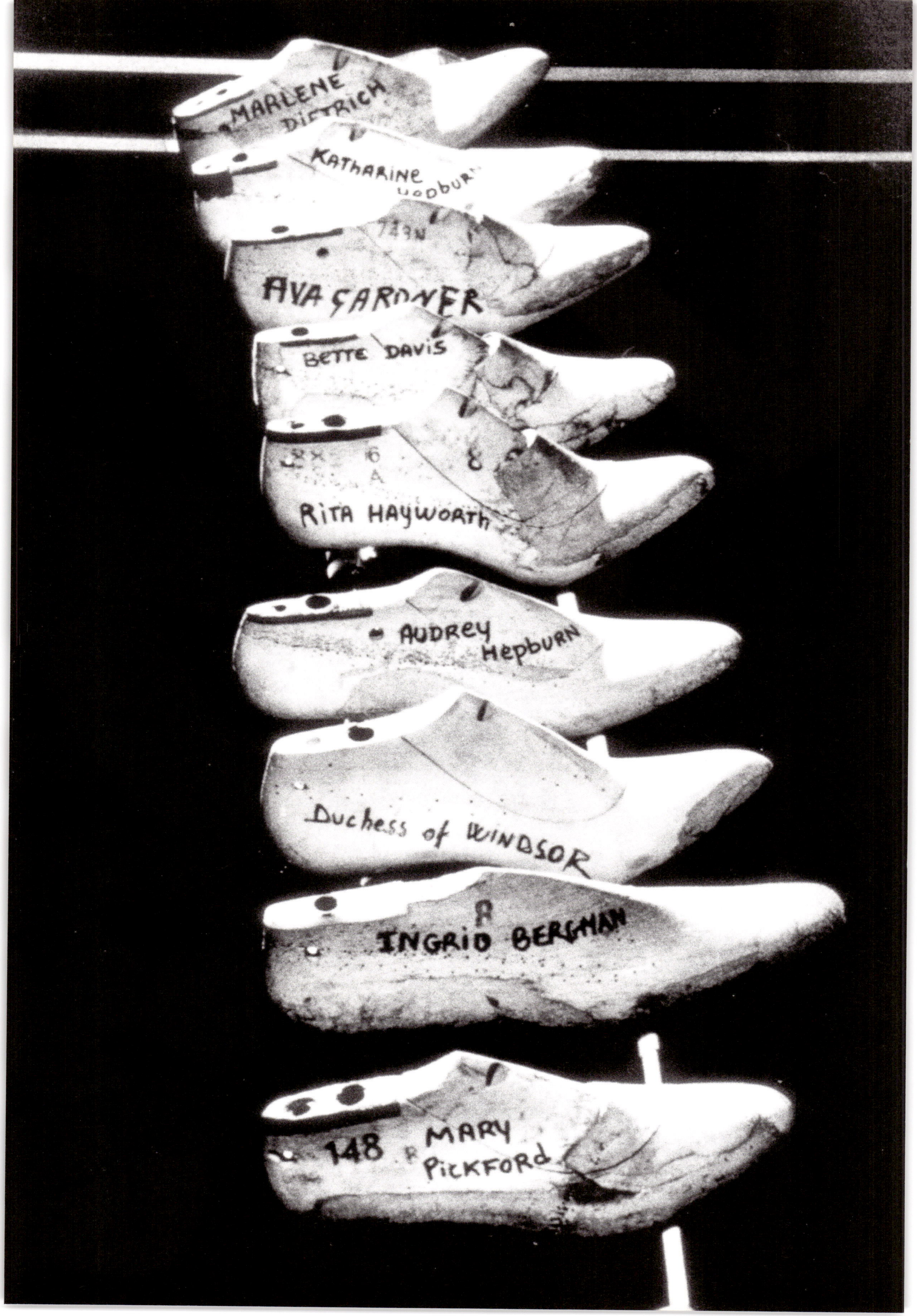
MARLENE DIETRICH
Katharine Hepburn
AVA GARDNER
BETTE DAVIS
RITA HAYWORTH
AUDREY Hepburn
Duchess of WINDSOR
INGRID BERGMAN
148
MARY PICKFORD

SHOES AND FAMOUS FEET

P. 324
WOODEN LASTS OF THE FEET OF SOME FAMOUS SALVATORE FERRAGAMO CLIENTS, 1950s

MARLENE DIETRICH, 1940s

ANTARTIA, SUEDE AND KIDSKIN, 1938; CALFSKIN PUMP, 1950. BOTH MODELS WERE DESIGNED FOR MARLENE DIETRICH

CALFSKIN AND SUEDE CLOSED SHOE WITH WEDGE HEEL IN COVERED CORK, 1940. MODEL DESIGNED FOR KATHARINE HEPBURN

KATHARINE HEPBURN WEARING FERRAGAMO SHOES IN *THE PHILADELPHIA STORY*, DIRECTED BY GEORGE CUKOR, 1940

Indira Devi
1934

INDIAN PRINCESS INDIRA DEVI, MAHARANI OF COOCH BEHAR, 1934

SILK SATIN AND KIDSKIN SANDAL WITH CORK PLATFORM COVERED IN VELVET AND BRASS FRAMEWORK STUDDED WITH STONES, 1938. MODEL DESIGNED FOR INDIRA DEVI

RAINBOW, KIDSKIN AND SUEDE WITH LAYERED HEEL AND PLATFORM IN COVERED CORK, 1938. MODEL DESIGNED FOR ACTRESS JUDY GARLAND

JUDY GARLAND AT GRAND CENTRAL STATION, NEW YORK, 1939

20

THE SINGER AND ACTRESS CARMEN MIRANDA WITH HER COLLECTION OF SHOES, 1944

SILK SATIN AND KIDSKIN SANDAL WITH CORK HEEL AND PLATFORM COVERED WITH MOSAIC-PATTERNED MIRRORS, 1939. MODEL DESIGNED FOR CARMEN MIRANDA

GHILLIE, SUEDE AND KIDSKIN WITH LAYERED WEDGE HEEL IN COVERED CORK, 1937. MODEL DESIGNED FOR PEGGY GUGGENHEIM

PEGGY GUGGENHEIM IN HER ART OF THIS CENTURY GALLERY, NEW YORK, OCTOBER 22, 1942

PRINCESS MARIA JOSÉ OF SAVOY IN A RED CROSS NURSE'S UNIFORM, LATE 1930s

GHILLIE, ANTELOPE AND KIDSKIN WITH WEDGE HEEL IN COVERED CORK, 1938–40. MARIA JOSÉ OF SAVOY ENSURED THE MODEL BECAME PART OF THE RED CROSS UNIFORM

RAFFIA SANDAL WITH
SHAPED CORK HEEL, 1938.
MODEL DESIGNED FOR
ACTRESS LORETTA YOUNG

LORETTA YOUNG,
LATE 1930s

CLARETTA PETACCI,
C. 1940

CROCODILE SANDAL
WITH LAYERED WEDGE
HEEL AND PLATFORM IN
COVERED CORK, 1938–39.
MODEL DESIGNED FOR
CLARETTA PETACCI

KIDSKIN SANDAL WITH LAYERED WEDGE HEEL AND PLATFORM IN COVERED CORK, 1939; SUEDE SANDAL WITH LAYERED WEDGE HEEL AND PLATFORM IN COVERED CORK, 1939. BOTH MODELS WERE DESIGNED FOR CLARETTA PETACCI

EDDA MUSSOLINI CIANO,
LATE 1930s

CALFSKIN CLOSED
SHOE, 1938. MODEL
DESIGNED FOR EDDA
MUSSOLINI CIANO

SIRIA, SUEDE WITH LAYERED WEDGE HEEL IN COVERED CORK, 1942–44. MODEL DESIGNED FOR PALMA BUCARELLI, DIRECTOR OF THE GALLERIA NAZIONALE D'ARTE MODERNA IN ROME

PALMA BUCARELLI VISITING THE 24TH VENICE BIENNALE, 1948

AVA GARDNER IN *THE KILLERS*, DIRECTED BY ROBERT SIODMAK, 1946

VELVET AND SILK SATIN SANDAL WITH COVERED WOODEN PLATFORM, 1947. MODEL DESIGNED FOR AVA GARDNER

SUEDE LACED SHOES
WITH WEDGE HEEL IN
COVERED CORK, 1946.
MODEL DESIGNED FOR
ACTRESS LAUREN BACALL

LAUREN BACALL WEARING
FERRAGAMO SHOES, 1946

EVA PERÓN WITH
HUSBAND JUAN DOMINGO
PERÓN, PRESIDENT OF
ARGENTINA, 1951

RABY, SUEDE, 1948–50.
MODEL DESIGNED FOR
EVA PERÓN

TORIA, CALFSKIN, 1949.
MODEL WORN BY GRETA GARBO

GRETA GARBO AT THE PLAZA HOTEL,
NEW YORK, 1946

GRETA GARBO IN LONDON WITH PHOTOGRAPHER CECIL BEATON, NOVEMBER 17, 1951. THE ACTRESS IS WEARING HER FAVORITE FERRAGAMO SHOES

CLOCKWISE, FROM TOP: SUEDE TWO-PIECE SHOE, 1950–55; *ZITA*, SUEDE AND KIDSKIN, 1949; CALFSKIN LACED BALLERINA SHOE WITH SHELL SOLE, 1960; *GRETA*, ANTELOPE, 1959; CALFSKIN LACED SHOE WITH WEDGE HEEL IN COVERED CORK, 1946; *GRETA*, SUEDE, 1959. SHOES WORN BY GRETA GARBO

EMBROIDERED TAVARNELLE LACE AND KIDSKIN SANDAL, 1950. MODEL DESIGNED FOR BALLET DANCER ALICIA MARKOVA

ALICIA MARKOVA WITH SALVATORE FERRAGAMO AT PALAZZO SPINI FERONI, 1949

THE DUKE AND DUCHESS
OF WINDSOR, 1950

CISTIA, CORD AND
CALFSKIN, 1950. MODEL
DESIGNED FOR WALLIS
SIMPSON, DUCHESS
OF WINDSOR

HEMP, RAFFIA STRIPS, AND CALFSKIN SHOE WITH WEDGE HEEL IN COVERED CORK, 1948. MODEL DESIGNED FOR ACTRESS VALENTINA CORTESE

SALVATORE FERRAGAMO WITH VALENTINA CORTESE AT PALAZZO SPINI FERONI, 1950

SALVATORE FERRAGAMO
WITH ACTRESS GENE
TIERNEY AT PALAZZO
SPINI FERONI, 1951

OXALIA, SUEDE, 1950.
MODEL DESIGNED FOR
GENE TIERNEY

AQUILA, ANTELOPE WITH GLOVED ARCH, 1952

CLAUDETTE COLBERT WEARING FERRAGAMO'S *AQUILA* SHOES ON THE SET OF THE MOVIE *VERSAILLES*, DIRECTED BY SACHA GUITRY, 1953

SALVATORE FERRAGAMO WITH AUDREY HEPBURN AT PALAZZO SPINI FERONI, 1954

SUEDE AND KIDSKIN BALLERINA SHOE WITH SHELL SOLE, 1954; *ARTIA*, SUEDE WITH GLOVED ARCH, 1952. BOTH MODELS WERE DESIGNED FOR AUDREY HEPBURN

ALICIA
RSYC

GRACE KELLY AT THE
CANNES FILM FESTIVAL,
APRIL 1, 1955

SUEDE CLOSED
SHOE, 1952–55.
MODEL DESIGNED
FOR GRACE KELLY

RANINA, TAVARNELLE LACE AND SILK SATIN WITH SEQUINS, VINYLITE LINING, 1955. MODEL DESIGNED FOR ANNA MAGNANI

SALVATORE FERRAGAMO WITH ANNA MAGNANI AT PALAZZO SPINI FERONI, 1955

MADONNA, TAVARNELLE LACE AND KIDSKIN WITH BEADED APPLIQUÉ, 1955. MODEL DESIGNED FOR SOPHIA LOREN

SOPHIA LOREN AND SALVATORE FERRAGAMO AT THE OPEN GATE CLUB IN ROME, FEBRUARY 28, 1955

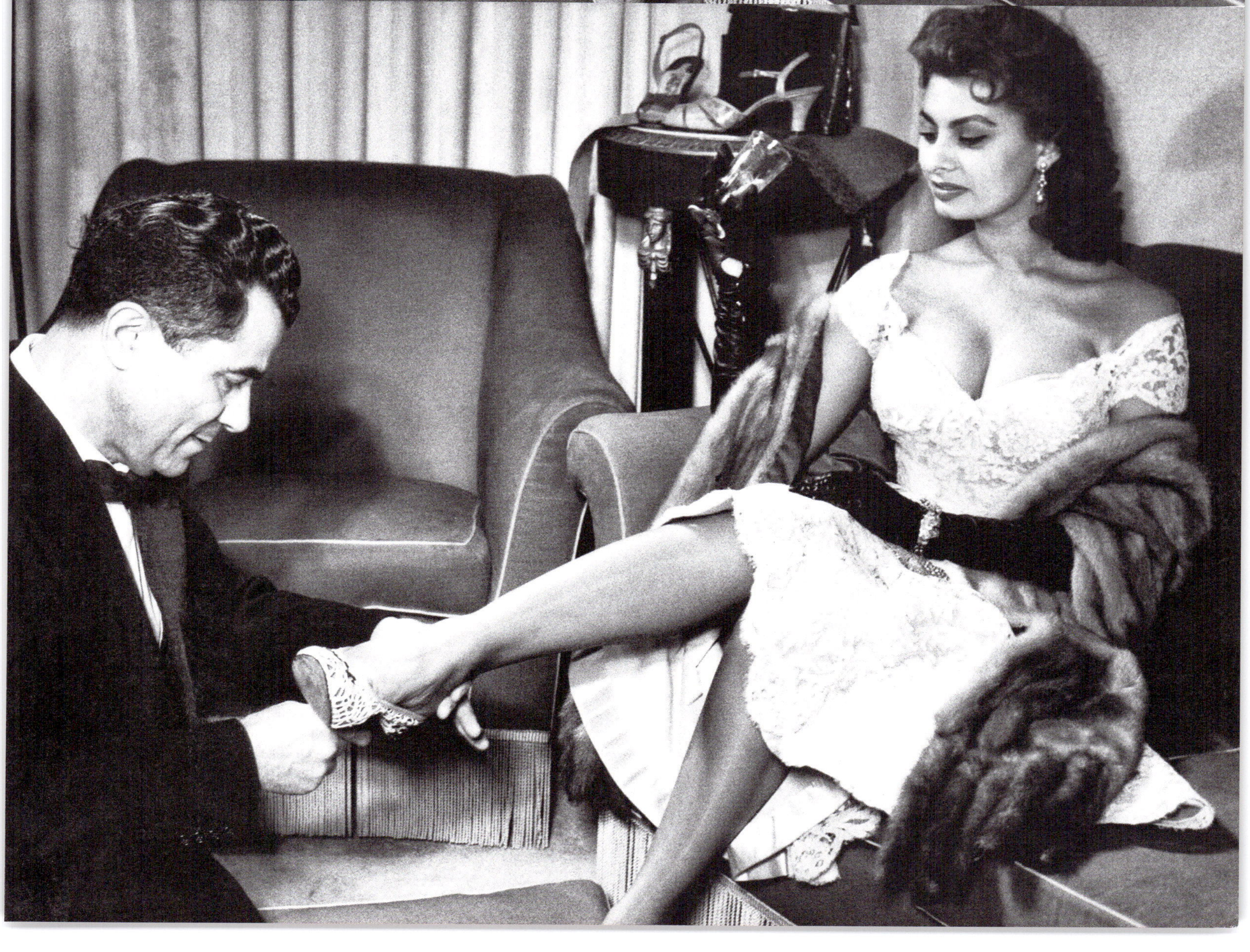

DAMIGELLA, STRETCH BROCADE FABRIC, 1957. MODEL DESIGNED FOR SOPHIA LOREN

CROCODILE PUMP, 1959–60. MODEL DESIGNED FOR MARILYN MONROE

MARILYN MONROE WEARING THE FAMOUS FERRAGAMO PUMP MODEL, 1962

MARILYN MONROE WEARING FERRAGAMO SHOES IN *SOME LIKE IT HOT*, DIRECTED BY BILLY WILDER, 1959

PUMP COVERED IN SWAROVSKI RHINESTONES. MODEL DESIGNED FOR MARILYN MONROE IN *LET'S MAKE LOVE*, DIRECTED BY GEORGE CUKOR, 1960

PUMP MODELS DESIGNED BY FERRAGAMO, PART OF MARILYN MONROE'S PERSONAL WARDROBE, 1956–60

MARILYN MONROE
PHOTOGRAPHED
BY WILLY RIZZO IN
BEVERLY HILLS, 1962

BERTILLA, SUEDE
AND CALFSKIN, 1960.
MODEL WORN BY
MARILYN MONROE

PIC NIC, SUEDE AND CALFSKIN WITH SHELL SOLE, 1957. MODEL DESIGNED FOR ARTIST GEORGIA O'KEEFFE

GEORGIA O'KEEFFE WEARING HER *PIC NIC* SHOES, ABIQUIU (NEW MEXICO), 1966

SALVATORE FERRAGAMO
WITH ACTRESS PAULETTE
GODDARD AT PALAZZO
SPINI FERONI, 1959

SALVINA, SUEDE AND
CALFSKIN, 1959. MODEL
DESIGNED FOR PAULETTE
GODDARD

ARBIA, SUEDE AND CALFSKIN WITH SHELL SOLE, 1960; SUEDE BALLERINA SHOE, 1960. BOTH MODELS WERE PURCHASED BY INGRID BERGMAN

INGRID BERGMAN, 1958

LANA TURNER IN
IMITATION OF LIFE,
DIRECTED BY DOUGLAS
SIRK, 1959

TEXTURED SILK FABRIC
PUMPS, 1960. THE
MODEL WAS DESIGNED
FOR LANA TURNER
AND WAS PART OF HER
PERSONAL WARDROBE

AGNOLA, SUEDE, 1960.
MODEL DESIGNED
FOR PRINCESS MARIA
GABRIELLA OF SAVOY

SALVATORE FERRAGAMO
WITH MARIA GABRIELLA
OF SAVOY AT PALAZZO
SPINI FERONI, 1958

SALVATORE FERRAGAMO

1898–1960

Salvatore Ferragamo 1898–1960
Museo Ferragamo
Palazzo Spini Feroni, Florence
October 27, 2023
November 4, 2024

Exhibition promoted and organized by
Fondazione Ferragamo, Florence
Museo Ferragamo, Florence

Under the Patronage of
Ministero della Cultura
Regione Toscana
Comune di Firenze

Exhibition curator
Stefania Ricci

With the scholarly contribution of
Chiara Fucci

Museo Ferragamo Scholarly Committee
Arturo Galansino
Davide Rampello
Angelica Visconti

Exhibition design
Green Spirit

Scenic design of first room
Leonardo Filippini

Multimedia installation
"La man che ubbidisce all'intelletto" M. Buonarroti
Produced by Rampello & Partners for Museo Ferragamo
Concept: Davide Rampello; Producer: Daniele Rampello; Production Manager: Guja Montanari; Director: Andrea Longhin; Administrative Coordinator: Erika Bignami; shooting crew: Nubifilm Studio; filming: Niccolò Corti, Adamo Scieghi; editing: Claudio Spanu
Craftsmen: Enrico Tallone, Elisa Tallone (Alberto Tallone Editore); Juri Cavallini, Fabio Conti, Jody Baldacci (Salvatore Ferragamo S.p.A.); Katia Maratea, Oriana Castagnozzi, Anna Ciccone (Fondazione Arte della Seta Lisio); Luca Ciaccheri, Daniela Messeri (Nerdi Orafi Firenze); Riccardo Bisazza, Laura Tonicello, Valentina Baldin, Matteo Baldini, Manuela Bonicelli, Domenica (Monica) Bottalico, Michele Giuman, Sara Rollo, Viviana Stefani, Williams Vianello, Rossella Zanninello (Orsoni Venezia 1888); Mariagiovanna Casagrande, Annamaria Bacolla, Blesila Borja, Laura Bosinon, Silvana Macciò, Maria Maddalena Zurletti (Cooperativa Lou Dzeut)

Video
First room videos and *Hollywood Boot Shop*, edited by Rocco Gurrieri

Graphic design
RovaiWeber design

Exhibition installation
Opera Laboratori Fiorentini

Shoe restoration
Opera Laboratori Fiorentini
(Antonio Frenna, Head of Restoration Center and Carla Molin Pradel, Technical Director)
Salvatore Ferragamo S.p.A.
(Daniele Talini, Production Manager and Juri Cavallini, Internal Shoes Factory Coordinator)

Organization secretariat
Bianca Arcangioli
Benedetta Bonfigli
Marta De Michelis
Eleonora Geppi
Ottavia Guenzi
Paola Gusella
Giulia Pettini
Tommaso Pieri

Education
Maria Ida De Ioanni

Multimedia
AVUELLE

Lighting
Watt Studio

Insurance
AON

Shipping
Apice Firenze

MINISTERO DELLA CULTURA

REGIONE TOSCANA

COMUNE DI FIRENZE

FERRAGAMO MUSEO

FONDAZIONEFERRAGAMO

Catalogue

Edited by
Stefania Ricci

Contributors
Chiara Faggella
Arturo Galansino
Elisabetta Nardinocchi
Davide Rampello
Stefania Ricci
Elvira Valleri

Graphic design
RovaiWeber design

Coordination
Ludovica Barabino

Copy editor
Emanuela Di Lallo

Translations
Adam Victor for *Scriptum*, Rome

Photographs of shoes
Roberto Quagli

Photographs of artworks
Arrigo Coppitz
Antonio Quattrone

This project would not have been possible without the unconditional support of the Ferragamo family and Salvatore Ferragamo Company.

The shoes designed by Salvatore Ferragamo, the components, and the leathers belong to the Historical Archive of the Museo Ferragamo.

The photographic reproduction of Salvatore Ferragamo's patents was kindly granted by the Archivio Centrale dello Stato in Rome.

Fondazione Ferragamo and Museo Ferragamo, promoters and organizers of this exhibition, together with the exhibition curator and the editor and contributors to the catalogue, wish to thank the institutions, museums, and private collections that have taken part in the project:

Archivio Centrale dello Stato, Rome
Associazione Museo della Paglia e dell'Intreccio "Domenico Michelacci," Signa (Florence)
Biblioteca Nazionale Centrale di Firenze, Florence
Gallerie degli Uffizi, Tesoro dei Granduchi, Florence
Museo Archeologico Nazionale (Direzione regionale musei della Toscana), Florence
Museo di Arte Sacra, Tavarnelle Val di Pesa (Florence)
Museo di Arte Sacra della Basilica di Santa Maria dell'Impruneta, Impruneta (Florence)
Museo Civico della Paglia, Signa (Florence)
Museo Nazionale del Bargello, Florence
Museo Stibbert, Florence
Sistema Museale di Ateneo, Università degli Studi di Firenze, Florence

Archivio Bice Lazzari, Rome
Archivio Tullio d'Albisola
Atelier degli Artigianelli collection – Fondazione CR Firenze, Florence
Fondazione Massimo e Sonia Cirulli, San Lazzaro di Savena (Bologna)
Fondo Julia & Giangio Banfi
Loretta Caponi collection, Florence
Private collection, Milan. Courtesy Giò Marconi

All private collectors who wished to remain anonymous.

Our gratitude goes to Archivio Foto Locchi of Florence, which in 2024 celebrates 100 years since the founding of the Bottega Foto Locchi, for its important contribution to the iconography of this project.

Our most sincere thanks to Valerio Massimo Miletti for reconstructing Salvatore Ferragamo's family tree and for his kind availability.

In particular, we wish to thank:
Daniela Aleggiani, Giulia Arecco, Jody Baldacci, Rubina Baldi, Giuliano Banfi, Fausto Barbagli, Maria Isabella Barone, Chiara Baroni, Ilaria Bartocci, Angelita Benelli, Luca Bochicchio, Roberto Boddi, Teti Bonsignore, Laëtitia Braquenié-Viot, Klara Bredlow, Federica Brivio, Andrea Brugnoni, Laura Buonocore, Francesco Cacudi, Giuseppe Cacudi, Lorenzo Calcinai, Candida Calosi, Letizia Campana, Lucia Capponi, Stefano Casciu, Piero Castri, Michele Cecchini, Maria Sara Cellai, Elena Chiti, Giulia Ciappi, Sabrina Cicogna, Gianni Cinali, Massimo Cirulli, Sonia Cirulli, Vittoria Cirulli, Ilaria Ciseri, Enrico Colle, Lucilla Conigliello, Paola Conti, Valentina Conticelli, Beatrice Cuniberti, Lorenzo Cusimano, Paola D'Agostino, Deborah D'Ippolito, Gaia Danieli, Daniela De Palma, Roberto De Rose, Franco Del Grosso, Simona Di Marco, Giulia Donini, Stefano Fiordi, Francesca Fiori, Anna Floridia, Marco Fortini, Letizia Franceschini, Riccardo Franci, Simone Frosecchi, Bianca Fugaldi, Simona Fulceri, Angelo Galiotto, Marcella Gastini, Erika Ghilardi, Maria Giannini, Federica Giovannola, Claudio Girasoli, Marco Graziano, Fabio Guadagno, Claudia Guasti, Erin Harris, Antonella Ielpo, Aldo Innocenti, Luciano Iorio, Mario Iozzo, Jasmine Kennedy, Paolo La Morgia, David La Spina, Giovanna Lambroni, Nicoletta Lanciano, Donatella Lapadula, Elisa Lazzerini, Anna Loengard, Cecilia Lorenzoni, Anna Lucarelli, Andrea Madrigali, Barbara Mangione, Giorgio Marconi, Federico Marretti, Roberta Masini, Maria Maugeri, Duccio Mazzanti, Niccolò Mazzoni, Simone Monticelli, Andrea Moresi, Tiziano Mugnai, Niccolò Nava, Alessandro Nencini, Lucia Nocera, Chiara Onniboni, Luigi Oropallo, Giovanna Pecorilla, Francesco Pergolini, Gianni Piolanti, Susi Piovanelli, Giuseppe Poeta, Muriel Prandato, Claudia Ricchieri, Camilla Rizzo, Oriana Rizzuto, Maria Gloria Roselli, Giovanni Rossello, Stefano Rovai, Vincenzo Russano, Sauro Sallei, Susanna Santoni, Massimo Sanzani, Fabrizio Saska, Cristiana Savoia, Eike D. Schmidt, Bruna Scognamiglio, Lapo Sergi, Raffaella Serra, David Speranzi, Chiara Squarcina, Andrea Staderini, Alessandro Tedesco, Mia Torres, Elisa Vanni, Michele Vasta, Catherine Vautrin, Massimo Vercesi, Silvia Vettori, Marco Vianello, Giuseppe Viesti, Davide Zandomeneghi, Luigi Zanini, Monica Zavattaro, Susanna Weber.

Photo credits

AF Archivi Farabola: p. 369

© Allan Grant / Life Magazine: p. 383

Archivi Alinari, Florence: pp. 2, 438, 449 (bottom and right), 461

Archivio Centrale dello Stato, Rome: pp. 172, 174–176 (patents), 179, 180 (right), 183, 184, 187 (patent), 189, 190, 193, 194, 197 (patent), 198, 201, 202 (bottom), 203–209 (patents), 211 (patent), 213, 214, 216–217 (patents), 219, 221 (left), 223 (bottom), 225, 226, 227 (patent), 229 (patent), 230, 233, 234 (top), 236, 238 (bottom), 240–245 (patents), 247 (patent), 249, 250 (bottom), 253–257 (patents), 259, 260 (patent), 263, 264, 267 (left), 268, 271, 273 (left), 275, 277 (patent), 279, 280, 283, 284 (patent), 285, 286–287 (patents), 288, 289 (patent), 291, 292 (patent), 294, 296, 299, 444 (center and bottom), 445, 452, 460, 462 (top), 489 (top), 497, 498

Archivio di Stato di Firenze – courtesy Ministero della Cultura. Photo Paola Conti: p. 244 (bottom)

Archivio Fondazione 3M. Photo Ghitta Carell: p. 338

© Archivio Foto Locchi, Florence: pp. 70, 150 (center right and bottom left), 153, 361, 365, 366, 370, 371, 377, 392, 399, 412, 449 (center), 469 (bottom center), 470, 477, 490, 492 (top center)

Archivio Fotografico del Sistema Museale di Ateneo, Università degli Studi di Firenze, Florence: pp. 44, 45, 74, 77

© Archivio Storico della Biennale di Venezia, ASAC: p. 349

Biblioteca di Storia Moderna e Contemporanea, Rome: p. 457

Biblioteca Nazionale Centrale di Firenze, Florence – Courtesy Ministero della Cultura. Any further reproduction by any means is prohibited: pp. 36, 53, 91 (top)

Cecil Beaton Studio Archive at Sotheby's: p. 357

© Contrasto, Rome: pp. 9, 10, 432 (top)

Courtesy Archivio Bice Lazzari: p. 99 (top)

Courtesy Archivio Fotografico Fondazione Massimo e Sonia Cirulli: pp. 87, 89, 96

Courtesy Giò Marconi, Milan. Photo Fabio Mantegna: pp. 91 (bottom), 95 (bottom right)

Courtesy Santa Barbara Historical Museum: pp. 423, 424 (bottom), 425 (bottom)

Courtesy The State Hermitage Museum, St. Petersburg: p. 149

Direzione regionale Musei del Veneto – Collezione Salce, Treviso: p. 410

© Ezra Stoller / Esto: pp. 144, 171

Fondazione Musei Civici di Venezia, Museo di Palazzo Mocenigo: pp. 120, 472 (top center)

Foto Fulvio Rosso, Calice Ligure (Savona): p. 93

Foto Scala, Florence – Courtesy Ministero della Cultura: pp. 492 (bottom), 493

Gabinetto Fotografico delle Gallerie degli Uffizi: p. 495 (bottom left). Photo Antonio Quattrone: pp. 307 (right), 495 (bottom right)

Getty Images. Bettmann: pp. 11, 326, 329, 333, 362, 428 (bottom); Corbis Historical: p. 342; Corbis Historical / Photo David Lees: p. 156; Gamma-Keystone: pp. 346, 374; Hulton Archive: p. 8; New York Daily News: pp. 21, 433; The Chronicle Collection / Photo David Lees: p. 324; Ullstein bild: p. 22

Los Angeles Public Library: p. 429 (bottom)

Museo Archeologico Nazionale (Direzione regionale musei della Toscana). Photo Antonio Quattrone: pp. 55 (bottom), 65

Museo di Arte Sacra della Basilica di Santa Maria dell'Impruneta (Florence). Photo Antonio Quattrone: p. 496 (bottom)

Museo Ferragamo, Florence: pp. 13, 14, 18, 25, 26, 30, 55 (top), 57, 63 (top left), 95 (top left), 118, 137, 147, 150 (top, center left, and bottom right), 151, 157, 160 (top left), 161 (right), 166 (bottom left),169, 180 (top left), 202 (top), 206, 210, 221 (right), 223 (top), 224, 228, 234 (bottom), 238 (top), 247 (background), 250 (top), 253 (background), 267 (right), 273 (right), 276, 330, 334, 341, 353, 354, 358, 379, 395, 396, 406, 408, 416, 418–423, 424 (top center), 425 (top), 426, 428 (top center), 429 (center), 430, 431, 432 (bottom), 434–436, 440, 441, 442 (center), 444 (top), 446, 447, 448 (top), 449 (top), 450, 451, 453 (bottom), 454–456, 458, 459 (right), 462 (bottom), 463–467, 472 (bottom), 473–476, 482, 484–486, 488 (bottom), 489 (bottom), 500. Photo Arrigo Coppitz: pp. 63 (top right and bottom), 81, 100, 103, 126, 129, 132, 146, 306 (right), 462 (center), 496 (top), 502–507. Photo Christopher Broadbent: pp. 439, 443, 448 (bottom), 453 (top), 459 (bottom), 487 (bottom), 489 (center). Photo David Lees: p. 300. Photo Giuseppe Palmas: pp. 150 (bottom right), 152. Photo Marco Palermo: pp. 468, 469 (left and top right). Foto Roberto Quagli: pp. 4–7, 12, 15, 16, 19, 20, 23, 24, 27–29, 31–34, 37–43, 46–52, 54, 56, 58, 59, 61, 62, 64, 67–69, 71–73, 75, 76, 78–80, 82–86, 88, 90, 92, 94, 97, 98, 99 (bottom), 101, 102, 104–117, 119, 121–125, 127, 128, 130, 131, 133–136, 138–140, 148, 154, 155, 160–161 (center), 162–163 (top), 164, 165, 166 (top), 167, 168, 170, 174–176 (shoes), 178, 181, 182, 185, 187 (shoe), 188, 191, 192, 195, 196, 197 (shoe), 199, 200, 203 (shoe), 204, 205 (shoe), 207 (shoe), 208–209 (shoes), 211 (shoe), 212, 215, 216 (shoe), 217 (shoe), 218, 220, 222, 227 (shoe), 229 (framework), 231, 232, 235, 237, 239, 240–243 (shoes), 245, 246, 248, 251, 252, 254–257 (shoes), 258, 260 (shoe), 261, 262, 265, 266, 269, 270, 272, 274, 277 (shoe), 278, 281, 282, 284 (shoe), 286 (shoe), 287 (shoe), 289 (shoe), 290, 292 (shoe), 293, 295, 297, 298, 302–305, 306 (left), 307 (left), 308, 310–323, 327, 328, 331, 332, 335, 336, 339, 340, 343–345, 347, 348, 351, 352, 355, 356, 359, 360, 363, 364, 367, 368, 372, 373, 375, 376, 378, 380–382, 385–387, 389, 390, 393, 394, 397, 398, 442 (top and bottom), 487 (top), 494, 495 (top center)

Museo Stibbert, Florence: pp. 60, 141, 143

Ninfa Valvo papers regarding the M. H. de Young Memorial Museum, 1930–1973. Archives of American Art, Smithsonian Institution: pp. 487 (bottom right), 488 (top)

Photo John Loengard: p. 391

Shutterstock: pp. 350, 384

The Art Institute of Chicago / Art Resource, NY / Scala, Florence: p. 488 (center)

Tom Fitzsimmons / AP / LaPresse: p. 337

Vogue © Condé Nast. Photo André Durst: p. 177. Photo Anton Bruehl: p. 66. Photo Erwin Blumenfeld: p. 180 (bottom left). Photo Irving Penn: pp. 158, 186. Photo Nicolas De Molas: pp. 162–163 (bottom)

© Willy Rizzo: p. 388

Zuma Press: p. 17

STEFANIA
RICCI

INTRODUCTION

A hundred years have elapsed since Salvatore Ferragamo opened his first store in Hollywood in 1923, across from Grauman's Egyptian Theatre. Ever afterward, cementing his success in the United States (to which he had emigrated in 1915), the young man who hailed from Italy's Irpinia region became known as the "Shoemaker to the Stars."

Back then, Los Angeles aspired to become a major cultural and economic hub. Ferragamo was part of the wave of change that was transforming the area into a center of collective imagination. A firm believer in admixing art and industry, economy and culture, he helped transform Hollywood into the city the press of the day referred to as "the Paris of America" and "the art center of the world."

To celebrate this special anniversary, this project retraces the great craftsman's life story and recalls the first Salvatore Ferragamo retrospective exhibition held at Palazzo Strozzi in 1985—a pioneering traveling show that ushered in a new way of viewing fashion as the embodiment of value-led cultural messages. Back then, Ferragamo's shoes were displayed chronologically as artworks, featuring only marginal cross-references to the creative and social context in which he had conceived them. Today, these creations are being showcased not just for their aesthetic worth but as documents that attest to the entrepreneurial and innovative expertise, passion for colors, anatomical knowledge of the human skeleton and foot, extraordinary craftsmanship, research into materials, and a variety of inspirations drawn from the world of ancient and contemporary art and culture that were emblematic of Salvatore Ferragamo's work and life.

After that initial 1985 experience, the Ferragamo Archive was established to collect products and documentation about the company's journey and its key figures. The Museo Ferragamo first opened its doors to the public in 1995, dedicated to preserving and promoting the founder's and brand's history through roundtables, publications, workshops, and exhibitions, projecting past experience and chronicles into the present day to stimulate and influence contemporary debate and thinking.

Today's project is the culmination of retrospective research not just into Salvatore Ferragamo's work and life, but also the corporate museum's role and its underlying curatorial practice, drawing on new insights that on the one hand highlight Ferragamo's contribution to the revival of craftsmanship that defined post-war Made in Italy, and on the other emphasize how, partly thanks to Ferragamo's footwear, Italian design is the expression of a winning combination of decorative and artisan tradition, functionality, and technological innovation.

An analysis of Salvatore Ferragamo's personal library reveals a number of interesting aspects. The books it contains testify to his undeniable and innate propensity to perceive the latest developments in the society of his time, along with a philosophy of life and work that encompasses a broad and deep worldview, one governed by an over-arching, universal, divine wisdom.

SALVATORE FERRAGAMO WITH THE *DAMIGELLA* ANKLE BOOT DESIGNED FOR SOPHIA LOREN, 1959

ARTURO
GALANSINO

SALVATORE FERRAGAMO, A RENAISSANCE ARTIST-CRAFTSMAN

The major *Salvatore Ferragamo 1898–1960* exhibition offers visitors a chance to make countless connections and find many similarities between the life of this Florence-based fashion house's founder, his creative techniques, and various aspects of Renaissance culture and artistic practice.

Salvatore's lyrical autobiography, *Shoemaker of Dreams*, chronicles his educational journey, following time-honored traditions passed down through the generations. Like an aspiring artist driven by a desire to create beautiful and comfortable "shoe-masterpieces," when he was just nine, Salvatore apprenticed himself to the cobbler Luigi Festa at his workshop in Bonito, Irpinia, learning this ancient handmade craft that, at that time, lacked any social prestige.

The tasks young Salvatore was expected to perform would not have been so very different from practices in Renaissance workshops, where learning and production went hand in hand. Beginning in childhood, apprenticeships were long and grueling. For example, Paolo Uccello apprenticed at Lorenzo Ghiberti's workshop, and Giovanni Antonio Sogliani at Lorenzo di Credi's, starting from the simplest tasks to learn the trade step-by-step.

Prospective painters learned how to grind paints; shoemaking apprentices prepared thread for stitching shoes. Salvatore meticulously described the ancient tradition of waxed thread—which was recalled by Franco Sacchetti at the end of the fifteenth century in his *Trecentonovelle*—and, when he finally succeeded in managing it, he felt he was "truly learning the craft."

Under their masters' guidance, young workshop apprentices diligently copied existing works. As they copied, they picked up the diverse techniques that, as part of a comprehensive education, enabled Renaissance artists to be as eclectic as possible. Among the many examples, we can recall that many prominent painters, sculptors, metallurgists, goldsmiths, and other craftsmen learned their trade at Verrocchio's workshop before moving on to expertly fulfill their clients' vision.

Workshop owners' primary duty was to mentor and train their young charges, to give them the skills they needed to start up their own workshop or to take over an existing one. Although such a broad and generous vision was a world away from the petty self-interest of shoemaker Festa, Salvatore's genius did not quail in the face of early challenge. He voraciously continued learning, spurred on by a desire to grasp every technical aspect. Through curiosity, tenacity, and cleverness, he meticulously improved every part of his designs and in a short time started producing true masterpieces in the field of footwear.

Like shoemakers in Salvatore's time, for long centuries artists suffered low social standing. But in fifteenth-century Florence, as artists began studying mathematics,

PIETRO ANNIGONI, *PORTRAIT OF SALVATORE FERRAGAMO*, 1949, OIL ON CANVAS. MUSEO FERRAGAMO, FLORENCE

ALLACCIATURA VARIABILE A VOLONTÀ
PER SPIAGGIA PER PASSEGGIO PER CASA
VENNA
COTVRNO
FERRAGAMO
AUT. DALLA R. Q. DI FIRENZE
NUOVE CREAZIONI VENNA
LIT. P. BENAGLIA - FIRENZE

geometry, and optics, their role gradually diverged from pure craftsmen. This distinction was based on intellectual value and sanctioned by the dedication to Brunelleschi of Leon Battista Alberti's treatise *De pictura* and by Lorenzo Ghiberti's *Commentari*, which initiated the conceptual and scientific theory of artistic activity. This would soon result in lofty achievements such as Leonardo's anatomical drawings, which significantly drove scientific exploration forward.

Salvatore Ferragamo's creative pathway somehow replicated this complex blend of art and science. He knew that to elevate footwear designs to unprecedented heights would take technical expertise, scientific examination, and deep-seated conceptual understanding. Well aware that he had to undertake research, analysis, and experimentation to uncover the "secret" of the "perfect shoe," he felt the need to sign up for an anatomy course at the University of Southern California in Los Angeles. He also studied chemical engineering at the international school in Scranton, Pennsylvania, and attended mathematics courses at the University of Berkeley, California.

The life story of Salvatore Ferragamo that we retrace today in the magnificent rooms of this museum, narrated with expertise and passion by director Stefania Ricci, represents an example—unique in the fashion world—of how, following in the footsteps of Renaissance culture, the combination of exceptional technical skill, boundless creativity, and profound theoretical understanding led to the creation of extraordinary shoes that have become—in every sense—timeless works of art.

LUCIO VENNA, *COTURNO FERRAGAMO*, 1930, ADVERTISING POSTER, CHROMOLITHOGRAPHY ON PAPER. DIREZIONE REGIONALE MUSEI DEL VENETO, COLLEZIONE SALCE, TREVISO

DAVIDE
RAMPELLO

SALVATORE FERRAGAMO. DESIGN CULTURE

Every success story has its special byword, a magic ingredient without which no venture would ever see the light of day. Ferragamo has two: preservation and innovation, holding on tightly to its roots, storied traditions, and the values that paved the way for its reputation and fueled the brand's identity. Ferragamo is one of the world's most iconic fashion names for good reasons: commitment to uncompromising quality, the boldness to deploy that quality right across its shoes, outfits, and accessories, constantly breathing new life into the brand's legacy to ensure resonance with the evolving rhythms of the now. Yes, because fashion keeps a finger on the pulse of new trends, anticipating societal shifts and reshaping them according to the evolving cultural matrix.

Most recently, the Ferragamo brand has seamlessly integrated inclusivity and mindfulness into its production chain, heralding an era deeply rooted in social, environmental, and economic sustainability. This journey of self-reflection is no deviation from the path taken by the company's legendary founder, Salvatore—a path that he and his lineage have pursued with passion for over 60 years now.

Wanda Ferragamo masterfully took the reins of the company after Salvatore passed away in 1960, adding value to the brand with the same spirit of innovation so cherished by her dear departed husband. The results speak for themselves: soaring revenues, a diversified product range, and a global reputation as one of the beacons of Italian haute couture. Wanda artfully merged handcrafted precision with industrial evolution, all with the unwavering support of her children and grandchildren, whom she brought up with love and discipline.

Wanda was deeply in love with her husband. In a bond that transcended his charisma, generosity, and elegance, she loved and was fascinated by the things about him that made him a pioneer of Made in Italy and a founding participant in post-war Italian design.

From a very young age, Salvatore's calling for shoemaking was without equal. His parents struggled to keep him away from the workshop of local cobbler Luigi Festa, where Salvatore learned the basics of his trade. One night, before he reached ten years of age, despite having no practical experience whatsoever, Salvatore sneaked into the basement and crafted a pair of shoes for his sisters' First Communion ceremony the following morning.

These innate skills flourished so triumphantly and successfully because of another vital character trait: curiosity. Salvatore's impulse to care for things (the word *curioso* in Italian stems from the Latin *cura*, meaning "care" or "promptness") spurred him on to research, investigate, and try to understand the world, most notably themes and disciplines related to his art. Without this trait, Salvatore would never have pursued his dreams with such determination and skill. Without this trait, he would never have embarked on the journey that changed his life. In 1915, not yet 17, Salvatore set sail for the United States in search of fortune. On arrival, he found particularly fertile ground for nurturing, developing, and establishing his creative flair: the cinema, a bustling industry, in rapid expansion during the first decades of the twentieth century.

Movie stars put Salvatore on the map as one of the most ingenious and innovative shoemakers of all time. After creating footwear for countless films, he shifted his focus to screen goddesses, landing

SALVATORE FERRAGAMO WITH ONE OF HIS CRAFTSMEN, 1955

top American movie stars as clients, followed by famous Italian actresses Anna Magnani, Franca Valeri, Silvana Mangano, and Sophia Loren, and royalty like the Queen of Italy and the Duchess of Windsor—clients and, in many cases, friends with whom he spent leisure and personal time.

Mingling with California's superstar elite not only brought Salvatore the fame that propelled the Ferragamo brand into the stratosphere, it put him in the midst of a milieu of unparalleled appeal and unique taste. Intellectual interactions and cultural stimulation brought Salvatore new challenges on a daily basis, allowing him to hone his analytical spirit and drive for perfection. He attended anatomy classes at the University of Southern California in Los Angeles, embarking on an academic journey that led to mastery of balancing comfort and creativity, functionality, and aesthetic beauty in shoe design. To ensure utmost comfort and eliminate any discomfort or pain, Salvatore evolved his shoemaking approach to focus not just on foot length but also foot width.

His fame spread throughout the Hollywood film industry and the majors commissioned him to make shoes for their movies. Yet there was still, he felt, something missing.

Between the spring and summer of 1482, Leonardo da Vinci moved to Milan, a rapidly evolving "city under construction" abundant in resources, governed by enlightened, art-loving ruler Ludovico il Moro. There in Milan, Leonardo had the opportunity to work with a field-leading class of engineers and design urban, military, and architectural masterpieces. There in Milan, he found human capital, skills, and technical expertise that welcomed and translated his inventiveness and design vision into tangible works. Something similar was true for Salvatore: America offered nearly everything... everything except genuine craftsmanship. In 1926, this prompted him to return to Italy. He chose Florence to grow his business: its traditions, craftsmanship, beauty, intimacy, and the order of a Renaissance-flavored city provided an ideal environment to build the present and design the future.

Salvatore scoured the entire city and its surroundings for skilled shoemakers. Leveraging his entrepreneurial vision, he divided the staff into specialized groups and assigned each group a specific phase of production, creating a bustling "artisanal factory" in which Italian art and American techniques came together to make the perfect fit.

The first few decades of the twentieth century brought a succession of swift, unpredictable, epoch-changing events: major Futurist-inspired movements, the Russian Revolution, World War I, the Wall Street Crash, the rise of Socialist and Catholic currents in Italian politics, the advent of fascism, Italy declaring war on Ethiopia in 1935, and the subsequent economic sanctions.

The great challenge to find resources and shoemaking materials may have daunted Salvatore, but it certainly did not deter him. Open to and influenced by artistic and cultural currents of varied origins and makeup, kept abreast of and uniquely educated in aesthetic tastes through his Hollywood connections, he started experimenting with materials and form. Supply bottlenecks forced him to come up with unique models using extraordinary materials: paper, cork, felt. He devised special procedures for preparing leather substitutes and for making uppers from raffia, *rascello* (bark of poplar left to soak in chrome), lace. Combined with his innate foresight and entrepreneurial boldness, his movie world experience made him supremely adaptable.

During Italy's post-war economic recovery, he applied for patents for genuine works of structural engineering far removed from shoemaking. The "Sea fortress" and "Multiple-launch torpedo" were just two examples of the revolutionary military designs he conceived during World War II. A highway accident in California, a tragedy in which one of his brothers perished and he risked losing a leg, presented him with another significant challenge: to design a machine that could stretch the injured limb, helping to more easily and swiftly regain the lost inch.

Drawn to engineering, mechanics, anatomy, and architecture, much like in the Renaissance workshops of Florentine masters such as Ghiberti or Verrocchio, Salvatore embodied and radiated a "sense of everything." He cultivated the very same inclination for depth that, in the classical-humanistic era, had freed man's thinking and led to true knowledge. Salvatore's penchant for change, pursuit of knowledge, deep understanding, and a curiosity for everything enabled him to transcend the role of mere shoemaker. Renewing and enriching his craft with a multidisciplinary vision, while at the same time steadfastly preserving its essence and values, Salvatore Ferragamo rose from being a mere skilled artisan to a luminary in the renaissance of Italian design.

STEFANIA
RICCI

SALVATORE FERRAGAMO 1898–1960

Throughout the centuries, stories have guided human evolution toward greater knowledge. Few of them, however, manage to evoke emotions while conveying facts, thoughts, and values. The life and deeds of Salvatore Ferragamo do all this and more. So full of event, feelings, and meaning was his life that it reads like fiction, with all the right ingredients for a movie plot.[1]

The various chapters of this story encompass a real life that spanned the first half of the twentieth century, two wars, and the two worlds of Italy and America. Numerous documents bear witness to his journey, not least documents produced by Salvatore himself, who in lengthy audio recordings in English recounted the milestones in his life, without shying away from the hard times, mistakes, and disappointments he had to cope with.[2] The reason for this audio recording was neither vainglory or self-promotion; it was a desire to convey to his children, and indeed to anyone who appreciated his shoes, the deeper significance of his journey—a journey veined through with his incredible dedication to work as he followed his passion from childhood.

Ferragamo's words also clearly convey what one of the world's humblest professions, that of the shoemaker, meant to him. It was not just about making shoes and selecting quality leathers; it was also knowing about human anatomy and foot structure, finding the creativity to design original models ahead of fashion trends, and having the sensitivity to understand not just customers' tastes but their character and personality. Ferragamo's "autobiographical pact," as he referred to his oral memories,[3] foreshadowed and substantiated the publication of his autobiography, *Shoemaker of Dreams* (1957),[4] in which Salvatore expressed the narrative of his life more fluently, chronologically, with deeper reflections and, most importantly, engaging with time, place, and society—in a word, with history. English writers John Desmond Currie and Elizabeth Warner[5] helped Salvatore write the book. Little is known about them, what we might surmise is that Ferragamo met them through the film industry.

More details of Salvatore's life came out in radio interviews he gave in 1958 in four Australian cities—Melbourne, Adelaide, Sydney, and Brisbane[6]—and became visible through the moving images of the many film reels he shot, starting from when he returned to Italy from the US in 1926 on the *Roma* ocean liner. His home movies capture the journey across the ocean, arrival in Florence, factory

PORTRAIT OF SALVATORE FERRAGAMO, 1958

life, bankruptcy, meeting his wife, their honeymoon, the birth of their children, intimate family moments, birthday parties, and seaside vacations...[7] Every piece of this intense story is genuine: documents, letters, photographs, historical films, press clippings, patents, prototypes, and work tools attest to its authenticity. Effectively his own first archivist, Ferragamo collected all this; after his death, his family carefully preserved these testaments, adding more content through research conducted over the years for various exhibitions dedicated to this great craftsman and artist. Professionally organized, catalogued, and restored for future generations, this precious heritage is preserved in the Ferragamo Archive in Florence and is the cornerstone of the Museo Ferragamo, dedicated to the company founder. The life and works of this "amazing shoemaker" in the museum's halls are more than just a nostalgic recollection of an alluring past, they shine a light on the present day and offer insights into the future. Every day, people come for seminars, lectures, study courses, exhibitions, publications, or to research articles and interviews. Without this documentation and its analytical study, Salvatore's life story would probably not have fallen into obscurity, but it would certainly not have been as vibrant and cherished as it is.

From Bonito to Ellis Island

Salvatore Ferragamo was born on June 5, 1898 in Bonito, Irpinia, around a hundred kilometers from Naples. He grew up in a three-story building on the road that cut through the village, near the main square where the Town Hall stands. Destroyed in a devastating earthquake in 1980, it was subsequently rebuilt in popular housing style. The original appearance of Salvatore's house is documented by some old postcards and a few photos from villagers, proud of their renowned fellow citizen.[8]

Salvatore was the eleventh of fourteen siblings. The majority of the community, including his parents, were farmers. They fed themselves with their own harvest and made a little money selling wine, wheat, and oil from their land, which was around four hectares or slightly more. Back then, life in the South of Italy was a struggle: people barely made enough money to cover their debts. However, with great sacrifice, Antonio and Mariantonia Ferragamo managed to educate their eldest son, who graduated from Naples University. Blessed with extraordinary intelligence, Agostino quickly secured a teaching position at the University of Florence. Sadly, he would never start work: he fell ill with pneumonia and died at the age of 21.[9] As Salvatore recalled in his memoirs, it was as if a door had slammed shut on the whole family.[10] There was no more money to educate any other children; the only viable option was emigration, a painful fate common to many Italians in that period, as we know from migratory chains. Between 1812 and 1915, over 220,000 Irpinians emigrated to various parts of the world, followed later by their families.[11] Salvatore's elder brothers and sisters set off for the United States, hoping to live a life with greater dignity.[12]

There was no option to continue education beyond elementary school in Bonito at the turn of the twentieth cen-

VIEW OF BONITO; MAIN STREET, WITH SALVATORE FERRAGAMO'S HOUSE; THE TOWN HALL SQUARE

tury. Aged just nine, Salvatore was too young to leave, so he had to get a job. Since his youngest years, he had felt an immense passion for one profession: shoemaking, for centuries regarded as the humblest of jobs—practically, a misfortune. And yet in all world mythologies, shoemaking has a special aura, closely bound up with its evident ability to transform materials, to change the appearance of leather and hides. Shoemakers' stores have always been places where people meet and discuss life's great mysteries.[13]

From the time he was a little child, Salvatore spent his days watching Luigi Festa, the village cobbler, as his hands worked their quotidian artisanal magic. His parents tried to dissuade him from taking up this occupation: first, they sent him to work as an apprentice tailor, then to a barber, then to a carpenter's workshop—but to no avail. Salvatore got the chance to show this was his vocation almost by chance when his younger sisters, Giuseppina and Rosina, were scheduled to take their First Communion. Tradition dictated that the girls should wear white shoes to church, but their older sisters' shoes were too worn, and the family had no money to buy new ones. Certain dishonor awaited. Salvatore felt duty-bound to resolve the problem. He procured some white cloth, glue, a handful of nails, a piece of cardboard, two forms, and everything he needed from Mastro Luigi. That night, he secretly made his first-ever pairs of shoes. The next morning, the girls proudly wore their new little white shoes, surprising the whole village.[14]

This early event in Salvatore's life, so evocative it could be the start of a fairy tale, reveals so much about his character, his determination to always move forward, to overcome every obstacle, not to mention how much he loved this work, which he thought of as his "mission."

So it was that Salvatore began an apprenticeship with the town's cobbler, working seven days a week. He started out at the bottom, doing the most humble tasks: straightening nails and cleaning the shop up. His duties occasionally included taking care of Mastro Luigi's kids. Salvatore quickly mastered the art of shoemaking: sketching out designs on the mold, cutting leather, sewing uppers, preparing shoe bases, attaching the heel and sole. His talents soon helped the shop branch out: in addition to repairs and shoes for farmers, they began crafting women's designs. Before long, Salvatore had taken over measuring feet from his master, and while doing this, he noted a peculiar inconsistency: even with the same foot measurements, sometimes shoes fit, sometimes they didn't. This challenge led him to seek answers, first beyond Bonito, then beyond Italy.

In 1912, Salvatore's father suddenly died[15] and the family was plunged into penury. Salvatore's modest earnings, added to savings that his siblings sent from America, were no longer enough. Although he had a stable job and was beginning to reap some success, and despite his awareness that his mother depended completely on him, Salvatore felt that he had learned everything he could from Luigi Festa, and decided to leave Bonito for Naples. Attractive to many, Naples was a city of stark contrasts, as seen in a rare 1911 film: streets and shops oozing elegance, a nod to its past as the Bourbon Kingdom's capital, with grand theaters and

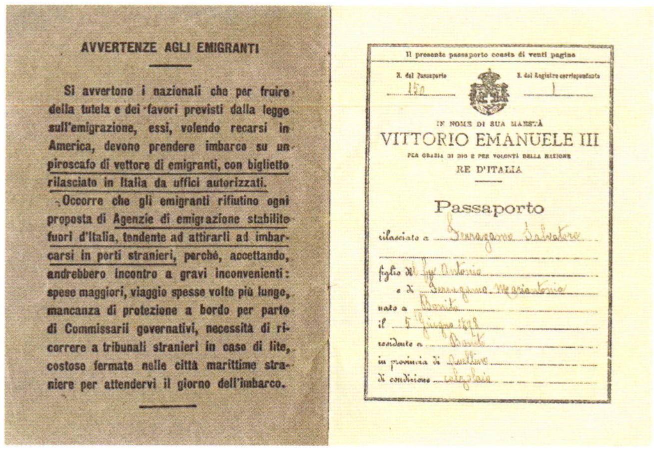

AVVERTENZE AGLI EMIGRANTI

Si avvertono i nazionali che per fruire della tutela e dei favori previsti dalla legge sull'emigrazione, essi, volendo recarsi in America, devono prendere imbarco su un piroscafo di vettore di emigranti, con biglietto rilasciato in Italia da uffici autorizzati.

Occorre che gli emigranti rifiutino ogni proposta di Agenzie di emigrazione stabilite fuori d'Italia, tendente ad attirarli ad imbarcarsi in porti stranieri, perchè, accettando, andrebbero incontro a gravi inconvenienti: spese maggiori, viaggio spesse volte più lungo, mancanza di protezione a bordo per parto di Commissarii governativi, necessità di ricorrere a tribunali stranieri in caso di lite, costose fermate nelle città marittime straniere per attendervi il giorno dell'imbarco.

Il presente passaporto consta di venti pagine

N. del Passaporto 150 — N. del Registro corrispondente 1

IN NOME DI SUA MAESTÀ
VITTORIO EMANUELE III
PER GRAZIA DI DIO E PER VOLONTÀ DELLA NAZIONE
RE D'ITALIA

Passaporto

rilasciato a Ferragamo Salvatore
figlio del fu Antonio
e di Ferragamo Mariantonia
nato a Bonito
il 5 Giugno 1898
residente a Bonito
in provincia di Avellino
di condizione calzolaio

SALVATORE FERRAGAMO'S FIRST PASSPORT, 1915. MUSEO FERRAGAMO, FLORENCE

THE *STAMPALIA* OCEAN LINER (PREVIOUSLY *OCEANIA*)

cinemas, and yet, right next door, stench-filled neighborhoods mired in poverty.[16]

Life in Naples turned out to be a real challenge for Salvatore. From a small village and with mere cents in his pocket, he shared lodgings with other villagers, all apprentices, all battling similar penury. "In Bonito we had never lived luxuriously," Salvatore penned, "but we had never gone without food. In Naples there were many days when I missed meals."[17] This is what it was like to make the arduous transition from rural to urban in the lead-up to World War I, the living conditions precarious to say the least, especially in southern Italy.

Driven by an insatiable and lifelong thirst for knowledge, young Salvatore did not give up. We do not know where he began his apprenticeship in Naples. It may have been in the Fontanelle neighborhood, a bustling artisan workshop district, or on Via dei Calzolai in the San Pietro a Patierno district. Nor do we know which shoe shop he ended up in —in his words, one the finest in town—in the attempt to finally discover the secret of the perfect shoe.

The young man learned everything there was to know about artisanal shoes in just a few days. Ferragamo later speculated that his rapid learning was perhaps a sign that, in a previous life, he had been a shoemaker—a recurring theme in his autobiography. "It simply seemed to me that when they had pointed out the work that must be done, the knowledge came back as if I had been reminded of a task I had forgotten, as if I was undergoing a refresher course of things I had learned in the past. Perhaps it was absurd, but that is how it seemed to my mind."[18] These words, which he wrote when he was 59, referred not to mere memories, they were the reflections of a man in his maturity, a man who had come to understand the true essence of life and wished to share what he'd learned with others. References to Plato's theory of Anamnesis, part of many Eastern religious disciplines and echoed in the Theosophical doctrine popular in the US when Salvatore was beginning to make his way in the world, abound in books preserved in his Florentine library, the culmination of an investigative journey Ferragamo had begun during his early years in California, where, as elsewhere in the US, a wide array of religious practices denoted an openness to various forms of spirituality, underpinned by a belief in a single, universal "divine wisdom" that lay at the heart of all religions.[19]

Salvatore did not stay in Naples for long; certainly not long enough to resolve the mysteries of shoe fitting—a secret that not even the most skilled local artisans could reveal to him. He decided to return to Bonito and, thanks to a small loan from Uncle Alessandro, a priest in Cervinara (another village in Irpinia) who would help him out again in the future, he managed to open his own store. A modest space carved out of his home, between the front door opening onto the street and the kitchen, the store was a far cry from the luxurious setting of Salvatore's Naples apprenticeship. But it was good enough to start. Salvatore hired two assistants: an 18-year-old with some experience at another shoemaker's, and a young lad whose job was to straighten nails. "It was like a fairy-story, my dreaming; and, of course, it *was* a fairy story. Instead of playing the comedies with the other boys of my own age, I was playing at work."[20] An artist at heart, Ferragamo's life knew no boundary between private and public.

In a very short span of time, he became a successful entrepreneur with six employees, all older than him. But that wasn't enough for this ambitious young man. His siblings kept telling him to travel out to the United States and join them. Not only was wealth and fame apparently within reach out there, the shoe industry had made significant strides and brought in innovative new methods.

This was too much for Salvatore to resist, and he resolved to leave Bonito again. On March 24, 1915, his name appeared on the passenger list of the *Stampalia* ocean liner, departing from Naples for New York. He purchased a third-class ticket for 200 lire, entitling him to a berth in a dingy, smelly, six-person cabin. So he decided to stump up more than half of his remaining funds, an additional 75 lire, to upgrade to second class. This came with perks more important than just a cleaner bed for the 15-day journey: it had the advantage of bypassing the lengthy arrival inspections at Ellis Island, because, considered wealthy enough not to be a burden on the American state, first- and second-class passengers underwent on-board inspection.

To gain entry to the US, Ferragamo had to prove to the immigration office that he possessed at least 20 dollars and that, being underage, he was traveling with an adult. He recalls wrapping what little money he had left, only one dollar, around a paper roll secured with a rubber band, hoping customs officials busy with the stream of migrants would fail to notice his subterfuge. He asked a kind stranger on board to act as his accompanying adult, only to lose sight of him on disembarkation. Nonetheless, he managed to bluff his way through the inspections.[21] It was April 7, 1915. Salvatore was just one of many Italians arriving in New York; a lot of them, like him, were shoemakers or cobblers, others were leather workers, tailors, seamstresses, masons, barbers.[22] Gifted with bravery and a miraculously positive mindset, Salvatore did not feel lost in the least: "America beckoned me. I felt at

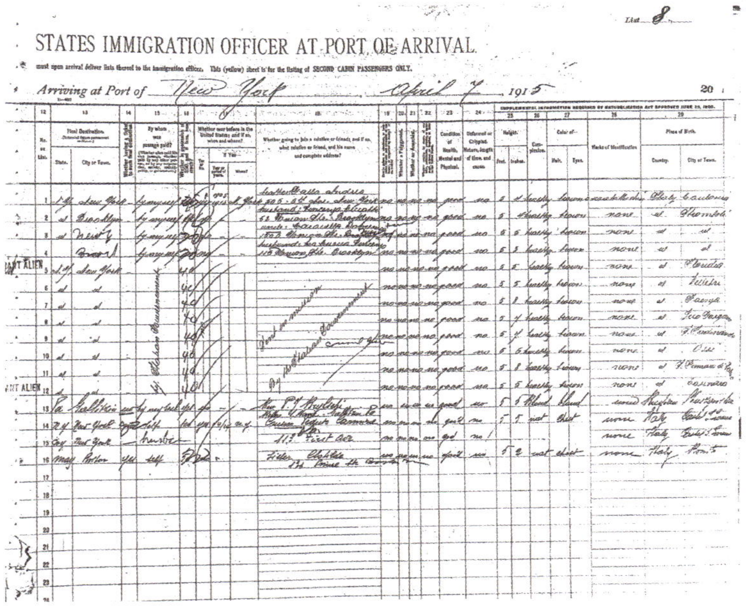
STATES IMMIGRATION OFFICER AT PORT OF ARRIVAL
Arriving at Port of New York April 7 1915

ARRIVAL AT ELLIS ISLAND,
APRIL 7, 1915

THE THOMAS G. PLANT SHOE FACTORY IN BOSTON AND ITS MANUFACTURING DEPARTMENT

SALVATORE FERRAGAMO'S FIRST SAVINGS BOOK, 1915. MUSEO FERRAGAMO, FLORENCE

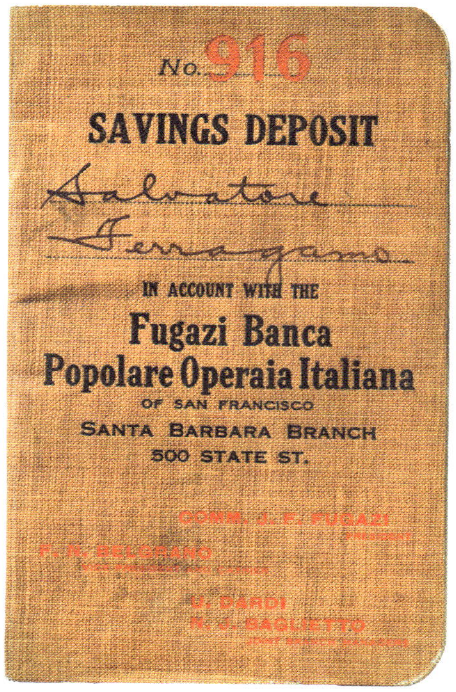

home there even before my feet touched soil. It was all new, huge, and impressive; and I remember thinking that here I could carve a way for myself. It was a country, I knew instinctively, in which I could be at home."[23]

The Santa Barbara years

Salvatore traveled on to Boston, where his sister Clotilde and brother-in-law Giuseppe Antonio Coviello hosted him.[24] He found work at the Thomas G. Plant Factory, which produced the then-famous Queen Quality Shoes; it was a leading East Coast company, which his brother Alfonso described enthusiastically. But Salvatore's approach to industrial production was very different: "This was not shoemaking. This was an inferno, a bedlam of rattles and clatters and whizzing machines and hurrying, scurrying people."[25] Salvatore saw for himself that machine-made shoes were qualitatively inferior to shoes he or any other Italian craftsman could make by hand. So, after just 15 days of employment, disappointed by the experience, he resigned and moved to Santa Barbara in California, joining his other siblings who had been attracted by more favorable conditions on the West Coast for immigrants, including greater tolerance for their origins.[26]

The Ferragamo brothers were adept at switching professions. Documentation shows that in 1912, Girolamo worked as a tailor at the P. A. Swanson store in Santa Barbara. Three years later, he went into business with his brother Secondino as a shoemaker in a small shop at 1033 State Street, near one of the city's oldest brick houses, owned by the Janssen-Orella family.[27] The store's opening likely coincided with their younger brother's arrival; indeed, Salvatore had been in California since at least September 20, 1915, when he opened a savings account at the Santa Barbara branch of the Fugazi Banca Popolare Operaia Italiana of San Francisco.[28] In 1916, Girolamo went back to work as a tailor. Alfonso was listed in the Santa Barbara residents' directory sometimes as a shoemaker, sometimes as a tailor. They moved house practically every year, essentially staying at small boarding houses specialized in accommodating extended families. From 1919, the Ferragamo family, including Secondino's wife, Jennie, lived under the same roof in a rented house in Mission Canyon, not far from the American Film Company headquarters. They moved several more times after that[29] until, in 1922, they settled at 719 California Street.

Salvatore's description of the train journey to California is literally epic. In our fully connected world, it's hard to imagine the awe of this teenager, born in a small Italian village, when he first set eyes on the Arizona desert with its vast expanse of sand and cacti, the grandeur of the Rocky Mountains, and the beauty of Santa Barbara: the beaches, grand hotels, splendid villas, and blooming gardens that made it a tourist attraction, aided by the Southern Pacific Railroad that traversed the state of California and was often used as the setting for photography and advertising, symbolizing everything that was modern and progressive about America. The southern California movie industry took advantage of vastly varied local landscapes, from plains to forests, mountains and sea views, offering the perfect setting for every movie genre. By 1920, 80 percent of all US films were produced in Santa Barbara and the area around Los Angeles, employing not just a great many professionals but people who worked in hospitality and related businesses, from logistics to catering and entertainment.[30] Salvatore immediately intuited that the movie business could offer his shoes the perfect platform. Up there on the big screen, clothing, details, and accessories were highly visible and, worn by A-list actors, they could set new fashion trends and define styles.

Girolamo, who was a tailor, had found a job as ironer of actors' costumes at the American Film Company (also known as Flying "A" Studios); in all likelihood it was him who gave Salvatore his entrée to the movie world.[31] In his autobiography, Salvatore describes feeling immediately at home among all these clothes, cloaks, hats, and shoes. His first commission was for several pairs of cowboy boots for one of many westerns shooting—a genre moviegoers loved very much. Until that point, footwear for films had been made up in Eureka, Northern California, albeit without too much skill: when the shoes were comfortable, they looked wrong for the film, and when the models were right for the film, they weren't right for the actor's feet. Despite his young age, Salvatore immediately offered to improve on these boots, and that first job for a film studio led to more.[32] Thanks to his cousin Jerry, who had also migrated from Bonito to Santa Barbara and landed a supporting role in the serial *The Diamond from the Sky* (1915), Salvatore supplied shoes for the film's lead, the whimsical Lottie Pickford, sister of Mary, one of the most famous of all silent film actresses.[33] Crafting shoes for the stars on set meant winning business offset as well: because the studios did not yet have their own in-house costume or footwear makers, historical film costumes had to be rented from theatrical costume designers, or sometimes from European productions, while in cases of films set in the present, actors brought in their own clothing and shoes from home to wear on screen.[34]

THE JANSSEN-ORELLA HOUSE, 1027 STATE STREET, SANTA BARBARA

THE BUILDING OCCUPIED BY THE FERRAGAMO STORE, 1033 STATE STREET

SALVATORE FERRAGAMO'S HOME, 719 CALIFORNIA STREET, SANTA BARBARA

LILLIAN GISH IN *WAY DOWN EAST*, DIRECTED BY D. W. GRIFFITH, 1920. FERRAGAMO MADE SHOES FOR THE STAR

A SCENE FROM *THE DIAMOND FROM THE SKY*, 1915

SET FOR A WESTERN PRODUCED BY THE FLYING "A" STUDIOS IN 1916

It was abundantly clear to Salvatore that to connect with locals and pursue naturalization, he had to learn English. In practically no time at all, the Santa Barbara store became known not just for quality repairs but for the Ferragamo brothers' ability to entertain their customers and speed of service. The store frequently took orders for new designs from an increasingly sophisticated and demanding clientele, primarily movie stars. Lottie and Mary Pickford, Pola Negri, the Costello sisters, Helen Hayward, Barbara La Marr, Douglas Fairbanks, and Lolita Lee were just some of the celebrities who visited the small Santa Barbara shop, each with a specific, often eccentric request.

Salvatore's success was attributable not just to the beauty and creative flair of his designs; above all, it was down to the comfort of his footwear. We are accustomed to thinking of Ferragamo as an artist, a skilled craftsman, a competent entrepreneur who revolutionized the very idea of shoemaking. But the true fulcrum of his entire world was his understanding of the relationship between foot and shoe. It is in this realm that he took on the aura of a sorcerer, a magician, a healer, an architect, an engineer, a visionary scholar... He wrote, "I love feet. They talk to me. As I take them in my hands I feel their strengths, their weaknesses, their vitality or their failings. A good foot, its muscles firm, its arch strong, is a delight to touch, a masterpiece of divine workmanship."[35] The Archive abounds with photos of Salvatore's hands on customers' feet. The unique quality of his footwear was ultimately a result of his extraordinary ability to feel and love the harmony of the foot. He refined this sensitivity during his early years in America, studying anatomy at evening classes at the University of Southern California in Los Angeles.[36] The confidence in individual capabilities—an attitude that was widespread at the time in California and,

JERRY FERRAGAMO, SALVATORE'S COUSIN. HE WAS A CHARACTER ACTOR IN THE FIRST MOVIES SHOT IN SANTA BARBARA

SIDE VIEW OF THE FLYING "A" STUDIOS, SANTA BARBARA

To
Salvador Ferragamo
Creator of exquisite footwear
Bruno Hollywood

more generally, in America—allowed young immigrants like Salvatore, with no formal education, no knowledge of the language, and more importantly, no citizenship, to attend university. He built up a foundational awareness that shoemaking was in dire need of renewal, informed by new concepts, especially technical. He traveled 40 miles to attend lectures three or four days a week. He dedicated what little free time he had from work to study, so he could make shoes that were not just desirable but comfortable to walk in. He wrote in his autobiography: "When I began studying human anatomy, I found my first clue to the problem in the distribution of the weight of the body over the joints of the foot. I discovered the interesting fact that the weight of our bodies when we are standing erect drops straight down on the arch of the foot. A small area between one and a half and two inches on each foot carries all our weight. As we walk, the weight of our bodies is swung from one foot to the other."[37] In traditional shoemaking, both artisanal and industrial, the focus was on making shoes that provided adequate support to the knuckles and heels, but the arch was left suspended, as in nature. "Yet the fact remains," Ferragamo continues, "that many feet are injured by shoes. Does the answer lie, then, in the fact that when the foot is inside the shoe it is no longer allowed to perform its natural functions? . . . If that is so, does this imprisonment affect the arch? Again, if this is so, does this mean that the arch not only should but *must* be supported?"[38] Or, "Nature, the supreme architect from whom Man has borrowed and adapted so many of his ideas, has created the human foot in that shape and did not allow it to develop without an arch because, as any architect will tell you . . . an arch can support more weight than a flat surface. This arch, however, has to do more than carry a stationary weight, like the arch of a church door: it has to carry our moving weight as we walk."[39]

Ferragamo's research enabled him to manufacture revolutionary forms that, supporting the plantar arch with a steel plate, the shank, allowed the foot to move like an inverse pendulum. Like an architect, Salvatore used a plumb line to find the body's median line, running from the head to the center of the foot's arch. Metatarsal joints and heels no longer bore any weight: rather than being in opposition, his shoes guided the body's balance while walking—a balance that, Ferragamo argued, was not just physical but mental.

In audio recordings, Ferragamo said that before the academic year was out, "I had learned a lot and had a perfect understanding of the relationship between the human body and the feet . . . I knew I had new knowledge. Then my customers told me my principles worked, that they felt the shoes different, and so I made my fortune . . . My new discovery maintained the line of the shoes . . . I combined anatomical research with the fitting experience."[40]

Every day in the shop, Salvatore observed and examined hundreds of feet: long, short, very narrow and arched like those of Spaniards and Mexicans, the slender American feet, or the small-at-heel feet of South Africans. All feet were different, he realized: they varied not just in length but in width, based on how slender or not a person is.

Realizing that taking a single measurement was not enough, he developed a new approach that, for each foot length, could be combined with six different widths distinguished by the letters of the alphabet, from narrowest (AAAA) to widest (D). Although this practice was already in use in the United States, the American fitting system was calibrated for industrial rather than artisanal production. This meant that the wooden forms on which Ferragamo created his shoes, which were available on the market, had to be adapted to manual and custom work. The form had to continuously be corrected, planing the wood, adding and removing plaster . . . The end result was more like making a sculpture than a shoe.

Producing high-quality footwear also required knowledge about materials: that's why Salvatore enrolled in chemical engineering courses by correspondence from the University of Scranton (Pennsylvania), and in mathematics courses from the University of Berkeley.[41]

The Hollywood Boot Shop

Aware that the American Film Company's relocation to nearby Hollywood might impact his business, Salvatore decided to leave Santa Barbara. He suggested to his brothers that they stop doing repairs and focus on bespoke production. Neither Alfonso, Girolamo, nor Secondino were keen to leap into a venture that required significant investment in equipment and materials, skilled personnel, meticulous organization, and, most importantly, carried great risks in a small town like Hollywood prior to the 1920s. In the end, they compromised and decided to move the repair shop to Los Angeles. However, their plans unraveled on February 4, 1920, when driving his Hudson Six through Ventura en route to Los Angeles, Salvatore was involved in a severe accident on the Rincon Highway with a fast train from the Southern Pacific line. His youngest brother, Eliodoro, who only recently had arrived in the United States, was killed.[42] "His death was like the end of the world,"[43] Salvatore recalled. And he

PHOTO OF ACTRESS
LOLITA LEE, DEDICATED
TO SALVATORE
FERRAGAMO

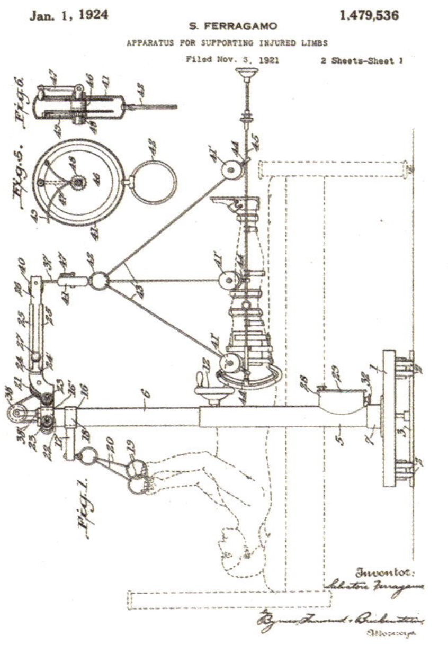

nearly lost a leg in the accident. At Bard Memorial Hospital in Ventura, he underwent very painful yet ineffective limb traction treatment; orthopedics at that time was still emerging as an independent discipline from general surgery, while physiotherapy was at a very early stage.[44] So Salvatore decided to apply what he had learned in anatomy lessons to his body. During six months of hospitalization, he started work on his first patents, based on a cylinder for limb traction and a screw device to regulate the pull.[45] He later turned this into an "Apparatus for supporting injured limbs," a product later marketed by a Chicago-based orthopedic products company.[46]

After convalescing, Ferragamo returned to Santa Barbara. He was ever more certain that they had to move to Hollywood. No longer a small village, it had transformed into the bustling center of US film production and was becoming the international capital of cinema, attracting talented artists from all round the globe.

Salvatore compiled two scrapbooks during his years in America. Today at the Ferragamo Archive in Florence, they include articles from April 1923 reporting John Bohannon transferring the license for one of the city's oldest shops, the Hollywood Boot Shop, specialized in footwear, to Ferragamo.[47] Via the Frank Meline Company real estate firm, Salvatore contracted to pay rent of $57,000 for ten years;[48] the contract was not, however, actually signed until October 1923. Salvatore, Secondino, and Jerome (Girolamo) Ferragamo set up a new company, and Salvatore was named store manager. After an initial clearance sale of stock items, by the end of May the Hollywood Boot Shop was promoting and selling elegant footwear, some by famous American brands I. Miller & Sons and the F. P. Smith Shoe Co. The two-story premises at no. 6687, on the corner of Hollywood and Las Palmas Boulevards, boasted an enviable location:

PATENTS NO. 1,479,536, JANUARY 1, 1924 AND NO. 1,399,606, DECEMBER 6, 1921: CYLINDER FOR LIMB TRACTION WITH DOUBLE SCREW TIGHTENER AND ORTHOPEDIC DEVICE

VIEW OF HOLLYWOOD BOULEVARD IN THE 1920s

it was right opposite Grauman's Egyptian Theatre, an imposing building containing a 1,700-seat movie hall that had opened the previous year. In addition to theatrical and variety shows, all film premieres were held at this venue.

From that moment on, Ferragamo began splitting his Hollywood output three ways: shoes for movies, custom-made shoes, and shoes for Grauman events.[49] He lived at 2222 North Beachwood Drive, not far downhill from Charlie Chaplin's villa and the Hollywoodland sign.

Articles in the press praised the new Hollywood Boot Shop management team, pointing out that Salvatore Ferragamo was active in city institutions (the Hollywood Chamber of Commerce, Hollywood Retail Merchants, and the Hollywood Credit Association) and played an important role for the city and its residents. The "Shoemaker to the Stars," as Salvatore was immediately nicknamed, did indeed have a clientele of and friendships with film idols of the day, from Rudolph Valentino to John Gilbert and Douglas Fairbanks, with whom he used to spend weekends.[50] As he consolidated his economic position, Ferragamo applied for American citizenship. He had already applied in September 1920, was rejected again in 1924, and his application was only accepted in 1926, when he finally obtained an American passport.[51]

In February 1925, Salvatore moved the store on a ten-year lease to 6683 Hollywood Boulevard, one door east of the old establishment.[52] Here, the refurbishment of the interiors took inspiration from Italian Renaissance, with rich, orange-toned drapes, furniture purchased from Fox film studios, chairs and sofas upholstered in amber, gray, and light burgundy, large mirrors, wrought iron display stands, and chandeliers. Meticulously designed lighting and a floor carpeted in light tones set off the colors of batiks on the walls—an analog imitation of Renaissance tapestries. An imposing colonnade led from the entrance to the fitting rooms.

SALVATORE FERRAGAMO DRIVING HIS HUDSON SIX

SALVATORE FERRAGAMO'S HOME, 2222 NORTH BEACHWOOD DRIVE, HOLLYWOOD

INAUGURATION OF THE GRAUMAN'S EGYPTIAN THEATRE, LOS ANGELES, OCTOBER 18, 1922

Hidden from external view, shoes were displayed on Ferragamo-designed shelves. The display windows along the sides of the entrance were made of Venetian walnut and Belgian marble. Ferragamo wanted the store to exude an atmosphere of luxury yet remain intimate and welcoming. The overall appearance was that of an Italian palazzo designed to cater to American interior and fashion magazines' taste, filled as they were with the myth of Florence and Renaissance art.[53]

Ever since the gold rush, Italian immigrants had flocked to the nascent State of California as fishermen, winemakers, or got involved in business and banking. Despite this consolidated history, WASP society had an ambivalent view on immigrants, sometimes manifested as outright hostility.

Italy's history, culture, and craftsmanship may have been held in high esteem, but certain stereotypical characteristics (impulsiveness, passion, excessive sentimentality, and lack of reliability) were still attributed to immigrants, especially from southern Europe.[54] Involved in several cultural and artistic promotional activities, Ferragamo was acutely aware of how important it was to associate his name with the high-end image of Italy.[55] He ran unique advertising campaigns and became closely involved with the opera world and the grand theater at the Hollywood Bowl, where maestro Pietro Cimini, a friend of his, often conducted the orchestra.[56]

On Thursday, February 19, 1925, the new store's grand opening attracted hundreds of guests, with queues around the block. The entire building was lit by Otto K. Olesen, with special effects that reverberated inside. The store was bedecked with floral decorations and gifts for guests, music, and entertainment. The event was so successful that it ran until midnight—indeed, the inauguration continued over the next three days,[57] with many film stars attending: a famous photograph from the inauguration evening shows Mary Pickford, Douglas Fairbanks, Gloria Swanson, Monty Banks, and Rudolph Valentino. So well-known was the Hollywood Boot Shop that it even appeared in the movies, in King Vidor's 1928 film *Show People*.

In his autobiography, Ferragamo reminisced about his designs for the stars and revealed some big-screen celebrities'

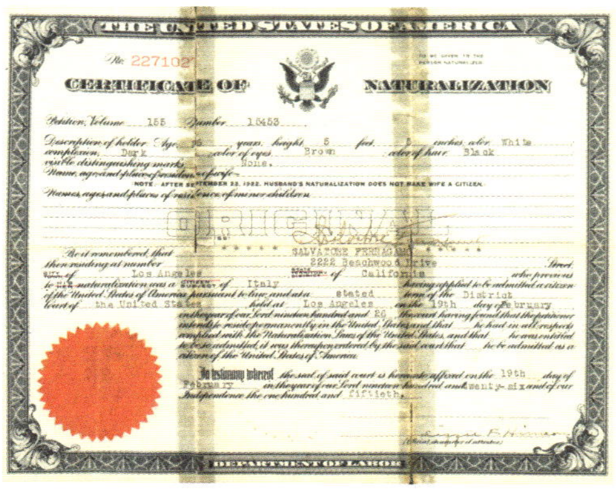

THE UNITED STATES OF AMERICA

CERTIFICATE OF NATURALIZATION

DEPARTMENT OF LABOR

CERTIFICATE OF NATURALIZATION, ISSUED ON FEBRUARY 19, 1926. MUSEO FERRAGAMO, FLORENCE

FRANK C. JORDAN, SECRETARY OF STATE

FRANK H. CORY, DEPUTY
ROBERT V. JORDAN, DEPUTY

STATE OF CALIFORNIA

DEPARTMENT OF STATE

I, FRANK C. JORDAN, Secretary of State of the State of California, do hereby certify that I have carefully compared the annexed copy of Articles of Incorporation of HOLLYWOOD BOOTSHOP, INC.

with the original now on file in my office, and that the same is a correct transcript therefrom, and of the whole thereof. I further certify that this authentication is in due form and by the proper officer.

IN WITNESS WHEREOF, I have hereunto set my hand and have caused the Great Seal of the State of California to be affixed hereto this 23rd *day of* October *A. D. 192*3

Secretary of State

Deputy

PURCHASE DEED OF LICENSE FOR THE HOLLYWOOD BOOT SHOP, OCTOBER 23, 1923

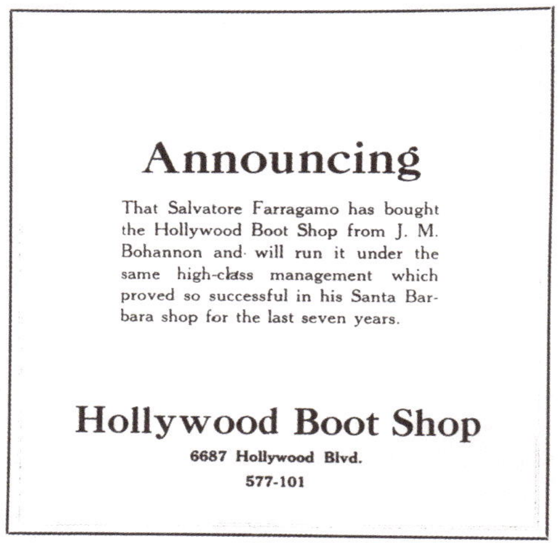

Announcing

That Salvatore Farragamo has bought the Hollywood Boot Shop from J. M. Bohannon and will run it under the same high-class management which proved so successful in his Santa Barbara shop for the last seven years.

Hollywood Boot Shop

6687 Hollywood Blvd.

577-101

ANNOUNCEMENT OF OPENING OF THE HOLLYWOOD BOOT SHOP AT 6687 HOLLYWOOD BOULEVARD

SIGN OF HOLLYWOOD BOOT SHOP

INTERIOR VIEW OF THE NEW SPACE AT THE HOLLYWOOD BOOT SHOP, 6683 HOLLYWOOD BOULEVARD, ONE DOOR EAST OF THE PREVIOUS LOCATION

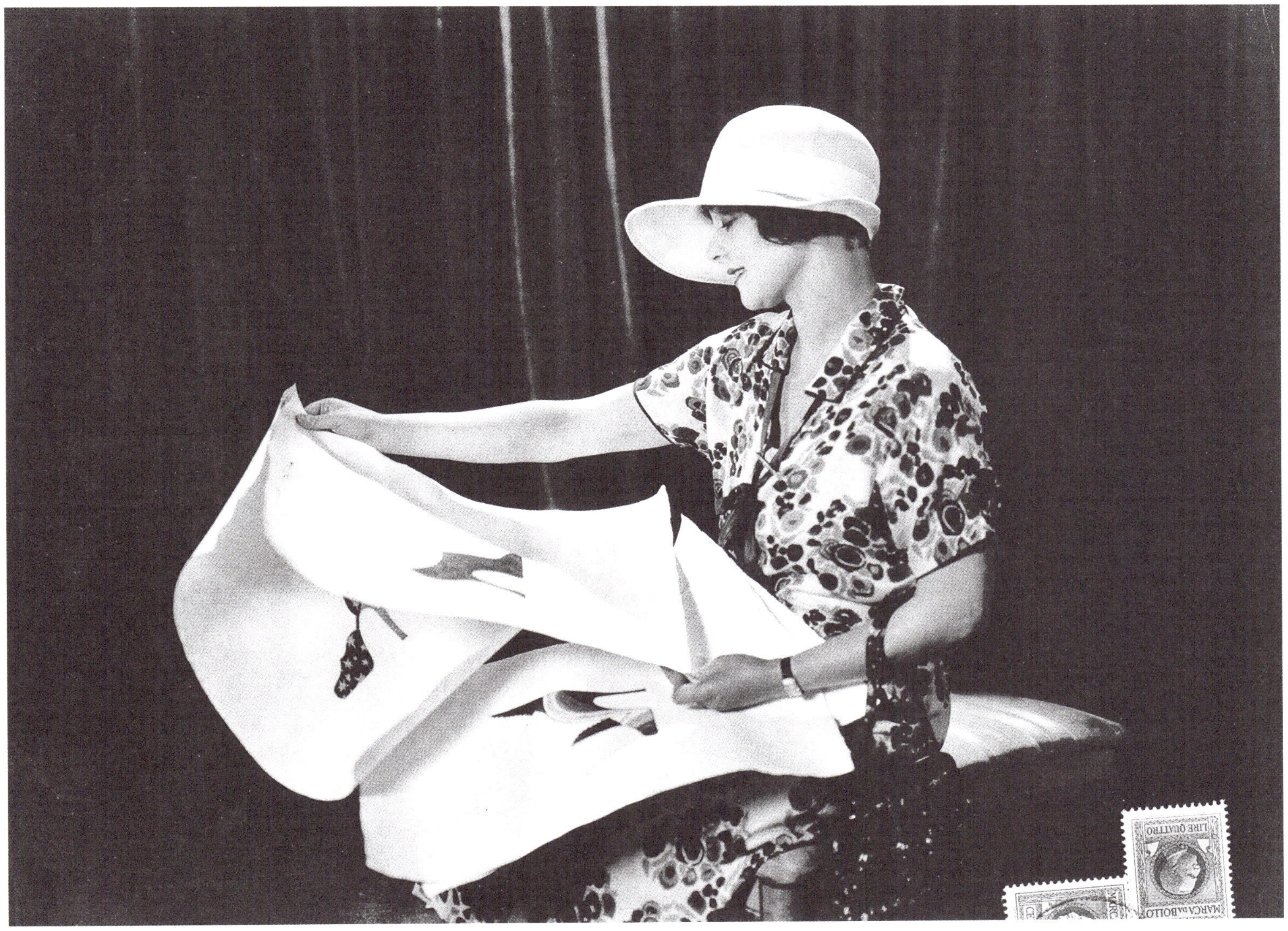

PICTURES OF
THE HOLLYWOOD
BOOT SHOP'S
INAUGURATION
AND CLIENTS

ACTRESS ALICE WHITE, ONE OF SALVATORE FERRAGAMO'S CLIENTS

A SCENE FROM *THE COVERED WAGON*, DIRECTED BY JAMES CRUZE, 1923. FERRAGAMO MADE THE STARS' BOOTS

idiosyncrasies. Pola Negri, for instance, had no love of extravagant footwear and always bought shoes in large quantities, because she hated cleaning them: she wore them a few times before discarding them. Rudolph Valentino was always magnificent and impeccably stylish, perhaps even overly meticulous in every detail. Alice White, who began her Hollywood acting career as Charlie Chaplin's secretary, was a true fashion enthusiast who favored two-tone shoes. In these years, Ferragamo designed a unique stage toe, an elevated sole for short clients, and his successful model *First*. He also designed a stretch boot resembling a sock to pair with leopard fur for Lola Todd, "corkscrew" heels adorned with faux pearls for Gloria Swanson, multi-colored silk satin slippers for Lillian Gish, evening lace-up shoes in rainbow colors with tall, gold heels for Dolores del Río, and for Esther Ralston, black and gold shoes with a pointed heel and a snake design on the upper, its glossy, flexible body, painted with golden scales, winding up to the middle of the actress's beautiful legs.

Ferragamo's creativity seemed to know no bounds. He fashioned an even more original and costly design ($500) for one American actress (who remains nameless), the uppers made of rare, tiny hummingbird feathers specially imported from Mexico.[58] Newspapers and fashion magazines publicized Ferragamo's evening shoes in silk satin, with sprinkled rhinestone powder in unique decorative patterns, high-ankled shoes in painted fabric, and antelope models with intriguing fan-shaped ornaments.

Ferragamo's burgeoning business during his 12 years in California cannot be explained away merely as a consequence of Hollywood's exponential growth. This was a time of rapid change through Western society, when women's roles were changing drastically; they featured more prominently on the public stage, which had significant consequences on women's fashion. Dress lines became simpler, hems got shorter; feet and legs, taboo for centuries, were now exposed for all to see, becoming a focus for magazines and leather/accessory manufacturers. Ferragamo drew on the latest innovations in the tanning industry, including special varnishes and dyes for leather that produced pearlescent and metallic effects, and prints in a variety of patterns to varied visual effect. He used reptile skins as well as traditional calf and kid leathers: python for its beautiful patterns, kalimanka with its design as regular as fabric, Calcutta lizards in the most unexpected colors, and small, oval-scaled Java lizards. As we have mentioned, Ferragamo took chemistry correspondence courses to learn more about leather tanning. The shoe design world was evolving swiftly as a plethora of new designs came to market: open shoes with or without straps, footwear fastened with laces, buckles, and buttons, boots in varying heights, and flat or high-heeled sandals, a style not in fashion since Neoclassical times.[59]

War in Europe led to another major shift: if until 1914, Paris had set all trends in women's fashion, a stifled flow of information about France and French creations during the war years prompted US magazines to start featuring clothing and accessories worn by film actresses, on and off-screen. By the early 1920s, the Hollywood studios had effectively become dream factories, operating complete production lines. Wardrobe departments were run by professionals who designed costumes for the main characters and oversaw everything else. Major Hollywood studio fashion became the new touchstone for female audiences, shaping style despite the odd, hard-to-replicate, exaggerated detail employed in two-dimensional filming or to emphasize a character's personality.[60]

Following the template adopted in his early Santa Barbara days, in Hollywood Ferragamo dedicated a portion of his output to films. In 1923, director Cecil B. DeMille commissioned Salvatore to design and produce shoes for his latest costume colossal, *The Ten Commandments*. This huge job sent Ferragamo scurrying to the city library to research and find solutions to go with the costumes designed by Clare West. Thrilled with the results, a few years later the director commissioned him to make shoes for his films *The Volga Boatman* (1926) and *The Deluge*, a story about Noah and the Great Flood that was ultimately never made. In 1927, he involved him once again, this time for the footwear for another epic, *The King of Kings*. Ferragamo also worked with D. W. Griffith on *Way Down East* (1920) and *The White Rose* (1923), with James Cruze on *The Covered Wagon* (1923), and with Raoul Walsh on *The Thief of Bagdad* (1924). Film work stimulated Salvatore's creativity, prompted him to learn even more about materials, and set him searching for new

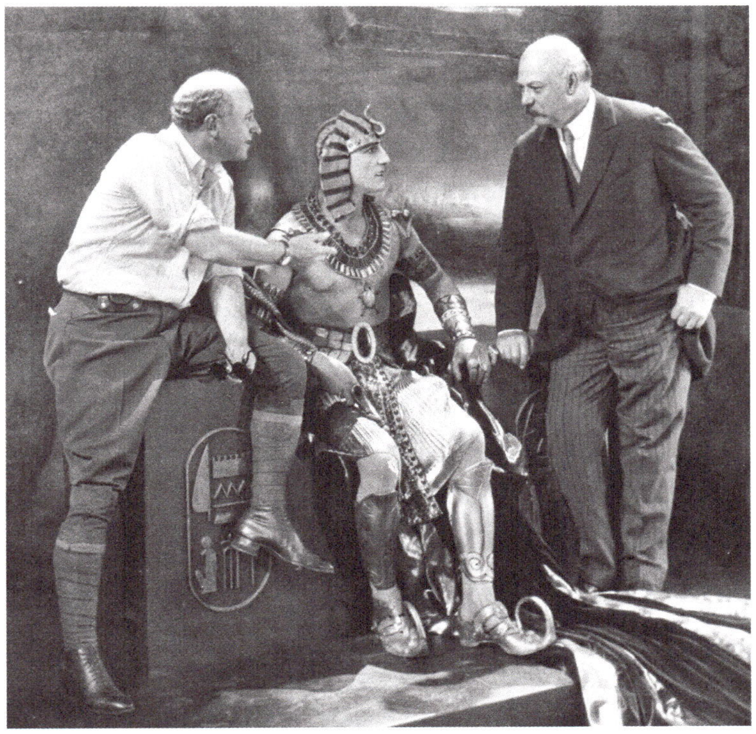

DIRECTOR CECIL B. DEMILLE WITH ACTOR CHARLES DE ROCHEFORT, PLAYING PHARAOH RAMESSES IN *THE TEN COMMANDMENTS*, AND WAR SECRETARY JOHN WEEKS, 1923

FRANK C. JORDAN, SECRETARY OF STATE

FRANK H. CORY, DEPUTY
ROBERT V. JORDAN, DEPUTY

STATE OF CALIFORNIA

DEPARTMENT OF STATE

I, FRANK C. JORDAN, Secretary of State of the State of California, do hereby certify that I have carefully compared the transcript, to which this certificate is attached, with the record on file in my office of which it purports to be a copy, and that the same is a full, true and correct copy thereof. I further certify that this authentication is in due form and by the proper officer.

IN WITNESS WHEREOF, I have hereunto set my hand and have caused the Great Seal of the State of California to be affixed hereto this 4th day of May A. D. 1926

Frank C. Jordan
Secretary of State.

By Frank H. Cory
Deputy

DEED OF INCORPORATION FOR FERRA-GAMO INC., FILED ON MAY 4, 1926

SALVATORE FERRAGAMO ON THE *ROMA* OCEAN LINER, EN ROUTE FROM NEW YORK TO ITALY, FALL 1926

sources of inspiration: classical antiquity for his Roman sandals, the sensational 1922 discovery of Tutankhamun's tomb for pyramid-shaped brass heels…

The fame of the talented artist and entrepreneur, who managed to combine glamour and anatomy, made it onto the airwaves. On August 11, 1926, in a speech he made on KHJ radio entitled "On Proper Footwear,"[61] he told the world that capturing the American film industry market was not enough, he wasn't going to limit himself to custom-made shoes for a small group of affluent clients. He wanted to expand production without giving up quality or style.

In February 1926, Salvatore founded Ferra-Gamo Incorporated with ten funding partners who contributed $250,000 in capital. He was designated company agent, general manager, and president. The company's five directors were Salvatore, sister Rosina, brother Girolamo, and two external partners whose identities changed over the years (initially, Ethel A. Haun and Jerome J. Mayo).[62] Salvatore felt that time was ripe to delocalize production: on the one hand, he wanted to cater to increasing demand from influential clients, and on the other, to pursue the growth plan he had in mind. He had a gut feeling that only in Italy would he find craftsmen able to satisfy his high standards of workmanship, while he firmly believed the Hollywood store should continue to handle product distribution.

Furthermore, we should not forget that, in the early 1920s, the American press showed a great deal of interest in Italy and post-war events, like the rise of fascism. As early as 1922, Mussolini expressed concern for Italians in America: "Emigrants," he said, "should be seen as means of radiating Italian ideas and products, and emigration an integral part of Italian foreign policy."[63] In line with this approach, Mussolini had already requested an increase in immigration visas, which was introduced in May 1921 as the *Immigration Quota Act*. Logically, Italian immigrants to the United States, such as Ferragamo, viewed the new political direction of their country positively, at a time when perceptions of Italy were beginning to shift in the States: from being a country of migrants, Italy started to be associated with positive characteristics, garnering ever-greater appeal until the Ethiopian War in the mid-1930s. US distribution of Margherita Sarfatti's biography of Mussolini, *Dux*, first published in English in 1925 and then in Italian the following year, further promoted the image of a modernist Italy gearing up for progress. Not surprisingly, this improving Italy would attract an enterprising entrepreneur like Ferragamo. Convinced he could make his dreams come true in his home country, in August 1926 he decided to go back to Italy.[64]

The return to Italy

With his home movie camera, 28-year-old Salvatore Ferragamo filmed his voyage on the *Roma* transatlantic ocean liner—this time, traveling first class. He was now an elegant and self-assured man: sister Rosina captured this image of him on the ship's deck, ready to embark on a new venture in which he would apply what he had learned from his younger years in two very different worlds: Italy and the United States.

The ship docked in Naples. After a brief period in southern Italy, in early 1927[65] he decided to settle down in Florence. As well as being globally acknowledged for its extraordinary craftsmanship and as the symbol of Italian culture, since the nineteenth century Florence had been a significant international tourism destination. Ferragamo focused his camera on the city's artistic beauties: Ponte Vecchio, the Uffizi Gallery from across the river, the Ponte alle Grazie and its chapels, destroyed during World War II bombings. He filmed his sisters Rosina and Giuseppina, arriving from Bonito with their mother, at Piazzale Michelangelo and, in the distance, the Fiesole Hills punctuated by villas, including "Il Palagio," the country home he would purchase as his residence a few years later.

Salvatore Ferragamo rented a large workshop at 57 Via Mannelli[66] from Guglielmo Vita, who since the turn of the century had been an interesting, multifaceted figure in the Florentine artistic and intellectual milieu,[67] as well as serving as president of the Jewish community. The workshop was in the Santa Croce district, a working-class area where the main traditional activities were leather tanning, wool spinning, and weaving. In the 1920s, progressive-minded artisanal stores and workshops moved their operations to Via Mannelli; among them was the Polloni artistic glassworks,[68] a company that, like Ferragamo, took advantage of its proximity to the Campo di Marte train station for shipments.

To run the workshop, Ferragamo established the S. Ferragamo & C. company,[69] which operated in tandem with American Ferra-Gamo Inc. The latter was responsible for the Hollywood store's operations, from which the majority of orders still came. Salvatore hired around 60 workers, all of whom were gathered under one roof. These skilled craftsmen soon made some of the most remarkable designs Ferragamo ever created, putting together an Italian collection of 18 prototypes to be shipped and presented in the United States.

On that trip, Salvatore's first meeting was with George Miller, president of the I. Miller & Sons footwear chain in New York.[70] Miller was expected to place orders for the American market based on the sample shoes, but the meeting went

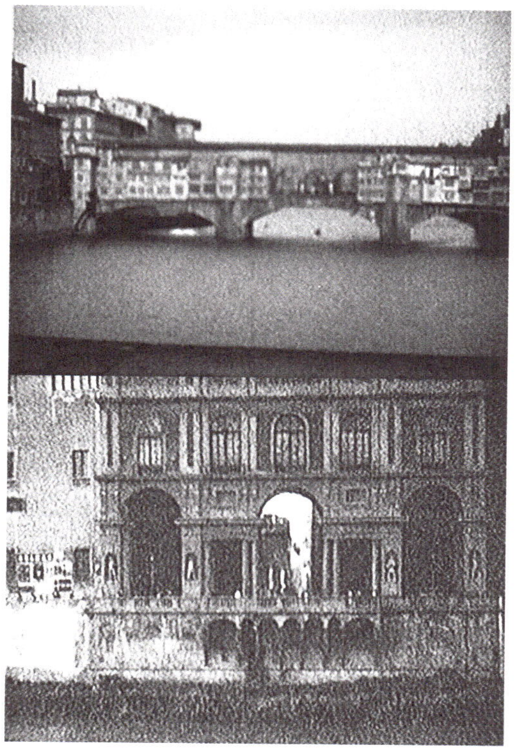

SALVATORE SHOOTS FLORENCE WITH HIS FILM CAMERA: PONTE VECCHIO AND THE UFFIZI

PROMOTIONAL POSTCARD OF CALZATURIFICIO FERRAGAMO & C., VIA MANNELLI 57, FLORENCE

FERRAGAMO'S PARTNERS IN THE NEW FLORENCE COMPANY

SALVATORE FERRAGAMO
TEACHING A YOUNG
APPRENTICE HOW TO
ASSEMBLE A SHOE

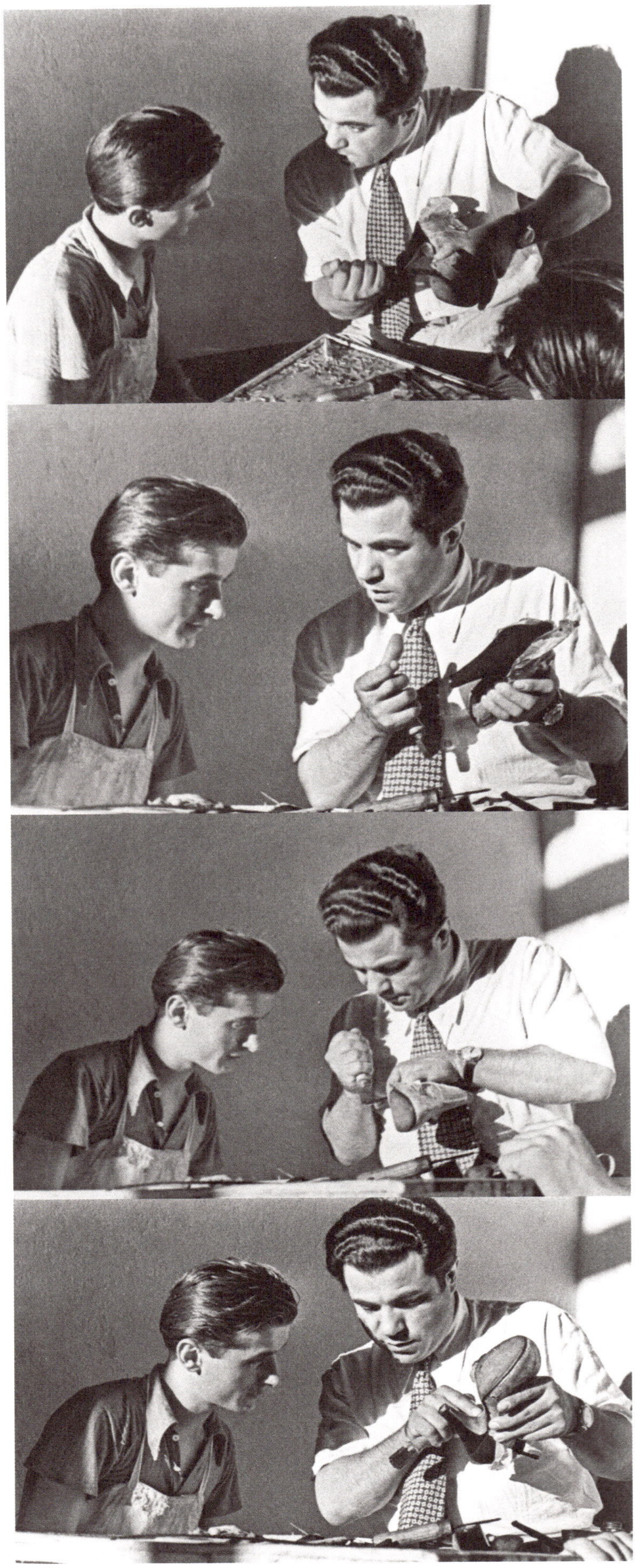

awry. Miller's judgment was not just negative, it was final. In his autobiography, Salvatore painfully recalls Miller's words: "you have got nothing, nothing! Forget about all this. Take my advice and go back to Hollywood and do the work you have been doing so well. You've got nothing here, absolutely nothing." Ferragamo was devastated. He could not believe that all their effort and dedication had come to nothing. "As I sat in my misery and looked at those beautiful shoes, I heard them speaking to me. They said: 'Don't be a fool, Salvatore. Forget that man's opinion. Look at what you have done already! Get busy. Work, work, work!'"[71]

Determined not to give up, Salvatore called Saks Fifth Avenue buyer Manuel Gerton.[72] He told Gerton about his experience in Italy and his samples, and then requested a meeting that went as differently as possible to the first. So impressed was Gerton with Ferragamo's shoe designs that he placed an order worth several hundred dollars. The scene was repeated with the Marshall Field's buyer in Chicago, and with major stores and department stores in Hollywood and Los Angeles. Ferragamo ended up staying in the US longer than expected, owing to the challenges of reorganizing the Californian corporation and managing his relationship with his partners. In his absence, capital had decreased so much that the company was short of cash to cover current expenses. Unable to understand the complexities Ferragamo faced setting up his new factory in Italy and fearing for their investments, his American partners started losing faith: they failed to realize it would take time to see a return. Ferragamo eventually prevailed, but the challenging negotiations kept him away from Florence and his work from March to May 1928.

When he finally got back to Italy, it was to yet more crisis management and disappointment. Despite being paid during his absence, many of the cobblers he employed had left, some had done nothing, and some of the older shoemakers openly questioned his working methods. They were all working independently, as accustomed. In consequence, the shoes they made were inconsistent and had defects that nobody, let alone the Italian partner, had been able to fix while Salvatore was away.[73] The young entrepreneur found the situation intolerable. He fired the old craftsmen and hired young apprentices who, although lacking technical expertise, were willing to learn, as well as believing in his innovations. He trained up 75 workers and established a production system that resembled a human assembly line, combining a hand-made production approach with industrial organization. Rather than each cobbler making a shoe from start to finish, tasks were divided up into individual steps, each of which was assigned to a worker specializing in operations that ranged from sole stitching to leather cutting, modeling, and finishing. His creative genius in overdrive, within a month Salvatore was shipping his first orders, leveraging his studies on fitting, a new approach to work organization, and his invention of the metal shank.

In a 1949 memoir at the Ferragamo Archive, Salvatore mentions actively promoting his designs to prominent American retailers during that period: Saks Fifth Avenue, Gimbel Brothers, Macy's, and Franklin Simon & Co. in New York; May Co. in Los Angeles, Baltimore, and Cleveland; Famous-Barr in Saint Louis; Wollch & Baner and Marshall Field's in Chicago; The White House in San Francisco.[74] A 30-pair shoe order from The May Department Stores Company for M. O'Neil Co. of Akron, Ohio, dated August 6, 1928, confirms the Via Mannelli-based footwear manufacturer's ongoing business relationship with major American retailers.

Ferragamo's passport stamps show he traveled extensively to Switzerland, France, and the Netherlands, seeking to rustle up European customers. His flexibility when forging international relationships was evident not just in business but in other groundbreaking initiatives. On June 23, 1928, *Shoe Retailer* published an article announcing a partnership between the Brooklyn School of Shoe Design and Ferra-Gamo Inc., with offices in both Hollywood and Florence. Significantly, this news revealed Ferragamo's interest in training the next generation of shoemakers, while highlighting shoe production features like "hand-painted heels" and other clothing accessories such as wool scarves and shawls. A pair of women's shoes with a hand-painted floral heel purchased on the antiques market is one fine example of Ferragamo's early Florentine output. The insole label reads "Ferra-Gamo Inc. Florence Hollywood," flanked by seared emblems of the US and the Kingdom of Italy.

In 1929, Ferragamo applied for Italian citizenship and residence in Florence. By January, he was registered on the city's municipal list as resident at Via Cavour 81. The 1931 census included family members Rosina, Giuseppina and her husband, as well as their mother, Mariantonia.[75]

Ferragamo's decision to stay on in Florence may have been influenced not just by increasing tensions with his American partners and early signs of the economic crisis that would sweep through the US in October 1929, but also by local political undercurrents. In 1929, Alessandro Pavolini, the undisputed leader of Florentine fascism, called Florence "Italy's most artisanal city," acknowledging its primary role in shaping the myth of the Renaissance through its artisan workshops, generators of so many amazing artists. Pavolini's promotion and development of the crafts through new trade bodies and promotional events were part of a broader national strategy. Seeking a modern-day revival, the fascist government saw the craft sector as the country's true industry.[76]

Clearly, Ferragamo was working in a context favorable to his business. Once again, he demonstrated not just his exceptional creative skills but a visionary ability to read the runes of society and upcoming change. He was quick to grasp the essence of the relationship between the city's artistry and craftsmanship, not to mention its allure to Italians and increasing numbers of foreign tourists who flocked to Florence. Ferragamo added the writing "Florence" to his name on shoe labels, positioning himself in the public's eye as a Renaissance artist handcrafting modern-day models. To highlight the artistic value of his footwear, he patented a slogan, "All hand-made artistic shoes." He wanted to convey that, as well as being entirely hand-made, the uppers were inspired by long-consolidated Florentine craftsmanship, even if they repurposed decorative patterns in new ways.[77] Most shoes made around that time sourced leather from top tanneries: Freudenberg of Germany provided calf leather;

BRAIDERS AT WORK
IN THE COUNTRYSIDE
AROUND SIGNA
(FLORENCE), EARLY
TWENTIETH CENTURY

Italy's Cornelia supplied printed calf leather; France's Grison and Salp from Rivarolo Canavese, near Turin, provided kid leather, while Switzerland's Alpina and France's Pomponne catered to reptile and other exotic skins.[78]

With the return to femininity and romance in fashion after the stylized designs of the 1920s, Ferragamo branched out into embroidered decorations and lace for his shoes. One of Florence's longest-established crafts, embroidery was alive and well in small workshops in the city and surrounding areas, supported by local noblewomen Countesses Edith Rucellai, Beatrice Pandolfini, and Donna Elisabetta Stori dei Principi Corsini, all of whom sat on the 1928 Florentine Committee of Italian Women's Industries. Loom and needlework embroidery were undertaken in white or colored thread, in various stitches. Chain stitch appeared frequently in Ferragamo shoes, performed either by hand or using mechanical needles, especially on kid leather or suede. Materials like beads, blown Venetian glass beads, and jet beads were all used alongside silk and cotton thread, which allowed for greater creative freedom and were well-suited to geometric designs.

Tuscany may not have been as renowned for lacework as Veneto, but it did see a resurgence of this high craft in the early twentieth century across Italy and Europe, taking advantage of economic benefits on emerging markets like the US. Crafted by contract workers in villages and countryside homes scattered throughout the area, Tavarnelle lace, primarily produced in Mercatale in Val di Pesa and Greve in Chianti, was the most renowned lace in the Florence region. Before Ferragamo started using it, it was employed almost exclusively for personal and household linens. Production had declined at the start of the 1920s, when excessive simplification of clothing rendered certain decorations superfluous. Even when lace reappeared in collections from 1927 onwards, its recovery was hindered by cheaper machine-made lace and workers' limited ability to refresh their ornamental repertoire. Ferragamo used the most common decorative motifs—scrolls, leaves, flowers, medallions, and fans on netted or checkered backgrounds—on his shoes, creating a distinctive style that emphasized not just the quality of the materials but the entirely handcrafted process, in contrast to growing generic industrial output. As part of the never-ending search for innovation and for the most current sensibilities characteristic of his entire career, he also experimented with geometric decorations both square and circular in form.

Lace-making techniques grew simplified in the 1920s, while retaining traditional stitches. New, thinner, sparser lace that could be churned out far more quickly was a boon to the Italian shoemaker, making it possible to create clever interplays of transparency on shoe uppers, subtly revealing a bare foot in contrast with a solid heel covered in leather

TAVARNELLE
LACE AND SILK SATIN
SANDAL, 1935

STRAW SANDAL
WITH CORK
HEEL, 1937

HAND-PAINTED
CANVAS PUMP,
1930–35

LUCIO VENNA, *SKETCHES FOR SALVATORE FERRAGAMO ADVERTS*, 1930, STENCIL ON PAPER. MUSEO FERRAGAMO, FLORENCE

LUCIO VENNA, *ADVERTISING POSTER FOR SALVATORE FERRAGAMO*, 1928, PRINT ON PAPER. MUSEO FERRAGAMO, FLORENCE

or fabric. Another significant innovation Ferragamo brought to traditional lace was color. Embroidery had traditionally been undertaken in white. By the late nineteenth century, colored threads were appearing in filet production, albeit for the most part limited to accessories and models of lesser elegance. To focus attention on his creations' modernity and artistic flair, Ferragamo designed his shoes using lace in colored threads.

Straw processing was another long-held Florentine tradition to which Ferragamo turned on arrival in Florence. Originating in the Signa area in the eighteenth century, with certain local variations, it spread to many areas near the Tuscan capital. Prato was known for braided designs; openwork and embossed designs were produced in and around Impruneta. In Fiesole, braids of straw mixed with horsehair were woven and used for edgings. After being processed and woven, straw was sold on Tuesdays and Thursdays in Florence at the loggia of Mercato Nuovo (also known as Loggia del Porcellino), and on Mondays in Prato at Piazza San Francesco. Not only was wheat straw available but *rascello* was too.[79] Grass from the Philippines was also on sale, along with Manila hemp made from banana leaf fiber, and East African palm raffia.

Straw had, for the most part, been used until then to make trademark Florentine hats known around the world, and a limited number of handbags. Ferragamo started using straw for the uppers of his summer shoes, crocheted in a single stitch, knitted, or embroidered onto hemp or canvas fabric.

One of the standout features of Ferragamo's shoes was color, an absolutely new development for accessory fashion. Salvatore loved primary colors. He used them either as the absolute stars or combined in unusual weaves or in bold fabric and leather patchworks. Although they might initially look geometric, it soon becomes evident that the surfaces follow a rhythm, the foundational element of any artistic expression. Generated by shifts or translations in which colors obey new laws of decomposition, such rhythms produce constantly new and unique designs.

Color was to the fore in early 1920s painting too. In Italy, the Futurists adopted moving color schemes as tools for interpreting the speed and energy of contemporary life. In her paintings and fabric designs, French art and fashion innovator Sonia Delaunay produced the first specimens of simultaneous colored contrast, the essence and foundation of this new use of color in art. Much-acclaimed *Vogue* and *Gazette du Bon Ton* magazines and other fashion outlets of the day all popularized the epoch's vast decorative repertoire, commissioning renowned illustrators who drew inspiration from various sources, from Cubism to Futurist experimentation, compositions by Kandinsky, Klee, and Mondrian, primitive simplifications of ethnic art, and exotic, sensual, and naive decorativism from China, India, and far-off Japan.

Salvatore Ferragamo learned quickly from contemporary artists, making their teachings his own and blending them with elements of his own lived experience: Mexican

LUCIO VENNA, *SKETCHES FOR SALVATORE FERRAGAMO ADVERTS*, 1930, STENCIL ON PAPER. MUSEO FERRAGAMO, FLORENCE

HAND-PAINTED ANTELOPE
PUMPS WITH SILK THREAD
EMBROIDERIES, 1930

INTERNAL SHOE
LABEL DESIGNED BY
LUCIO VENNA IN 1930

HAND-PAINTED KIDSKIN
PUMP WITH SILK THREAD
EMBROIDERIES, 1930

folklore from California, which influenced his American education, details from Florentine architecture, intricate mosaics found in a type of local goldsmithing foreigners seemed to love, in addition to sinusoidal, ornamental Art-Deco-style patterns and other motifs from the classical repertoire that were all the rage in 1924, after Amedeo Maiuri's archaeological excavations at Pompeii. These many different sources of inspiration creatively resulted in a definitive color palette combining twentieth-century avant-garde tones with pure colors from Giotto's frescoes and the early Renaissance that Salvatore saw and admired in Florence; they were also redolent of the strong colors in certain landscapes of southern Italy, where Ferragamo came from. Salvatore acted on an idea put into words by Ernesto Michahelles—more commonly known as Thayaht, a contemporary Florentine artist who also worked in fashion—in *Oggi e Domani* on June 23, 1930. In an article titled "Estetica del vestire. Moda solare. Moda futurista," he suggested the Italian clothing industry move away from "a style of dressing created under sad, gray northern metropolis skies," and instead forge an Italian way of dressing that had more to do with the local landscape, all that blue and warm Mediterranean colors.

Sinuous and curvilinear lines, Cubist-derived zig-zags, and abstract ornamental motifs dominated Ferragamo's design research. One of his most extraordinary models was a high-heeled pump from this period, the uppers embroidered with geometric decoration inspired by printed fabrics of the day, Cubist graphics, and tattoos from Africa. This decorative pattern was named *Labirinto*, a word that in the same years appeared as a trademark in the furnishing company established by Gio Ponti for the popularization of modern decorative arts, which saw among its collaborators Tommaso Buzzi, Michele Marelli, Paolo Venini, and Pietro Chiesa.[80]

GROSGRAIN AND KIDSKIN SANDAL, 1930

KIDSKIN SANDAL, 1930

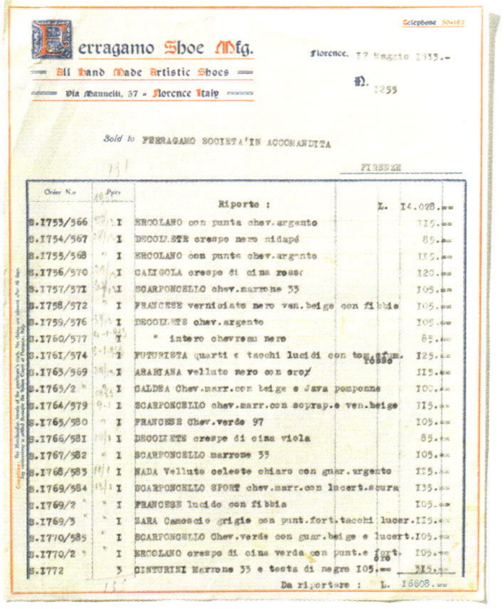
Ferragamo Shoe Mfg.
All Hand Made Artistic Shoes
Via Mannelli, 57 - Florence Italy

Telephone 50-102

Florence, 17 Maggio 1933.-

N. 1255

Sold to FERRAGAMO SOCIETA'IN ACCOMANDITA

FIRENZE

Order N.o	Pairs		
		Riporto :	L. 14.028.==
S.1753/566	I	ERCOLANO con punta chev.argento	115.==
S.1754/567	I	DECOLLETE crespo nero nidapé	85.==
S.1755/568	I	ERCOLANO con punta chev.argento	115.==
S.1756/570	I	CALIGOLA crespo di cina rossa	120.==
S.1757/571	I	SCARPONCELLO chev.marrone 33	105.==
S.1758/572	I	FRANCESE verniciato nero ven.beige con fibbia	105.==
S.1759/576	I	DECOLLETE chev.argento	105.==
S.1760/577	I	" intero chevreau nero	85.==
S.1761/574	I	FUTURISTA quarti e tacchi lucidi con tom.sfum. rosso	125.==
S.1763/969	I	ARABIANA velluto nero con oro	115.==
S.1763/2	I	CALDEA Chev.marr.con beige e Java pomponne	100.==
S.1764/579	I	SCARPONCELLO chev.marr.con soprap.e ven.beige	115.==
S.1765/580	I	FRANCESE Chev.verde 97	105.==
S.1766/581	I	DECOLLETE crespo di cina viola	85.==
S.1767/582	I	SCARPONCELLO marrone 33	105.==
S.1768/583	I	NADA Velluto celeste chiaro con guar.argento	115.==
S.1769/584	I	SCARPONCELLO SPORT chev.marr.con lucert.scura	135.==
S.1769/2	I	FRANCESE lucido con fibbia	105.==
S.1769/3	I	ZARA Camoscio grigio con punt.fort.tacchi lucer.	115.==
S.1770/585	I	SCARPONCELLO Chev.verde con guar.beige e lucert.	105.==
S.1770/2	I	ERCOLANO crespo di cina verde con punt.e fort. oro	105.==
S.1772	3	CINTURINI Marrone 33 e testa di negro 105.==	315.==
		Da riportare :	L. 15608.==

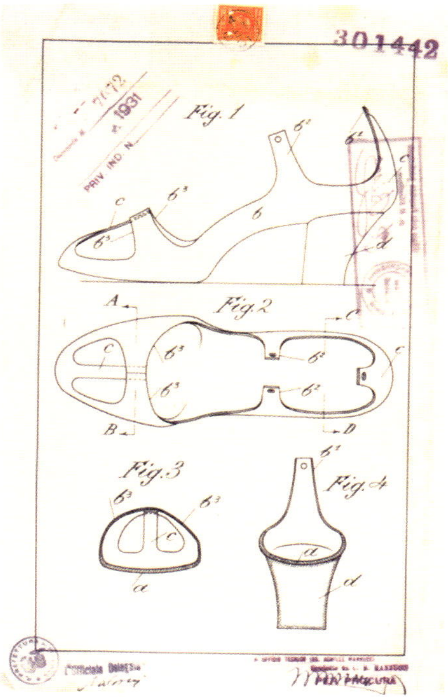

SALES ORDER FOR SHOES BY FERRAGAMO SHOE MANUFACTURING, VIA MANNELLI 57, FROM THE FERRAGAMO COMPANY, MAY 17, 1933. THE LIST INCLUDES THE *FUTURISTA* SHOE

PATENT NO. 6936: LADIES' SHOE WITH VERTICAL ZIG-ZAG PATTERNS, NOVEMBER 27, 1929

PATENT NO. 301442: SHOE SYSTEM MADE OUT OF ONLY ONE PIECE OF LEATHER, OCTOBER 4, 1932

It is not always easy to triangulate Ferragamo's relationship with specific artistic movements or prominent art world figures. We cannot say whether he embraced twentieth-century avant-garde arts through direct relationships, influenced by the contemporary press, or through his social connections. Something we do know is that Sonia Delaunay designed patchwork fabric clothing for American actress Gloria Swanson, a regular at the Hollywood Boot Shop. We also know that, after a triumphant exhibition at the 1915 Panama-Pacific International Exposition in San Francisco, Futurist artists were more famous in California than they were in Italy. Salvatore likely saw their work at that event.[81] Back in Florence, he formed a lasting partnership with Giuseppe Landsmann, who was part of the second wave of Futurism. Under the pseudonym Lucio Venna, Landsmann founded a graphics/advertising studio in the city, its offices on Borgo degli Albizi.[82] Between 1928 and 1930, he made numerous sketches, advertisements, and a promotional leaflet for Ferragamo footwear at the O'Connor & Goldberg chain in Chicago. He designed the iconic "Ferragamo's Creations Florence Italy" footwear logo, replacing the logo the American company had used until then. It is believed that he also conceived the design for one of Ferragamo's first shops on Italian soil, at Via Condotti 65, Rome.[83]

From the name *Futurista*, which Ferragamo assigned to a model appearing on a 1933 shoe order, we may infer that he shared the Futurists' world vision. This is confirmed by a number of influential, multi-talented artists from the time who expressed appreciation for his work. Thayaht remarked, "These shoes are the essence of Futurism! Originating in America, their unique blend of varied leather textures and colors, coupled with a distinctive design that seems to lend an air of forward momentum to each step, is genuinely captivating and exudes elegance. This ingenious fusion of tactile elements such as leather, canvas, and rubber drew inspiration from Italian Futurism."[84]

Salvatore Ferragamo had an innate ability to find inspiration in the world around him. Leveraging the latest technological advances, he was constantly dragging the boundaries of footwear into the present. In the summer of 1929, he began applying for his first patents for ornamental and functional designs, inventions, and company trademarks. With some, he sought to protect creations he had brought to the market a few years earlier, which had already won public acclaim. With others, particularly inventive constructions in which the primary requirement was that the idea was absolutely unique, the patent went hand-in-hand with the product's promotion and sale. Salvatore had adopted this strategy during his American years, and was still using it. Although he often crafted bespoke pieces, some of them one-of-a-kind, Ferragamo treated every concept as scalable. Like a quintessential industrial designer, without ever compromising on ornamental beauty, he created designs that always prioritized functionality. Every piece of footwear Salvatore crafted was a harmonious blend of artisanal skill and design philosophy, a true embodiment of the "Made in Italy" ethos (then as now).

Ferragamo's designs made footwear history. From 1929 to 1960, the year of his death, he applied for 368 patents for footwear, which are housed today at the Archivio Centrale dello Stato in Rome. The patents from the late 1920s to the early 1930s include invisible sole stitching methods, techniques for cutting uppers from a single piece of leather, decorations on leather obtained through top layer abrasion, and, of course, the incorporation of a metal shank into the shoe, a technique Salvatore first experimented with in his American years.[85] His 1929 patents range from innovative buckles to shoe molds, and a brilliant shoebox design in velvety blue paper, featuring a brass oval plaque on the lid (which showcased the brand) and incorporating a unique system, a slot on the short side that allowed a tab to be inserted or removed to indicate the shoe model name for the seller's convenience, allowing them to quickly identify stock in the warehouse. The box also appealed to the buyer, happy to reuse such a valuable container.[86]

Bankruptcy and the purchase of Palazzo Spini Feroni

Despite production numbers rising, tensions between Ferragamo and the American company boiled over in late 1928. Salvatore was critical of his partners' inability to manage US distribution; on their part, his partners wanted Ferragamo to move toward industrialization to increase profits, but were unable to persuade him. Salvatore was resolute, he would only handmake shoes because he was unwilling to sacrifice one iota of quality. Board meetings became increasingly fraught as the year wore on: a lawyer was brought in, and then one of the partners was tasked to audit the Italian company's ledgers and evaluate its assets and liabilities. Alas, liquidity was insufficient to cover debts. Despite Ferragamo's pressing objections, the Hollywood store was shut down.

The 1929 American economic crisis hit not just the US but Europe as well. Because industrialization in Italy lagged behind other European nations, Italy was less open to financial flows from the United States, but Ferragamo's strong American ties and Ferra-Gamo Inc. facing financial issues of

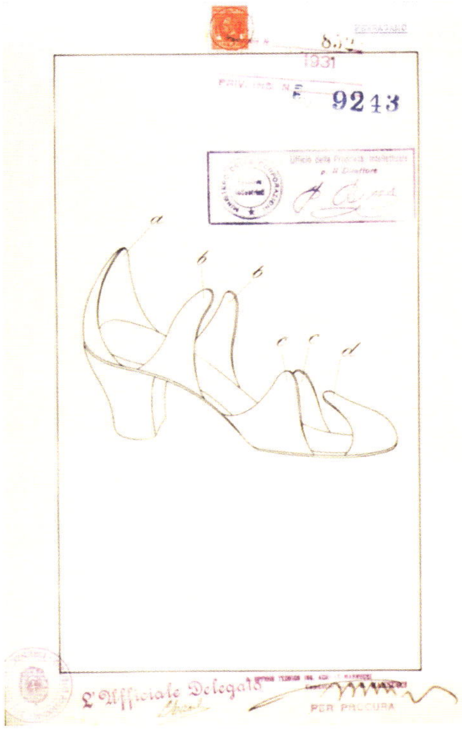

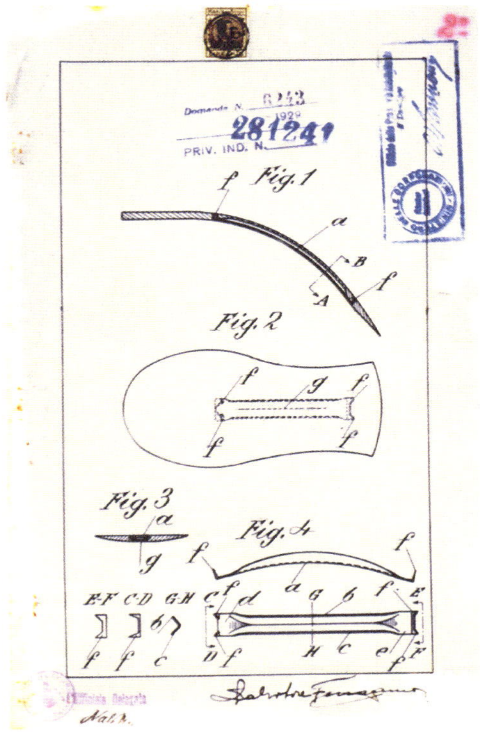

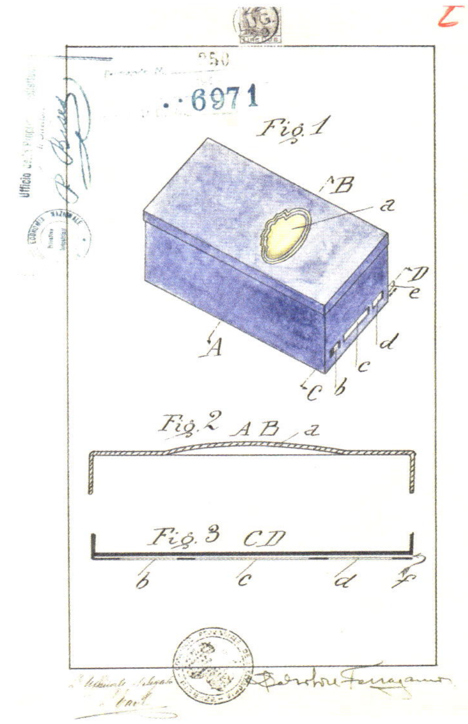

PATENT NO. 39243: SANDAL-STYLE FOOTWEAR, FEBRUARY 28, 1933

PATENT NO. 281241: SUPPORT DEVICE FOR THE SHOE SOLE ARCH, THE SO-CALLED WAIST, JANUARY 7, 1931

PATENT NO. 6971: SHOE BOX, NOVEMBER 27, 1929

its own proved to be a great setback. When production started to fall off, Salvatore set up an entirely Italian company of which he became sole owner, but in the early 1930s, the newly-founded company ended up suffering the ill-effects of the crisis. American and global economic instability only intensified the challenge for a company whose strategies and organizational processes were not fully formed.

Salvatore shifted his focus to the domestic market. On April 30, 1931, he set up a general partnership with his sister Rosina and Mario Testa to sell Ferragamo shoes, initially from a store at Via dei Fossi 2, owned by Testa. After Testa left the company, the store moved to Via Tornabuoni 14, in Palazzo Altoviti Sangalletti, as chronicled in topographic records at the Historical Archive of the Municipality of Florence and in a 1937 *Vogue* USA article.[87] Both stores sported minimalist decoration, comfortable customer seating, and stylish displays, with shoes arranged prominently against a checkered floor. Much of the furnishings were antiques, purchased from Florentine antique dealer Francesco Ciardiello. Exuding a cozy living-room feel, the store's overall ambiance was as elegant as its US counterpart.[88]

Despite his many efforts, Ferragamo fell into the hands of moneylenders and, on July 4, 1933, the Florence Court declared the shoe factory bankrupt.[89] With just a handful of loyal workers remaining, Salvatore set up a makeshift workshop at his home on Via Benedetto Varchi 15.[90] He then went about raising funds from prominent Florentines who admired his talent: Mario Vannini Parenti, a collector, art dealer, and promoter of art and tourism events in Florence; Savino Del Bene, owner of a family maritime transport business; and Francesco Ciardiello, whose antique gallery was in one of the city's most historic buildings, Palazzo Spini Feroni.

Thanks to their intervention, Salvatore repurchased patents, work tools, molds, and materials from the bankruptcy trustee, and was able to restart shoe production. Legally restricted by the bankruptcy from putting his name to products, on December 4, 1933 he set up a new company under his sister Giuseppina's name, located initially at Via Benedetto Varchi, then at Lungarno Corsini 6, and finally at Via Tornabuoni 12, just a short distance from the store.

PROMOTIONAL POSTCARD FOR THE FERRAGAMO & C. STORE, VIA DEI FOSSI 2, FLORENCE

THE FERRAGAMO & C. STORE AND SHOE FACTORY AT PALAZZO ALTOVITI SANGALLETTI, VIA TORNABUONI 12 AND 14

Business seemed to flood back. After two years of silence, Ferragamo began patenting his inventions again and actively resumed international trade, especially with the US. On September 18, 1937, he signed a significant contract, valid until 1945, with Saks in New York to make and deliver 5,000 pairs of shoes per year for sale across the American company's major US city outlets. The agreement featured a unique stipulation: Ferragamo-branded shoes would be sold in special sections bearing his name (a privilege Saks had never accorded any brand before), and be exclusive to Saks, with the exception of beach models made of raffia and similar materials.[91]

From then on, Ferragamo creations conquered an increasingly prominent place in American fashion press.

New stores opened in Italy under the Ferragamo name: in 1938 in Rome at Via Condotti 65; the following year in Milan at Via Montenapoleone 23. The company also improved its European distribution: Ferragamo shoes, which had been available in London since 1930 through Israel & Oppenheimer, could now be purchased in a new store that opened at 24 Old Bond Street in 1938.[92] Salvatore repeatedly showed a knack for choosing prestigious buildings in strategic locations. This particular building in London had belonged to the renowned Atkinson perfume brand; after significant fire damage in 1924, architect Emanuel Vincent Harris rebuilt it, adopting a more refined sense of "Britishness."[93] As early as 1929, Salvatore began selling his products in Berlin at a store managed by the Probat company at Kurfürstendamm 13,[94] a tree-lined boulevard dotted with luxurious restaurants, cafés, and elegant venues, with many cinemas where production companies premiered their films. Margaret Winter, the store's owner, set up the Italian Schuhegesellschaft company to do business with Ferragamo; later, in 1938–39, US-based Baroness Von Nagel purchased the rights to Italian Schuhegesellschaft for Europe and was represented in Germany by her son-in-law, Count Von Deyn. Thanks to her, Ferragamo managed to expand sales on German territory too. Salvatore recalls in his memoir that it was only when the United States entered the war that he severed all ties with Germany. During this period,

Ferragamo shoes were also sold on many transatlantic ocean liners—such as *Rex*, *Conte di Savoia*, *Conte Grande*, *Conte Biancamano*, *Duilio*, *Giulio Cesare*, and *Victoria Rex*—in stores managed by Maria Monaci Gallenga, the well-known owner of a Rome tailoring shop who also had a store in Via Tornabuoni, at Palazzo Spini Feroni.[95]

After going through bankruptcy, Salvatore knew all too well how important it was to nurture a local clientele and be part of Florentine high society, living among the people who could afford his footwear. Before long, he needed a more suitable workspace and larger salesroom. In his autobiography, Ferragamo wrote, "Long before I ever moved into the Palazzo Spini Feroni, it was one of the buildings of Florence that I most admired and loved."[96] He openly admitted it was love at first sight, triggered by an iconic revelation: "Below the palace there still stands the well of Dante's Beatrice. I suppose almost everyone must have seen a copy of Holiday's famous painting, *Dante's Meeting with Beatrice*. It shows the poet leaning on the parapet of the Santa Trinita bridge, gazing at Beatrice as she passes with her friends along the Lungarno on her way to the well. The Palazzo Spini Feroni stands on the left of the Lungarno, immediately beyond the frame of the picture."[97] Very much intertwined with the city of Florence's long history, this antique palazzo was built in 1289, after a flood destroyed the Spini family home. Featured in every cityscape because of

GRASS CLOTH WITH BROWN CALF

FOR EVENING—GOLD KID WITH RED SATIN

THOSE cork-soled clogs worn on Italian beaches were the first step. Those cork-soled evening shoes shown in December 1 Vogue the second. And now comes the newest step in the evolution: a sole that develops into a leather-covered cork heel—a sole for any walk in life—street, sports, evening. Ferragamo, shoemaker to many of the smartest women in Italy, made these new versions—keeping one eye on comfort and the other on looks. Saks-Fifth Avenue imports them directly

59

VOGUE USA, JANUARY 1, 1938. MUSEO FERRAGAMO, FLORENCE

SILK SATIN AND KIDSKIN SANDAL WITH LAYERED WEDGE HEEL IN COVERED CORK, 1937

its strategic riverside position and remarkable grandeur, only comparable to Palazzo Vecchio, the building changed hands multiple times over the centuries, with each owner leaving their mark on the interiors. From 1834 to 1843, it housed one of the city's international hotels, the Hôtel d'Europe. Then it was the Florence Municipality's headquarters when the city was the capital of Italy, from 1865 to 1870.[98] The Società Anonima Immobili Costruzioni of Milan bought the building in 1923; by 1928, the company became joint-stock company Società Anonima Palazzo Spini Feroni and relocated to Florence. In 1934, they revised their charter, specifying in Article 2 that in future they might oversee not just the building's regular and special management but also the "direct or indirect, temporary or permanent management of commercial enterprises."[99] Primary shareholder Arturo Campagnano, a Jewish merchant living in Florence, subsequently became the company's administrator.

On November 25, 1938, the Società Anonima altered its structure once more, in preparation for Campagnano's departure. Ahead of the worsening situation brought about by Mussolini's racial laws against Jews on November 17, 1938, Campagnano likely made plans to leave Italy. He did not actually depart for America until late 1939, selling up his share in the property to Ferragamo. Because of his bankruptcy, Salvatore used a number of proxies for the transaction, including his sister Giuseppina and his friend and attorney Gabriele Consolazio, who hailed from his hometown. Ferragamo's name first appeared on the tenant list on December 12, 1938.

In his autobiography, Ferragamo detailed the substantial cost of acquiring these shares: the property's total price was three million, four hundred thousand lire. He agreed to pay just under two million through a loan set to last until 1970, with the remaining one and a half million settled in nine monthly installments of approximately 170,000 lire each. These payments were due by 10 in the morning on the final day of each month, and Ferragamo risked losing all prior

PALAZZO SPINI FERONI
AND THE FERRAGAMO
WORKSHOP, 1938–39

payments if he missed just one.[100] This time, Salvatore managed to meet his obligations.[101]

When, on July 21, 1939, the Florence Court discharged him from bankruptcy, Salvatore Ferragamo could at last use his own name. On December 2, the now-41-year-old craftsman set up the new "Salvatore Ferragamo" limited partnership. Two years later, on December 25, 1941, he acquired the other partners' shares and converted the company into a sole proprietorship.

This brief overview of corporate change and the process of acquiring the palazzo that, to this day, is home to the Ferragamo name requires further investigation and examination to provide a clear understanding of the complexities of events in the lead-up to World War II, spanning not just our own historical scope but the entire country's. However, what emerges clearly is once again Salvatore's entrepreneurial prowess, his ability to navigate stormy seas, trusting in his work and creativity, and being steadfast in his choices, which in the end always saw him through his professional and human journey. Considering his humble beginnings and lack of professional training in complex spheres where legal and economic expertise are required, his story seems even more remarkable today.

Cork wedges and chocolate wrappers

Leading up to and during World War II, Salvatore Ferragamo's creativity was at its peak. Unstable economic conditions, challenges in sourcing high-quality materials, and extensive nationalization under fascism seemed to stimulate rather than inhibit his flair, prompting him to show astonishing versatility as he turned to materials not commonly or traditionally used in shoemaking.

After the League of Nations imposed trade sanctions on Italy in October 1935 to punish imperialist aggression in Ethiopia, Benito Mussolini, Italy's head of government, announced in March 1936 a radical protectionist policy known as "autarky." These "unjust sanctions"—albeit far milder and less well-enforced than initially feared—allowed the regime to formally adopt an autarkic economy, something already underway elsewhere in Europe, tangibly motivated to win

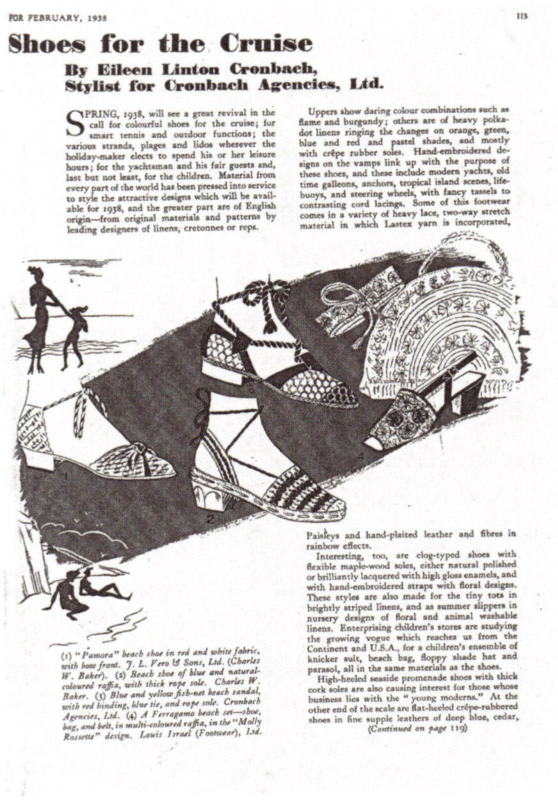

FOR FEBRUARY, 1938 113

Shoes for the Cruise

By Eileen Linton Cronbach, Stylist for Cronbach Agencies, Ltd.

SPRING, 1938, will see a great revival in the call for colourful shoes for the cruise; for smart tennis and outdoor functions; the various strands, plages and lidos wherever the holiday-maker elects to spend his or her leisure hours; for the yachtsman and his fair guests and, last but not least, for the children. Material from every part of the world has been pressed into service to style the attractive designs which will be available for 1938, and the greater part are of English origin—from original materials and patterns by leading designers of linens, cretonnes or reps.

Uppers show daring colour combinations such as flame and burgundy; others are of heavy polka-dot linens ringing the changes on orange, green, blue and red and pastel shades, and mostly with crêpe rubber soles. Hand-embroidered designs on the vamps link up with the purpose of these shoes, and these include modern yachts, old time galleons, anchors, tropical island scenes, life-buoys, and steering wheels, with fancy tassels to contrasting cord lacings. Some of this footwear comes in a variety of heavy lace, two-way stretch material in which Lastex yarn is incorporated, Paisleys and hand-plaited leather and fibres in rainbow effects.

Interesting, too, are clog-typed shoes with flexible maple-wood soles, either natural polished or brilliantly lacquered with high gloss enamels, and with hand-embroidered straps with floral designs. These styles are also made for the tiny tots in brightly striped linens, and as summer slippers in nursery designs of floral and animal washable linens. Enterprising children's stores are studying the growing vogue which reaches us from the Continent and U.S.A., for a children's ensemble of knicker suit, beach bag, floppy shade hat and parasol, all in the same materials as the shoes.

High-heeled seaside promenade shoes with thick cork soles are also causing interest for those whose business lies with the "young moderns." At the other end of the scale are flat-heeled crêpe-rubbered shoes in fine supple leathers of deep blue, cedar,

(Continued on page 119)

(1) "Pamora" beach shoe in red and white fabric, with bow front. J. L. Vero & Sons, Ltd. (Charles W. Baker). (2) Beach shoe of blue and natural-coloured raffia, with thick rope sole. Charles W. Baker. (3) Blue and yellow fish-net beach sandal, with red binding, blue tie, and rope sole. Cronbach Agencies, Ltd. (4) A Ferragamo beach set—shoe, bag, and belt, in multi-coloured raffia, in the "Molly Rossette" design. Louis Israel (Footwear), Ltd.

FOOTWEAR ORGANIZER, FEBRUARY 1938

BELLEZZA, APRIL 1941

national consensus and appeal to patriotic pride. As a matter of fact, ideological reasons subsequently served to politically justify an economic strategy initiated sporadically about a decade earlier, conceived to boost domestic Italian output of raw materials and capital goods, limiting imports to goods not available domestically, and encouraging the manufacture of replacements.[102]

Under autarky, rustic yarns such as broom, hemp (adopted for Parisian fashion shows with the eloquent name of "Balilla hemp"), local production, Casentino wool fabric, and Sardinian orbace were all promoted in the textile industry. Artificial fibers such as rayon, soft and as pliable as silk, also had a major role to play. Plant fibers and the skin of fish such as sharks and snappers, shiny and dotted with pearly scales, replaced traditional kid and calf leathers in footwear; the leather for soles was replaced by Cuoital, a mix of leather scraps, latex, and vulcanized rubber, or by Sapsa, which the Pirelli company produced using finely ground leather residue and rubber latex. Then there were Coriacel (made in paper mills from leather scraps, plant fiber, and glue), regenerated rubber, and a substitute made by kneading together leather cuttings and tannery shavings with rubber latex and resin.[103] Plastics also boosted the footwear and textile industries. The warm tones of Bakelite, transparent and easily dyed Plexiglas, synthetic resin, and polyvinyl chloride (PVC) were adaptively made into heels, soles, and woven uppers, offering moldability and high durability. Another widely used material was cellophane. Made from laminating viscose, itself derived from cellulose, it was versatile and lent itself well to various uses and combinations; available in a variety of colors, it could be mixed with cotton, rayon, or silk thread, woven or knitted.[104]

Experimenting with materials was just one part, albeit a rather successful one, of broader research to establish and provide an identity for Italian clothing and accessory production. The end-goal was to compete with French high fashion and English sportswear style, both dominant on the market, including in Italy. Industry magazines *Lidel* and *Per Voi Signora* teamed up with new regime bodies to run campaigns, seeking to persuade Italian women to purchase home-grown products rather than foreign ones,

GRAZIA,
APRIL 3, 1941

NOVUS,
SUMMER 1940

encouraging industry players to give up French haute couture and develop an Italian style that was creatively independent, supported by an equally independent manufacturing and commercial system.

Around this time, Salvatore Ferragamo patented his most famous invention of all: the cork wedge heel, created at least two years before it was widely adopted in international fashion and became a distinctive hallmark of that era's taste.[105] The wedge was primarily designed to elevate the heel and provide stable support for the arch. This clever and imaginative solution addressed shortages caused by sanctions on steel Ferragamo used for his metal shanks, which he had been importing from Germany even though at that time Italy's steel industry was in state hands, owned by IRI.

Duchess Visconti di Modrone was the first woman who let herself be convinced to wear wedge shoes, which in America people immediately started calling "lifties," or "wedgies." She found them a real to-do, but had no desire to offend her shoemaker. "She wore them for the first time to church one Sunday morning—the time chosen by all fashionable women in Italy to display their new clothes—and the effect was instantaneous."[106] Ladies loved them and the next day, many rushed to order a pair from Ferragamo. He quickly patented his idea but to no avail: all the shoemakers began copying him, their shoe factories churning out thousands of wedges daily—it was impossible to pursue everyone legally. Fashion magazines, including the American edition of *Vogue* and newspapers like *The New York Times*, vied to feature the new development.[107]

The wedge gave Ferragamo the artist a larger surface on which to express his creativity, a dimension that uppers and heels simply did not afford. Salvatore experimented with many wedge variants: heeled and platformed, layered and domed, carved and painted, decorated with glass mirrors assembled using ancient mosaic techniques, or with brass grates crafted with floral spirals or stone-studded. These designs seemed more akin to furniture, household items, or contemporary architectures, like New York's Chrysler Building, than fashion accessories of the time. The softened, aerodynamic shapes of some of these shoes looked like miniaturized versions of structures Florentine architect Cesare Augusto Poggi was designing for cars and planes around those years. Many eccentric designs had surreal influences—uppers perforated with elongated eyelets, toes in an unusual rhinoceros horn shape, impossibly high heels reminiscent of boots worn in ancient Greek tragedy, and very tall Renaissance wooden wedges—and were truly unique,

PATENT NO. 18453:
SUMMER FOOTWEAR FOR LADIES IN RAFFIA KNIT OR SIMILAR WITH EMBOSSING ON THE UPPER, OCTOBER 31, 1940

PATENT NO. 18366:
SUMMER FOOTWEAR FOR LADIES IN RAFFIA KNIT, OCTOBER 31, 1940

SUEDE AND CALFSKIN LACED SHOE, 1940

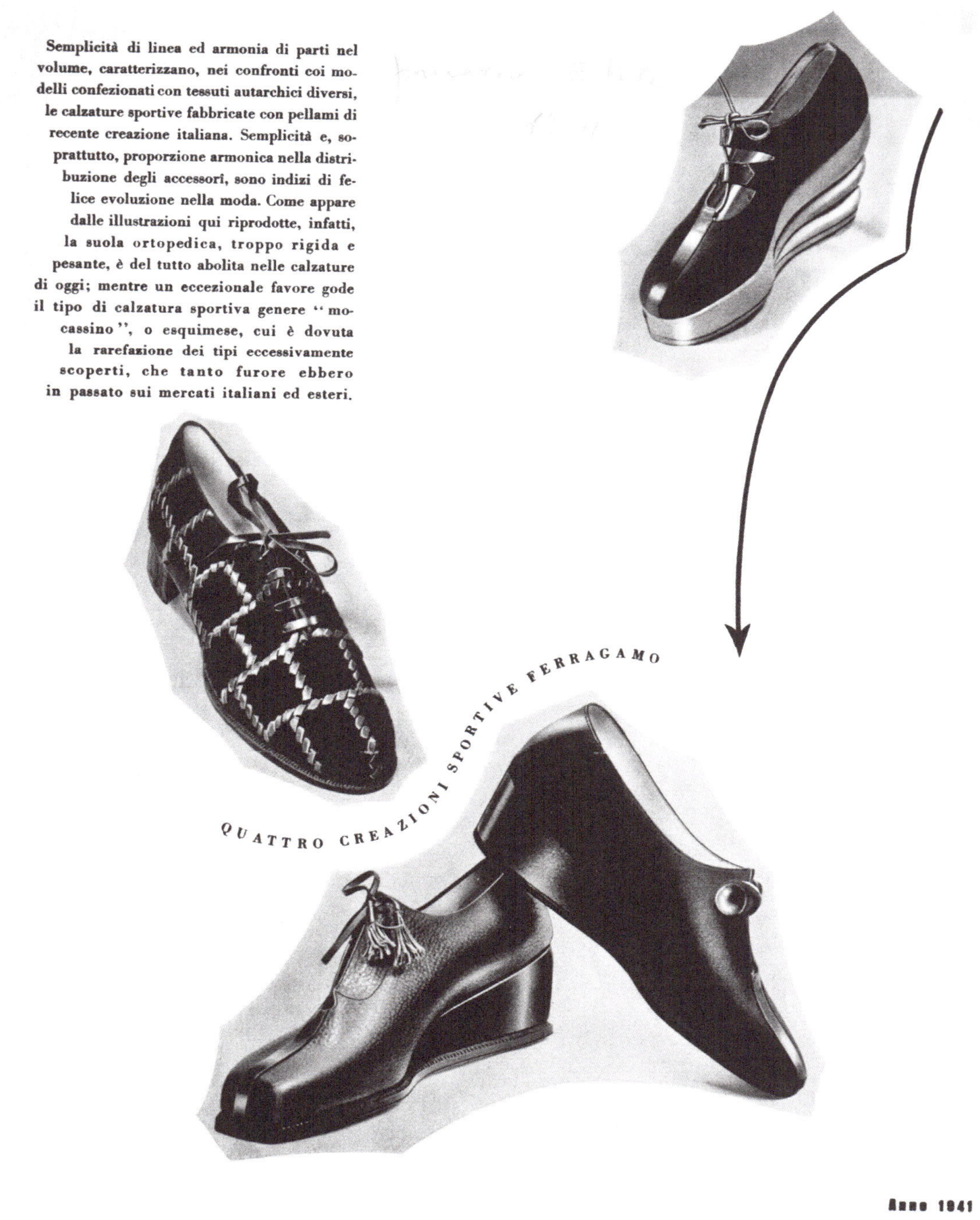

Semplicità di linea ed armonia di parti nel volume, caratterizzano, nei confronti coi modelli confezionati con tessuti autarchici diversi, le calzature sportive fabbricate con pellami di recente creazione italiana. Semplicità e, soprattutto, proporzione armonica nella distribuzione degli accessori, sono indizi di felice evoluzione nella moda. Come appare dalle illustrazioni qui riprodotte, infatti, la suola ortopedica, troppo rigida e pesante, è del tutto abolita nelle calzature di oggi; mentre un eccezionale favore gode il tipo di calzatura sportiva genere "mocassino", o esquimese, cui è dovuta la rarefazione dei tipi eccessivamente scoperti, che tanto furore ebbero in passato sui mercati italiani ed esteri.

QUATTRO CREAZIONI SPORTIVE FERRAGAMO

Anno 1941

DOCUMENTO-MODA,
SPRING–SUMMER 1941

except for creations by the most avant-garde fashion designers beyond the Alps, often working in tandem with artists: for example, French couturier Elsa Schiaparelli, who was a friend of Dalí, Bérard, and Cocteau, with her fabrics printed like newspaper pages, clothes decorated with raffia or cellophane, and buttons shaped like lips, demonstrated numerous similarities to Ferragamo's style. The two would only meet and work together after the war, so the reciprocal influences were entirely coincidental and were brought about through fashion magazines and a handful of shared clients such Claudette Colbert, Marlene Dietrich, and later Lauren Bacall.

Salvatore's creativity shone through not just in ornamental features but structural elements as well. He designed heels by sewing together wine bottle corks and then covering them in leather; patented special procedures for preparing leather substitutes; devised systems for producing raffia or mesh uppers, flexible wooden soles, transparent Bakelite heels, and heels made of galalith or glass resembling car wheels or sewing thread spools. He certainly enjoyed putting his creativity to the test.

Proving that luxury doesn't stem from the richness of the material used but the detailing, the creative originality of the idea, and high-quality craftsmanship, his natural penchant for humble materials prompted Ferragamo to make extensive use of hemp fabrics, straw, woolen threads, felt, pressed silk, and cellophane from the early 1930s onward. He wove pieces of chocolate paper together to make cellophane for shiny, thick, and pleated surfaces, a precursor of sustainable recycling far ahead of its time.[108]

That said, shape was always the dominant element in his creations. Every detail, the symmetry, the perfect balance between weight and measurements all drew on architecture—a connection that was the predominant feature of all Italian design during those years and that, serving as the nation's true cultural heritage, was ingrained in every kilometer of its landscape with a house, palazzo, or building.

The rollcall of international clients for Ferragamo's uniquely original footwear continued to grow during the years leading up to the war. He made Judy Garland's *Rainbow*

GRAZIA, MARCH 13, 1941

bricata con materiale tessile, attira dunque tutta la nostra attenzione, specie per il fabbisogno estivo, per il quale il tessuto delle massaie rurali cremonesi, dirette dalla illuminata perizia della Ispettrice del Partito, è stato studiato e creato da Fede Cheti, in collaborazione tecnica con Salvatore Ferragamo. Questo trinomio: Cremona, Ferragamo, Fede Cheti, costituisce dunque l'intesa nella collaborazione proficua delle forze vive atte a risolvere, con eleganza somma, le difficoltà contingenti del periodo di guerra, con una utilità indiscutibile per l'economia di materie prime nella fabbricazione delle calzature per il pubblico italiano.

cremonese

Creazioni FERRAGAMO

DOCUMENTO-MODA, SUMMER 1942. MUSEO FERRAGAMO, FLORENCE

sandals for *The Wizard of Oz* premiere in 1939, the film that made the actress famous. He created a high-platform shoe studded with jewels for the amazing Maharani of Cooch Behar, and a shoe with a cork platform and heel decorated with glass mosaic tiles for height-challenged Brazilian singer and dancer Carmen Miranda. We could go on, mentioning the cork-heeled raffia sandal for American Loretta Young in perfect autarchic style, or Claretta Petacci's numerous shoes, obsessed as she was with accessories. He made an antelope shoe for Princess Maria José of Savoy, with ghillie lacing and a wedge heel, which became part of the Red Cross uniform during the war. Even Eva Braun, the Führer's companion, fell for the allure of the Ferragamo footwear. Salvatore recalled that on a family trip to Florence in May 1938 with Hitler, she stopped in at Palazzo Spini Feroni.[109]

Able to make high-quality and elegant shoes out of any material, Salvatore Ferragamo was considered a national hero. A plethora of articles, including the summer 1940 issue of *Novus*, highlighted how his shoes upheld Italy's prestige

THE FERRAGAMO SHOE
FACTORY STAND AT
THE CRAFTS EXHIBITION,
FLORENCE, 1939

across Europe and in the United States.[110] *Documento-Moda*, the country's most prestigious and refined wartime magazine, published by the National Fashion Institute, featured Ferragamo in several pieces between 1941 and 1943. The summer 1942 issue ran a lengthy article featuring beautiful pull-out photos of lace-up shoes with lacquered wooden soles the color of the garment, along with patented footwear in armored felt with pressed silk bark soles, and shoes in woven synthetic straw in the garment's colors. In the article, Ferragamo's part in successful fascist-approved fashion creation was particularly praised. Under party inspector direction, the raw materials Ferragamo used for his sandals were woven by country housewives near Cremona on design by Fede Cheti. "This trio, Cremona, Ferragamo, Fede Cheti, laid the foundations for fruitful collaboration of active forces to solve contingent wartime difficulties with the utmost elegance, undeniably benefiting the raw material economy in manufacturing shoes for the Italian people."[111]

Not surprisingly, Ferragamo was invited to participate at events to enhance Italian prestige, not just locally[112] but abroad: his shoes were showcased alongside other textile products in the Italian pavilion at the New York World's Fair, which was held from April 30, 1939 to October 31, 1940.[113]

On the eve of World War II, Ferragamo's shoe production was up to some 200 pairs a day from his Florentine workshop and Schiavini Cassi Castle in the village of Buti, near Pisa. The company employed 400 workers. In the early months of the conflict, trade with England and America continued to thrive; however, when Italy joined the war, orders dropped off dramatically. Over the next few years, worker headcount tumbled to 50.[114]

War, marriage, and persecution

Not long after beginning the process of purchase of Palazzo Spini Feroni, after many years of renting different homes, Salvatore began considering purchasing somewhere permanent to live. He settled on a villa on a hill overlooking Florence, located on the slopes of Monte Ceceri, near Maiano. It was a place steeped in history: Leonardo da Vinci had tested his time machine here in 1506; local quarries had been extracting *pietra serena* here since the Middle Ages, which many architects used to erect Florentine palazzi. Built in the eleventh century as a towered dwelling, this tower house cum Renaissance palazzo featured a central layout between two massive towers (later converted into dovecotes) and a long frontal terrace supported by a barbican, which offered magnificent views out over Florence; dense woods spread behind the villa, replanted in 1929 to create a more natural look. Ferragamo's acquisition of the dwelling was preceded by the establishment of a new company, A.R.I.A., dedicated to purchasing and reselling real estate. He appointed the company's administrators and auditors and set about furnishing the property. It was big enough to host Giuseppina, Rosina, their respective husbands, and mother Mariantonia,

COVER OF THE CATALOGUE *ITALY AT THE WORLD'S FAIR NEW YORK 1939* AND THE TEXTILE AND FASHION DEPARTMENT BOOTH

all under the same roof: Salvatore's original family—indeed, the only family he had ever known—came to live with him in Florence.

Successful and the wrong side of forty, so completely had Salvatore thrown himself into his work that he had not settled down, married, or had children. In the summer of 1940, he, Rosina, and his brother-in-law went back to Bonito, to the house where all the Ferragamo siblings were born. His uncle, the priest who had helped him open his first store in the village, was now living there. Little did it matter fashion magazines circulated infrequently in the Irpinian village, everyone knew Salvatore had become a celebrity, and that his customers were movie actresses and queens. Fulvio Miletti, the village's physician and mayor, was one of the party who went to welcome the famous shoemaker. A handsome man from a notable local family, Miletti had a reputation for religious piety and immense generosity. His wife, Giovanna Pellegrino, had recently passed away. When Miletti invited Ferragamo to his beautiful home to discuss charity for the local poor, his younger daughter, 18-year-old Wanda, took on the hostess duties. Salvatore described this encounter in his autobiography. It was, he said, love at first sight when he saw young, nervous Wanda utter a few words of welcome. He decided there and then to marry her, something he whispered into his sister's ear in English. The doctor tried to send the guests away, but Salvatore did everything he could think of to extend the visit, attempting to engage Miletti

in topics of mutual interest: foot anatomy and perfect shoe fitting. Salvatore knelt before Wanda and asked her to slip off a shoe so he could measure her foot. Knowing she had a hole in her stocking, the young woman blushed. That moment was the start of an intense courtship, assisted by Wanda's trustworthy housemaid, Meneca, who acted as a messenger and go-between. Initially, Wanda's father would not hear of it, citing the significant age difference between the mature shoemaker and his daughter. Eventually, however, he had to relent.[115]

Wanda's account of that fateful day differed significantly from Salvatore's, both in interviews she gave the press and letters she wrote to her grandchildren. In the Wanda Ferragamo biography, written by her granddaughter Ginevra Visconti, Melania G. Mazzucco notes that in reality it was Wanda who took the initiative. She knew nothing about the fashion world, but she complimented Salvatore on elegantly outfitting women with his footwear, even if she had never actually seen any. Then, still unsure whether to accept or decline the man's advances, it was she who took the final step, sending a postcard after he left Bonito with the words "Thinking of you."[116] Whatever the case, Salvatore and Wanda married a few months later, on November 9, 1940, in the church of Santa Maria della Catena in Naples (also known as Santa Lucia). Their marriage was built on deep love and a shared vision: to have children who could work with their father in the family business and expand it, transforming it into a fashion house making not just shoes but clothing and accessories.

After a brief honeymoon in Sorrento and the Amalfi Coast, interrupted by aerial bombings of Naples, they returned to Florence to start their new life. Wanda immersed herself in her role as wife and perfect hostess, striving to integrate into the social fabric of a city that initially seemed so gray

ENGAGED COUPLE WANDA MILETTI AND SALVATORE FERRAGAMO IN BONITO, 1940

SALVATORE AND HIS WIFE ON THEIR HONEYMOON IN SORRENTO AND THE AMALFI COAST

SALVATORE FERRAGAMO AND WANDA MILETTI'S WEDDING IN THE CHURCH OF SANTA MARIA DELLA CATENA IN NAPLES, NOVEMBER 9, 1940

and cold compared to her hometown. Salvatore continued to navigate the challenges of footwear marketing and the search for alternatives to leather, all of which had been commandeered for army shoes. Their family expanded with the birth of three children: Fiamma, Giovanna, and Ferruccio, followed a few years later by Fulvia, Leonardo, and Massimo.

When Italy joined the war, regulations on making and selling shoes became much tougher. Army demand for soldiers' shoes accounted for the lion's share of what was available: the authorities only allowed limited quantities of bovine, equine, and ovine skins for civilian use, and put in place stringent rules on how they could be used.[117] Restrictions tightened once again in 1942: only felt, lined or padded fabric uppers, and soles made of wood, rubber, regenerated rubber, and synthetic resins, applied to uppers using a variety of systems, were permissible for civilian men's and women's shoes. Any footwear or tanning companies that had leather and leather goods in stock before the decree's date had to declare their inventory. These bans did not, however, prevent increasing smuggling of skins, or legal breaches.[118]

In January 1943, Salvatore opened in Bonito, at the former Casa dell'Assistenza, a shoe workshop that started making men's and boys' shoes with Cuoital soles, but unfortunately it was severely damaged by allied air raids on September 10 that year. His father-in-law kept Salvatore abreast by mail about developments regarding production, restoration work after the bombing, and the workers' mood.[119] Despite the host of problems the war brought, Salvatore strived to maintain a serene and family-friendly atmosphere at his workshops. He shared work and break times with his employees, and took a personal interest in their lives. During curfews, he organized impromptu meals in the basement of Palazzo Spini Feroni to distract his shoemakers—those who hadn't left for the war—from melancholic thoughts.[120]

SALVATORE FERRAGAMO WITH HIS FIRST CHILD, FIAMMA, BORN IN 1941

KIDSKIN LACED SHOE WITH FISH SCALE DECORATION, 1938–39. SALVATORE GAVE WANDA A BLACK VARIANT FOR THEIR ENGAGEMENT

The patents Ferragamo was filing were mainly for waterproof, antifreeze footwear systems, leather substitute preparation processes, military shoes, systems for stitching uppers to non-leather soles, and wooden soles.[121] Some of these ideas drew on his technological design skills in fields unrelated to the world of footwear: in 1942 and 1943, he invented an offensive and defensive anti-aircraft system, a sea fortress, and a multiple-launch torpedo.[122]

Italy's political situation deteriorated further on September 3, 1943, when the Italian government signed the Cassibile armistice, which was announced on the radio on September 8. Military leaders, King Victor Emmanuel III and his son Umberto, and the head of government Pietro Badoglio abandoned the capital and fled to Brindisi. The Italian army was left without orders and the nation suffered the fury of German troops, while anti-fascist forces formed a National Liberation Committee. The Germans were in control of Florence and its hills, and when the Americans realized the city was a crucial German logistics center and a danger to the allied army, they decided that it had to be bombed. On September 25, 1943, the Allies targeted the railway junction at Campo di Marte to weaken German army weapons provisioning, but due to an error, the Piazza Cavour area north of the old town center was bombed. Over 200 civilians were killed. After this massacre of innocents, Florence was not bombed for the rest of the year and it remained in German hands, as did Fiesole and the villa Il Palagio, where Salvatore and his family lived. Because of his former American citi-

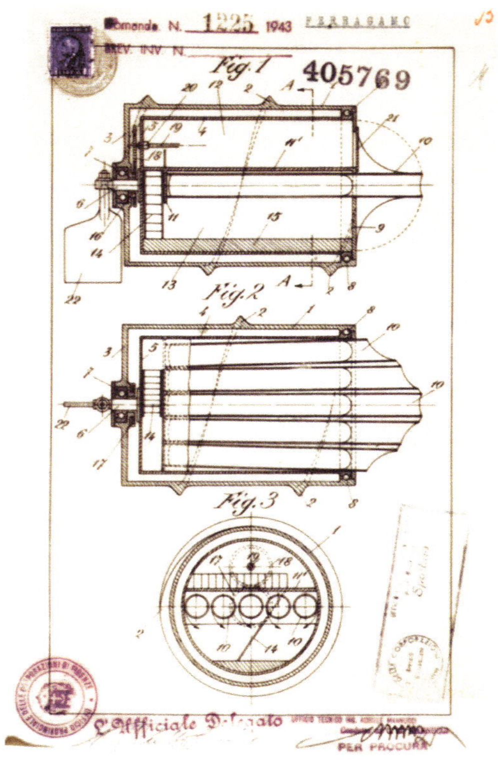

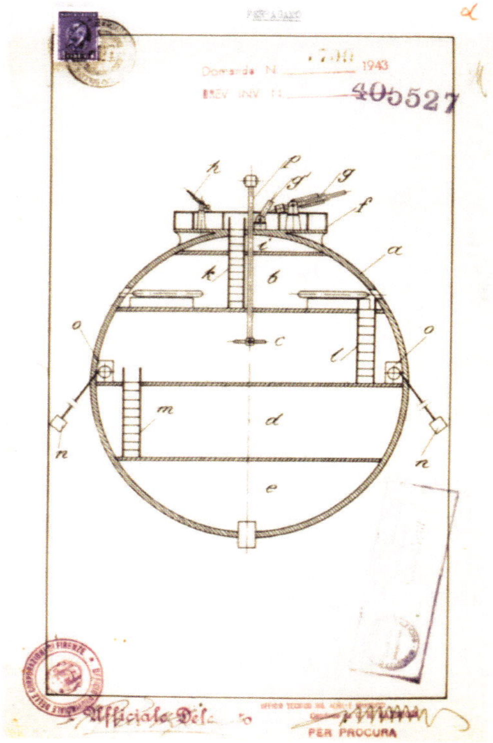

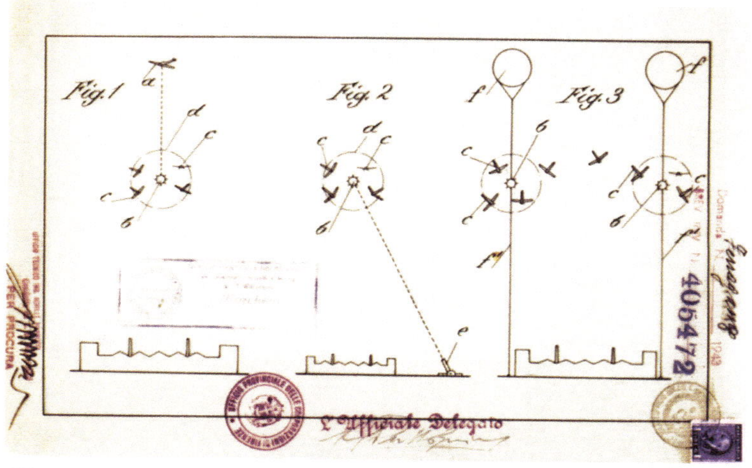

PATENT NO. 405769:
MULTIPLE-LAUNCH
TORPEDO, SEPTEMBER 7,
1943

PATENT NO. 405527:
SEA FORTRESS,
AUGUST 18, 1943

PATENT NO. 405472:
AIRCRAFT OFFENSE
AND DEFENSE SYSTEM,
AUGUST 14, 1943

VIEW OF SANTA TRINITA
BRIDGE IN FLORENCE,
DESTROYED IN
AUGUST 1944

zenship and trade with the United States, Ferragamo faced accusations of being an Allied spy. He managed to persuade the officers of his innocence and was spared, at the cost of food and his car being stolen. When soldiers expropriated other villas in the vicinity, the Ferragamo house became a place of shelter for many refugees. Salvatore continued to be persecuted: the Germans arrested him twice more on suspicion of spying; both times, he was released.[123]

On the night of August 3–4, 1944, to slow down the Allies' advance, the Germans mined and blew up bridges over the Arno, all except Ponte Vecchio. People heard the boom and saw the glare of explosions from miles away. Salvatore and Wanda watched the unprecedented destruction of Florence's historic center with horror from their terrace. The Santa Trinita bridge and their palazzo on Lungarno Acciaiuoli were hit too and suffered damage. When the war was over, Ferragamo and other citizens funded reconstruction of the bridge; a stamp issued on September 19, 1949 commemorated this moment, featuring the motto "It will be rebuilt as and where it was."[124]

After the bridges were destroyed, the entire city, from center to outskirts, became a theater of war, with battles and clashes occurring for the next 20 days or so. Bullets rained down on houses, causing death and injury; even the hospitals were under fire for a long time. The Allied army bombed the hills of Fiesole, where the German artillery had dug in. A nearby road to the Ferragamos' residence was hit: the windows at Palagio shattered, two gates and several walls collapsed. Salvatore, his wife, their children and some 50 evacuees took refuge for three days in the villa's cellars, listening to bullets and grenades as they whistled into the building's walls. Every now and then, a grenade flew through a window and destroyed everything in its path. Doors and stairways were damaged, but the villa's structure held firm.[125] Taking advantage of a truce, Salvatore and his family were finally able to flee to Florence, which had since been declared an open city. But Salvatore's problems did not end there. On August 31, the National Liberation Committee's control commission arrested him at Florence police station, after an anonymous tip-off that, through his commercial activities in Germany, he was involved in spying and collaborating with the Germans. The judiciary reviewed the case and found the allegations baseless. The authorities released Salvatore on September 8, 1944. He was arrested again on November 7 and, this time, was released after eight days of imprisonment. On August 20, 1945, the American Military Police imprisoned him for a third time on the basis of the original allegation. He proved his innocence and was released on September 6, just in time to witness the birth of Ferruccio, his third child and first son.[126]

The Neiman Marcus Award

The war may have been over, but Italy lay in ruins. Ferragamo's business was greatly diminished, Palazzo Spini Feroni had been damaged, the shops had nothing to sell, and the

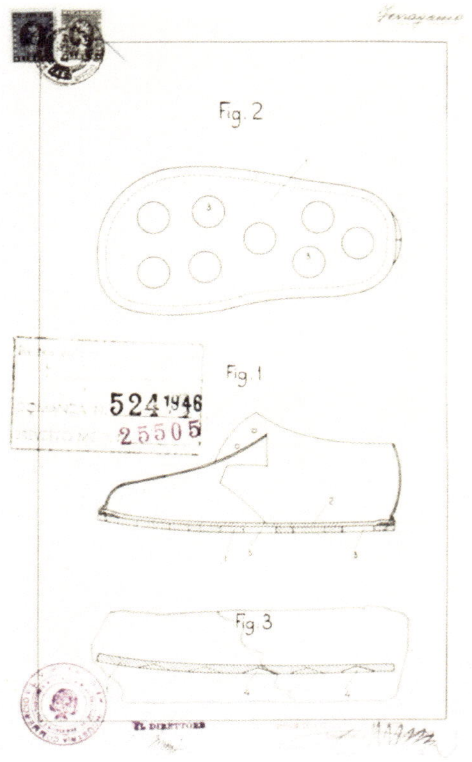

PATENT NO. 22505: SOLE FOR CHILDREN'S SHOES, WITH LIGHTENING AND TRACTION GROOVES ON THE WALKING SURFACE, NOVEMBER 16, 1946

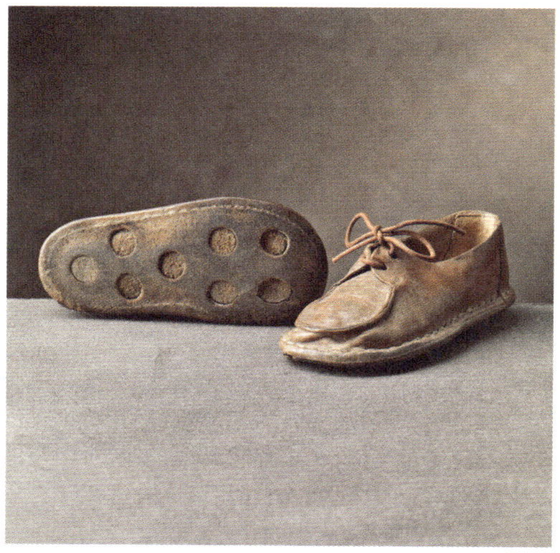

CHILDREN'S CALFSKIN DERBY WITH ANTI-SLIP SOLE, 1946

store in Lido di Venezia had been destroyed. Obtaining raw materials for shoemaking was touch-and-go, and chemicals for leather dyeing were in short supply. The cobblers who had stayed on during the war were no longer used to keeping up with their previous intense work pace—at most, they would make 25 handmade pairs of shoes per day during the war years. And those who had faced death at the front lost their passion for work.

Ferragamo did not lose heart. In 1945, he wrote the opening article for the November issue of Italy's main fashion magazine, *Bellezza*, in which, after the harrowing war years, he invited all fashion creators to resume production with optimism and energy. A few pages on, the magazine published a Riccardo Magni illustration of a Ferragamo shoe design displayed prominently, together with Brunelleschi's dome, against the backdrop of devastated Florence—a symbol of Italy's unwavering resilience.[127]

On November 15, 1945, Ferragamo established the limited liability company Esercizi Ferragamo & C., which from then on would exclusively trade products manufactured by Salvatore Ferragamo of Florence. Just a few months later, on May 29, 1946, it was converted into a joint-stock company: already employing over a hundred people,[128] it registered its first profit, 275,965 lire. A new line of children's footwear was launched: called *Primi passi*, it featured a special anti-slip sole.[129] The advertising brochure for models in this collection shows that Ferragamo already owned nine shops up and down Italy: in Turin, Milan, Venice, Genoa, Viareggio, Pisa, Florence, Rome, and Naples. Despite ongoing challenges for the Italian and world economies, trade relations were reestablished with European markets and the United States, and the company's business went from strength to strength. Esercizi Ferragamo & C. S.p.A. closed its 1947 accounts with a net profit of almost one million lire.

BELLEZZA,
NOVEMBER 1945

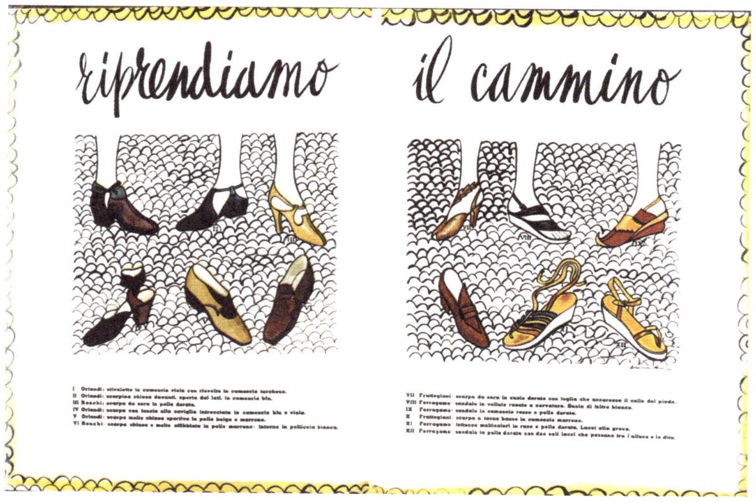

SALVATORE AND WANDA FERRAGAMO ON THE *QUEEN ELIZABETH* OCEAN LINER, 1947

THE NEIMAN MARCUS AWARD IN DALLAS: THE FASHION SHOW OF CHRISTIAN DIOR'S CLOTHES WITH FERRAGAMO SHOES

WHAT PRICE FOREIGN TRADE? continued

$1,077.43 British designer Hartnell's ball gown costs $1077.43. With these dollars, Britain could buy 13,417 gallons of oil.

$1,692.86 France can use the dollars this cocktail dress by designer Christian Dior brings. They could buy 5,287 pounds of cotton.

$45.00 One ounce of French perfume by Lanvin costs $45. France could use these American dollars to buy 17 bushels of wheat.

$29.75 Italian designer Ferragamo made these "invisible" shoes. With the dollars they bring, Italy can buy four tons of coal.

What Price Foreign Trade?

Neiman-Marcus Tenth Annual Fashion Award actually high-lights a lesson in international trade and good will

International winners of the Neiman-Marcus Fashion Award chat with H. Stanley Marcus, executive vice president of the Dallas store. Left to right, Frenchman Dior, American Irene, British Mitcheson–representing Norman Hartnell–Italian Ferragamo, and Mr. Marcus.

THE annual Neiman-Marcus award had more than local significance this year when Stanley Marcus, executive vice president of the Texas store, honored an Englishman, a Frenchman, an Italian, as well as the American designer, Irene. He was, in effect, asking America to foster international trade. Because, for every lush import (such as a $1,000 ball gown, $45 perfume, $30 shoes), some European country would get the benefit of the American dollars these goods brought in. These countries could use the dollars – which they need urgently – to buy critical emergency goods that would hasten the recovery of war-ravaged Europe.

LOOK took the extravagantly priced award-winning clothes, posed them against the tragically needed American raw materials which the money might buy – oil, cotton, grain, coal. Incidentally, such goods as these may figure largely in the Marshall Plan; thus, in its local Texas way, the Neiman-Marcus Awards may indirectly help international trade.

(Continued on page 71)

Figures are based on September–October, 1947, prices.

END

LOOK MAGAZINE,
DECEMBER 9, 1947

LABEL OF THE FERRINA LINE, 1949. MUSEO FERRAGAMO, FLORENCE

In the summer of 1947, Stanley Marcus, vice-president of US department store Neiman Marcus, invited Salvatore to Dallas to come and receive the Fashion Oscar, for "masterfully blending Italian classicism and artisan tradition with modern inventiveness in footwear." Since the prestigious award was established in 1938, only American designers had received it; but coinciding with the department store's fortieth anniversary, this latest accolade welcomed European fashion to celebrate the resurgence of creativity and revival of consumerism in countries directly affected by the war. Other awardees included Christian Dior, recognized as a leading figure in French fashion, Irene of Hollywood for her impeccable fashion taste in the American movie business, and Norman Hartnell, a royal tailor in England acknowledged for his versatile creation of sophisticated if more straightforward fashion styles.

On August 22, accompanied by his wife Wanda, Salvatore embarked on the *Queen Elizabeth* bound for New York; he would subsequently travel on to Texas. Christian Dior was also onboard; Salvatore had never met him before. The French designer asked Ferragamo if he could preview the shoes he was bringing along and was amazed that they perfectly complemented his outfits, which of course Salvatore had never seen before.

The September 8 award ceremony was followed by a fashion show at which Ferragamo shoes were paired with Dior designs. Salvatore had brought his *Invisibile* model to Dallas, featuring a leather-covered, wooden wedge heel shaped like an "F" (for his surname), with an upper made of transparent nylon thread, strung from one side of the foot to the other… actually, regular fishing line. Ferragamo had had the brainwave of using it as a material after meeting an employee, Alfonso Caldini, fresh back from a fishing trip on the Arno, on which he had caught a big fish using this new type of line. "The fish can't see it," he told Ferragamo.[130] The shoe model was an immediate and massive hit, soon endorsed in the international press. The sandals retailed at $29.75—a significant amount of money that could otherwise buy four tons of coal.[131]

Salvatore celebrated the award with his workers, giving them five kilos of sugar each upon his return to Italy: a precious gift for families that had experienced hunger during the war. He was well aware that his success depended in large part on the loyalty and hard work of his craftsmen.

Famous feet

Salvatore Ferragamo announced plans to open a factory for machine-made women's shoes in late 1947. Ever-greater demand, especially from America, surpassed what the Italian artisan workshops could produce. Salvatore was ready to embrace this new challenge, maintaining the high-quality and technical principles of his shoes despite moving to industrial production. He began establishing contacts with shoe factories in England and with the local Ministry of Commerce to initiate production of models to ship to the United States.[132] On October 26, 1948, in London, he founded Ferragamo Limited with Bernard Oswell, then technical director at the Fortnum & Mason department store, with whom he had been working for some time. The £5000 registered capital company was incorporated to manufacture ladies' shoes, make and market leather clothing, gloves, and tailored garments, and to undertake real estate transactions, monetary

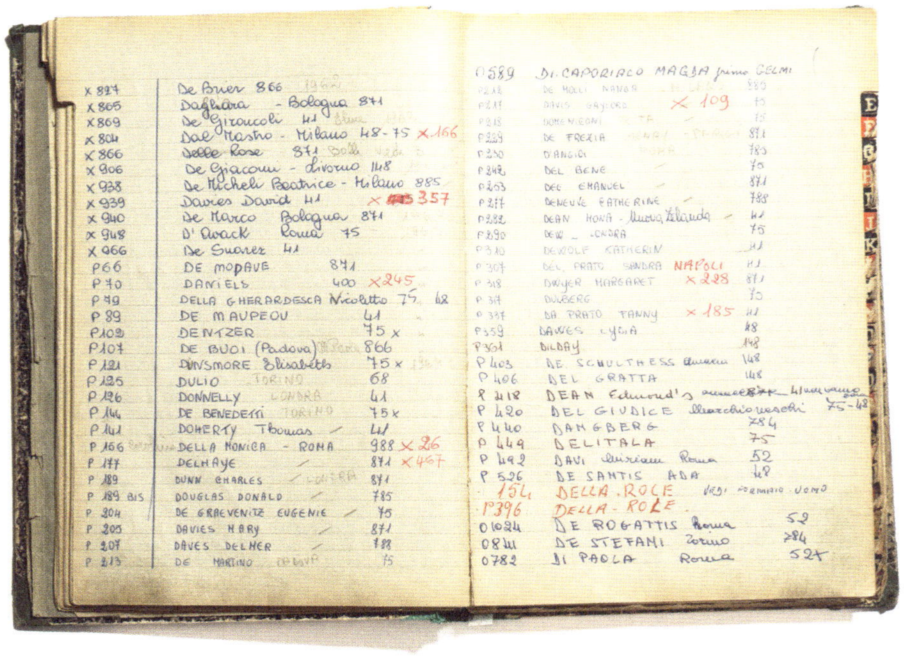

LIST OF FERRAGAMO CLIENTS IN THE 1950s. MUSEO FERRAGAMO, FLORENCE

SCARPETTE PER LA DUCHESSA

Passano gli anni, i capelli del Duca di Windsor sono ormai quasi tutti grigi, e la Duchessa non può nascondere le prime rughe. Ma la più fatale signora del secolo, Wallis Simpson, duchessa di Windsor, continua a essere la donna più elegante dei cinque continenti. Nei giorni scorsi, Edoardo e Wallis erano a Montecatini, per la cura delle acque. Ma Wallis non poteva star ferma: qualcosa la chiamava a Firenze. Il campanile di Giotto o Santa Maria del Fiore? Non questo. Qualcosa di più indispensabile e femminile. La duchessa di Windsor voleva comperarsi un paio di scarpette. Dopo breve consulto, il Duca marito (a sinistra) il "maestro di calzature" Ferragamo (al centro) non possono dire che sì a Sua Grazia la Duchessa.

OMNIBUS, SEPTEMBER 22, 1949

BELLEZZA, JANUARY 1950

investments, patent acquisitions and renewals, trademarks, copyrights, and publications.

In July 1949, Ferragamo registered a new brand, Ferrina, for women's and kids' shoes that were partially machine-made and produced in England. As he took the first step toward industrialization, custom orders continued to flood in from film celebrities and members of the international jet set, even if men's shoe production remained rather limited.[133] Ferragamo's list of famous clients was seemingly endless, as we may see from order books, photographs, receipts, and wooden foot measurement forms. Mary, Queen Mother of England, and her daughters Margaret and Elizabeth shopped for Ferragamo shoes at the London store. Ferragamo's *Elisabetta* model, with high heels, an ankle strap, and a butterfly upper in white silk satin or gold leather, was part of the future queen's bridal trousseau. The beautiful Ira von Fürstenberg commissioned Ferragamo to craft shoes for her wedding,[134] as did Princess Soraya for her wedding ceremony with the Shah of Persia. When Marilyn Monroe moved to New York in 1954 to attend the Actors Studio, she became a regular patron of the store at 424 Park Avenue, Ferragamo's first branded outlet in the city which had opened in 1948. Marilyn and Salvatore may never have met, but the Florentine archive holds orders for dozens of shoes, always the same models: *Filetia* and *Viatica*, two very similar pumps with an 11 cm heel, which the actress also wore on set to give her that particular and sexy walk, and the *Bertilla* laced ballet flat, which Marilyn wore in her free time along with pants and shirts made by another Italian master, tailor Emilio Pucci.[135]

Many of these famous clients visited his shop in Florence and Salvatore always took the opportunity to be photographed with them wearing his creations, fully aware of the influence that, published in magazines and newspapers, these images would have on every woman. Ferragamo extended hospitality beyond the store to many VIPs. From the late 1940s and throughout the 1950s, he hosted a great many celebrities at his home, where they spent time with his wife and children, dined together, and conversed.

Ferragamo cared deeply about people. This meant, in addition to his focus on high-quality shoes and precision measurement, that he attached much importance to sales service, inventing what was practically a ceremonial process for connecting with the customer. "There is no limit to beauty, no saturation point in design, no end to the materials a shoemaker may use to decorate his creations so that every woman may be shod like a princess and a princess may be shod like a fairy queen."[136] This quote from Ferragamo's autobiography reveals more than any other how well he understood the therapeutic function of purchase: a new item of clothing or a new pair of shoes have the power to transform the wearer into a happier person.

In his autobiography, Salvatore recalled models he crafted for VIPs and outlined the empathy-based relationship he had with his clients. He was able to discern the deepest truths of somebody's character just by touching their feet. He described Eva Perón as "one of the most intelligent women I have ever met"—most likely in Rome in 1947, when she was on the Italian leg of her European tour. "She had the wildness of the Andes in her feet and the wildness of extravagance in her demands. There are some skins that are uncommercial because they are too rare, or too heavy, or cannot be processed, or are too small. Eva Perón dismissed all difficulties. She must have the skins she demanded, not only the fairly common llama, but armadillo, lizard, and every rare reptile. Some of the shoes had to be painted with oils because the skins would not take the dye, and others had to be dusted with gold and silver."[137]

Ferragamo fondly remembers the Duchess of Windsor and her impeccable feet, when she visited Florence in 1949, not to mention Claudette Colbert's perpetually youthful feet. Audrey Hepburn's long, slender feet made an impression when she arrived at Palazzo Spini Feroni in 1954 after winning an Oscar for *Roman Holiday*. "Audrey is always natural and completely unaffected, whether she is acting or buying shoes or handbags. She can talk intelligently and knowledgeably on philosophy, art, astronomy, and the theater, and in my opinion she is in the same Scandinavian-British aristocratic tradition which began with Greta Garbo."[138]

Garbo had been a Ferragamo client at the Hollywood Boot Shop in the 1920s; after it closed down, she bought her Ferragamos from Saks in New York. She visited Florence

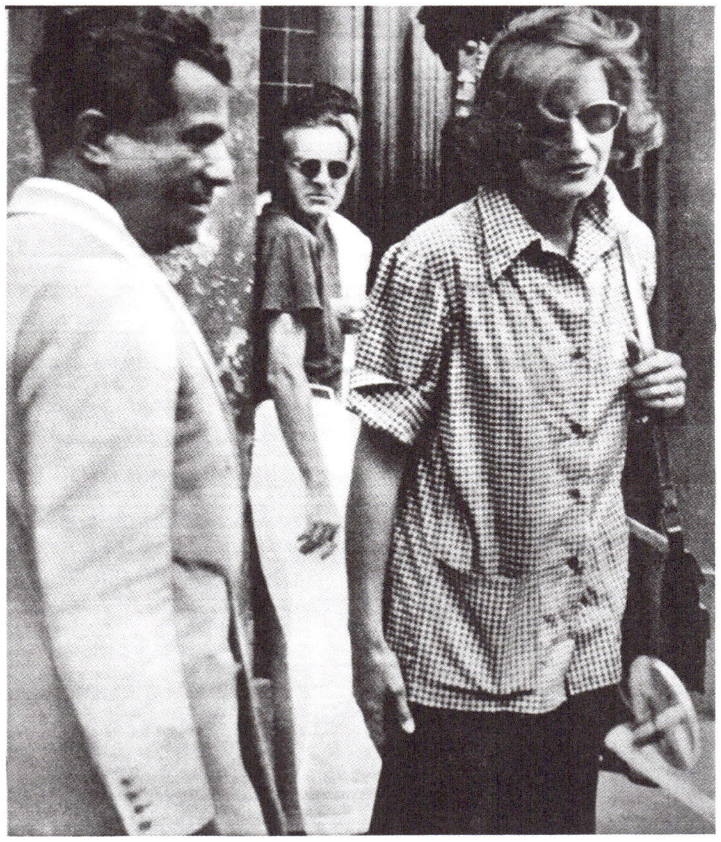

Prima di arrivare a Roma, Greta ha sostato brevemente a Firenze: qui la prima visita che l'attrice ha fatto è stata al "calzolaio" Ferragamo, che aveva già conosciuto a Hollywood. Ecco la diva (in camicetta a quadretti uso Capri) con il celebre "mago della scarpa", che l'accompagna sino all'auto in cui Greta prenderà posto. Ferragamo, al quale la Garbo ha ordinato una settantina di paia di scarpe (tra cui quelle per il prossimo film), sostiene che il piede dell'attrice, al contrario di ciò che si è sempre sostenuto, non è affatto grande; questa impressione deriverebbe dal fatto che ella usa scarpe con tacco molto basso. Poco dopo la visita a Ferragamo, Greta ha corso il rischio di essere investita da un ciclista.

OGGI, SEPTEMBER 15, 1949

QUASI UN'INTERVISTA CON LA "DIVISSIMA„

Greta vuol camminare tranquilla e si ordina settanta paia di scarpe

Primi ragguagli sul ritorno allo schermo - Dove si "girerà„ e chi saranno i suoi collaboratori

Greta Garbo è dall'altra sera ospite della nostra città. Come sempre, è giunta in strettissimo quanto vano incognito, accompagnata dal suo procuratore, Mr. Shillee.

L'abbiamo vista ieri mattina quando è uscita dal Grand Hotel, verso le 11. Indossava un abito di «shantung» nero, dalla linea sobria, ma elegante; in testa, il solito cappello di paglia nero, e un paio di occhiali da sole, quasi una maschera.

— «Buongiorno Miss Garbo. Sono un giornalista» — le abbiamo detto.

La «vecchia» Greta Garbo sarebbe rientrata di corsa nell'albergo, o montata velocemente in macchina. La «nuova» Miss Garbo, invece, ci ha guardato nervosamente, e:

— «O-o-h!» — ha esclamato, con uno sguardo spaventato, e poi: «Perchè è venuto qui?», ha continuato con quella sua caratteristica voce bassa e gutturale.

— «Per rivolgerle qualche domanda».

— «Ma a quale scopo?».

A questo punto Mr. Shillee ha messo in moto la bellissime «De Soto», azzurra, e «Gee-Gee» — come la chiamano gli americani — è partita.

Dopo esattamente due minuti l'abbiamo rivista in via Tornabuoni. Attendeva, dentro la macchina ferma dinanzi al palazzo Feroni, di salire nel laboratorio di Salvatore Ferragamo. Il suo pro-[illegible]ta per annunciarla.

E' stata lei, questa volta, che ha attaccato discorso. Ci ha fatto cenno di avvicinarci, e, con voce supplichevole, ha detto:

«Be a good boy, leave me alone» («faccia il bravo ragazzo, mi lasci in pace»).

Poi, è accaduto l'incredibile! La inavvicinabile Greta, che, per partire senza essere molestata da fotografi e giornalisti da New York, raggiunse la nave in alto mare, di notte, con un motoscafo, ha acconsentito a farci qualche dichiarazione.

— «Deve capirmi, io sfuggo i giornalisti perchè non desidero pubblicità. Io desidero avere una vita privata *mia*, che non appartenga al pubblico. Il fatto che come attrice io abbia avuto successo non giustifica questa continua persecuzione da parte vostra e, per conseguenza, anche del pubblico. Io non sono una donna misteriosa, come spesso mi dipingete, Voglio solo la mia tranquillità. Cosa che, finora, non ho mai avuto. A Londra, a Parigi, a Como, e ovunque, è sempre la stessa cosa. Giornalisti e fotografi mi fanno la posta fuori dell'albergo e mi seguono ovunque vada. La mia vita è una continua fuga».

Le abbiamo fatto notare che in parte tutto ciò è dovuto alla sua eccentricità. Quel cappello nero che le copre il volto, quegli occhialoni pure neri, il suo modo furtivo di camminare sono una specie d'«uniforme» che, invece di tener lontana la gente, fa da richiamo.

Nel frattempo si era andata radunando una considerevole folla di curiosi che cercava, senza successo, di ottenere autografi. La Garbo non ne concede mai.

Greta Garbo esce dal «Grand'Hôtel» (Foto Levi)

Finalmente, è disceso Mr. Shillee che l'ha accompagnata nel laboratorio di Ferragamo, dove si è trattenuta per oltre un'ora, ordinando ben settanta paia di scarpe. **«39» è la misura del suo piede**; preferisce i tacchi bassi.

A mezzogiorno, quando è uscita da Palazzo Feroni, prima di risalire in macchina, si è rivolta verso di noi, ed è stata lei, questa volta, ad intervistarci.

— «Dov'è Palazzo Pitti?» — ci ha chiesto.

* * *

E' rientrata in albergo verso le una e mezzo, e, contrariamente alle sue abitudini — la sua condotta a Firenze, in confronto al passato è stata addirittura rivoluzionaria — ha fatto colazione nella «dining room». Nel pomeriggio è uscita di buon'ora, verso le due, in macchina, e dopo aver fatto una girata per i dintorni, piazzale Michelangiolo e Fiesole, è tornata al Grand Hotel, ha lasciato la macchina, e, a piedi, si è avviata per Borgognissanti, ove ha visitato alcune botteghe di antiquari. Non è stata disturbata da nessuno ed ha continuato la passeggiata per il centro fino alle 19. Ha pranzato nel suo appartamento. Dopo cena, è rimasta lungamente affacciata sul balcone prospiciente l'Arno.

Partenza per Roma stamani alle nove.

Riccardo Ehrman

* * *

Intanto, l'«Ansa», comunica da New York che Greta Garbo ritorna al cinematografo. Il primo film della sua «rentrée» sarà girato in Italia e in parte finanziato da capitale italiano. Viene annunciata ora la costituzione della nuova Compagnia Internazionale «Wanger», che metterà in scena la versione cinematografica dei romanzo di Balzac «La Duchessa di Langeais». Il film verrà girato a Roma. Greta Garbo avrà a fianco James Mason, sotto la direzionel del francese Max Opul. Il lavoro avrà inizio il 15 settembre.

Walter Wanger della Compagnia omonima, in una conferenza-stampa, ha ieri annunciato questo progetto aggiungendo che sono associati con lui nel finanziamento del film il produttore Giuseppe Amato e Mario Rizzoli. Max Opul è atteso a New York, da Hollywood, tra pochi giorni. Ripartirà subito per l'Italia. James Mason s'imbarcherà il 14 settembre; Walter Wanger, con la moglie Joan Bennett, partiranno per Roma sabato prossimo in aereo.

IL MATTINO, AUGUST 30, 1949

ANDY WARHOL, FROM THE SERIES *À LA RECHERCHE DU SHOE PERDU*, SECOND HALF OF THE 1950s, MARKER AND WATERCOLOR DRAWING. MUSEO FERRAGAMO, FLORENCE

in 1949 to order 70 pairs of shoes at once: a series with low heels, including the *Zita* model—an afternoon suede shoe with a seamless upper, a simple buckle, and a soft toe—and a wine-red, calf-length, ankle-laced sandal. Ferragamo wrote: "Greta Garbo is charming, affable, intelligent—and knows exactly what she wants. In fact, our only difference of opinion occurred when I wanted to give her a heel, following up her arch in my own style, and she refused. She is the only person who has ever opposed my ideas. She has beautiful feet, and I imagine that her preference for low-heeled shoes reflects an intense desire to preserve her feet against any possible damage. In my shoes she does not need to worry. I did manage to give her a little heel—not as much as I would have liked but more than she wanted—and later, when I saw moving pictures of her, they convinced me that I was right. She walks beautifully on a small heel, and it shows off her ankles to perfection. Her temperament is truly aristocratic. I have never seen her in a bad temper and never expect to. I can tell from the reaction in her feet. There is none at all: the sure sign of an equable, assured personality . . . She has been endowed by Nature with a degree of acting quality which others do not possess, and she worked without cessation to transform it into a medium that could satisfy her own high standards. When she is acting, she possesses the film through and through; the film is her, her life, her personality."[139]

In his autobiography, Ferragamo divides women into Cinderellas, Venuses, and Aristocrats. "The Cinderella takes a shoe smaller than Size Six, the Venus takes Size Six, the Aristocrat a Seven or larger. The Cinderella, I have observed, is essentially a feminine person, a lover of jewels and furs, who must be in love to be truly happy. Venus is usually of great beauty, glamour, and sophistication, yet under her glittering exterior she is often essentially a homebody, loving the simple things of life. Because these two characteristics are mutually contradictory, the Venus is often misunderstood. People accuse her of too much luxury-loving and frivolity. The Aristocrats are sensitive, even moody, but possess a great depth of understanding."[140]

Winning that award in Dallas boosted Salvatore Ferragamo's renown and expanded his reputation among a network of journalists and young artists, some of whom worked as illustrators for magazines like *Vogue* and *Harper's Bazaar*. Andy Warhol, for example, dedicated some shoe drawings from the famous *À la recherche du shoe perdu* portfolio to Ferragamo in the mid-1950s; they are now housed at the Ferragamo Archive. Ferragamo also connected with other European fashion figures. In June 1948, French designer Elsa Schiaparelli, who had already talked with Ferragamo about tastes and ideas, visited Florence for an event at Palazzo Strozzi, *La donna italiana nei secoli*, in which her and Salvatore Ferragamo's designs were showcased.[141]

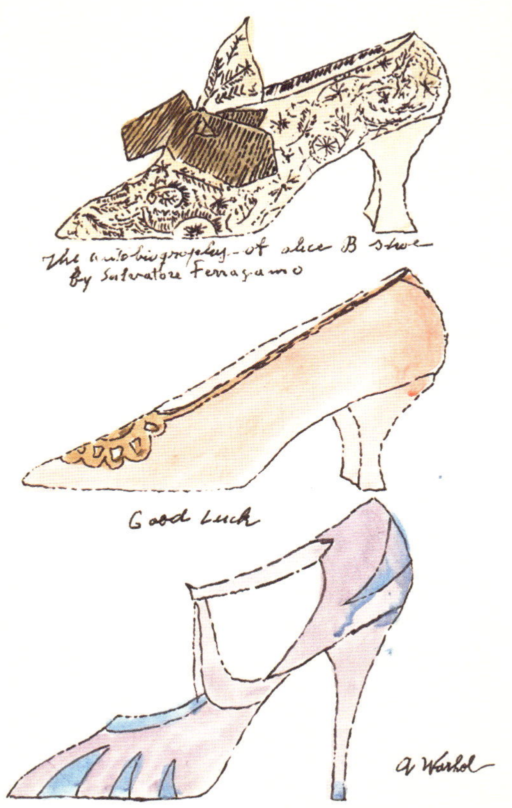

ANDY WARHOL, FROM THE SERIES *À LA RECHERCHE DU SHOE PERDU*, SECOND HALF OF THE 1950s, MARKER AND WATERCOLOR DRAWINGS. MUSEO FERRAGAMO, FLORENCE

SALVATORE FERRAGAMO WITH ELSA SCHIAPARELLI IN FLORENCE, 1948

CHRISTIAN DIOR WITH WANDA AND SALVATORE IN FLORENCE, 1949

At Salvatore's invitation, the following April, Dior attended a fashion event that took place at multiple locations all over Florence. The two mulled over establishing an international fashion hub at Palazzo Spini Feroni, akin to the Venice Biennale for art, but the ambitious idea, which ended up being leaked to the press, never got off the ground, perhaps because of opposition from cities like Turin and Rome, and internal disagreements in Florence concerning the launch of a distinct Italian fashion style, for which Ferragamo's support was deemed essential.[142] Still, Salvatore had significant US experience and a deep understanding of the American market and consumer preferences. His creations spearheaded the "new Renaissance," as the post-war Italian design revival was known overseas, in which material knowledge combined with artisanal skills.[143] A 1949 portrait of Ferragamo by Pietro Annigoni depicts the shoemaker as a painter, capturing the essence of this artisan/artist reminiscent of a Renaissance master.[144]

In the early 1950s, Salvatore Ferragamo represented Italy at the *United Europe* exhibition at the Piccadilly Tea Center, London. With some of the prominent tailors of Florence, he also attended the *Florentine Fashion Evening* at the Teatro della Pergola on May 21, 1950, an event conceived to establish the city as a hub of Italian fashion.[145] On November 29, 13 Ferragamo shoe designs, today partly owned by the Metropolitan Museum in New York, were displayed along with ceramics, glassware, furniture, fabrics, and other Italian

crafts at the *Italy at Work: Her Renaissance in Design Today* exhibition in the Brooklyn Museum, New York. The show traveled on to twelve other American cities, emphasizing the resurgence of post-war Italian design led not just by the country's architects and designers, but by its artisans too.[146]

It should come as no surprise that Giovanni Battista Giorgini, mastermind behind events that led to the birth of Italian fashion in Florence, sought Salvatore Ferragamo's assistance for the first fashion show at his Via dei Serragli residence. Giorgini had been running a buying office in Florence since 1923, sourcing high-quality Italian craftsmanship and fashion accessories for major US stores. He knew Salvatore well, they had been friends for a long time, and Ferragamo readily agreed to be part of the initiative. He designed a high-heeled, kid-leather sandal for Emilio Schuberth's dresses, to be worn with contrasting leather or silk satin socks. Called the *Kimo*, this sandal blended a Japanese Tabi and fifteenth-century soled stocking and was an example of that propensity for transformism peculiar to certain garments and accessories, which would shortly be defined as typically Italian.[147] Much lauded by the industry media, this inventiveness provoked the envy of local rival Edoardo Frattegiani, who owned a shoe shop in Via Tornabuoni and had had disputes in the past with Ferragamo over wedges. Frattegiani claimed Salvatore's design was inspired by one of his earlier shoes, the *Pinturicchio*, a two-piece item of footwear that had featured in *Bellezza* magazine. Ferragamo promptly responded by asserting that similar designs can emerge independently. A case in point was his 1937 cork wedge, which was found to resemble fourteenth-century footwear discovered in Boccaccio's house at Certaldo.[148]

Kimo's role was not just to protect the foot but to add a whimsical new element into women's fashion, which was achieved by varying colors and materials, while at the same

PRESENTATION OF THE *KIMO* AT PALAZZO SPINI FERONI, WITH CLOTHES BY EMILIO SCHUBERTH, FEBRUARY 12, 1951

time offering cost-reduction opportunities: indeed, buying one *Kimo* sandal with several socks in different colors made it possible to have numerous sandals for practically the cost of one. A few years later, Salvatore leveraged the same concept to invent heels with interchangeable sheaths: depending on the occasion and type of clothing, the sheaths, whose toes attached to the upper part of the heel, could be swapped.

Ferragamo's design interest remained on heels and soles over the decade, for shoes' architectural build and stability depended largely on these two elements. One of his most successful patents was for a silk embroidered boot, which, although seemingly flat-soled, concealed a small cork wedge heel. Its upper part was notable too: the embroidery was inspired by a dress worn by an eighteenth-century *Maharata Bride* figure, as displayed at the Stibbert Museum in Florence—a collection with which Ferragamo was familiar.[149]

In 1952, Salvatore crafted a high-heeled shoe with a unique feature: the foot's arch was covered in the same leather as the upper, restricting the sole to foot support areas only, the front and heel, in a glove-like design that was both durable and flexible. The patent was globally acclaimed as the "gloved arch."[150] A few years later, Ferragamo's design focus shifted to intricately constructed metal soles. Despite its rigidity, this material offered the comfort of a leather shoe and at the same time allowed the surface to accommodate almost neo-baroque decorative exuberance through techniques of metal engraving and chiseling, as applied to one of Ferragamo's most precious creations, an 18-karat gold sandal ordered by an American client who wished to remain anonymous.[151] Crafted with Florentine goldsmiths from Ponte Vecchio, the sandal epitomized Italian design's long-standing reverence of ornamental richness and the decorative repertoire of its cultural heritage. Redolent of Art Nouveau, Ferragamo's 1955 steel-cored cage-like heels bring to mind ephemeral architectural structures conceived for world fairs or Gaudí's studies for arches' funiculars; they are one example of myriad inspirations and trends that influenced Italian design during the 1950s.[152]

Ferragamo's final significant patent for a shell-like sole evoked associations with organic architecture. It appeared in a popular range of models, from ballet flats to boots, even classical dance shoes. Inspired by the construction of Indian *opanke* (a Native American moccasin in which the sole rises up the heel to become the upper), Ferragamo's shell enclosed and caressed the foot in a curved, enveloping shape reminiscent of Arne Jacobsen's 1958 "egg chairs"—a far-from-arbitrary citation.[153]

Alongside his structural footwear innovations, Salvatore continued to experiment with materials for making uppers. As well as weaves of various types of straw, he used an artificial type of viscose raffia named *pontova*, which was processed at the Bonito factory, and silk trim braiding in various colors, the soutache, sometimes mixed with cellophane or leather threads. The unique technique for stitching and attaching these thread-like elements to a base lining, which remained hidden, resulted in a new invention patent.[154] Between July 1954 and October 1956, Ferragamo had a productive and collaborative dialogue with Elda Cecchele related to this strand of his creative research, mirroring one he had had with another textile artisan, Fede Cheti, in the late 1930s. A talented and inventive weaver, Cecchele made at her Galliera Veneta workshop, near Padua, artisan tradition-inspired fabrics with a distinctly contemporary finish based on raw or colored materials like hemp, rope, or maize leaf. Correspondence between Ferragamo and Cecchele reveals a mutual understanding that drove the two designers to continuously explore and advance their craft. Samples of weaves attached to the 14 preserved letters highlight

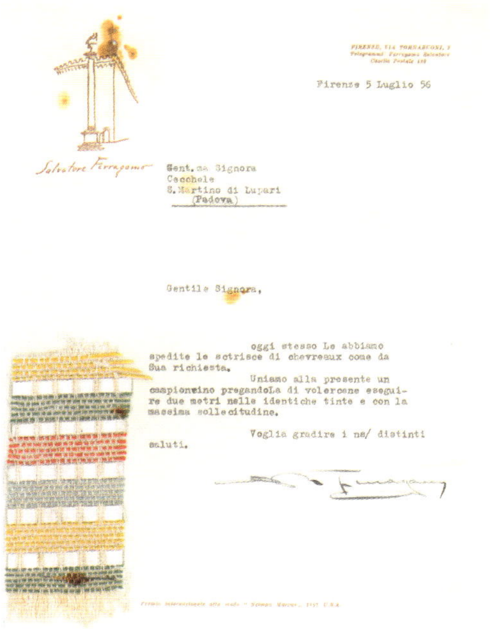

Salvatore Ferragamo

Firenze 5 Luglio 56

Gent.ma Signora
Cecchele
S.Martino di Lupari
(Padova)

Gentile Signora,

oggi stesso Le abbiamo spedite le sctrisce di chevreaux come da Sua richiesta.

Uniamo alla presente un campioncino pregandoLa di volercene eseguire due metri nelle identiche tinte e con la massima sollecitudine.

Voglia gradire i ns/ distinti saluti.

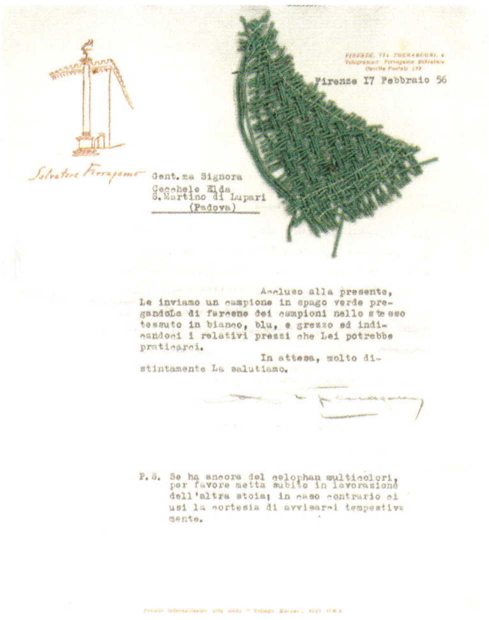

Salvatore Ferragamo

Firenze 17 Febbraio 56

Gent.ma Signora
Cecchele Elda
S.Martino di Lupari
(Padova)

Accluso alla presente, Le inviamo un campione in spago verde pregandoLa di farcene dei campioni nello stesso tessuto in bianco, blu, e grezzo ed indicandoci i relativi prezzi che Lei potrebbe praticarci.

In attesa, molto distintamente La salutiamo.

P.S. Se ha ancora del celophan multicolori, per favore metta subito in lavorazione dell'altra stoia; in caso contrario ci usi la cortesia di avvisarci tempestivamente.

LETTERS WRITTEN BY SALVATORE FERRAGAMO TO ELDA CECCHELE WITH FABRIC ORDERS, 1956. THE ORIGINALS ARE PRESERVED AT MUSEO DI PALAZZO MOCENIGO, VENICE. ATTACHED ARE THE SAMPLES CECCHELE SENT FERRAGAMO FOR REVIEW

THE FERRAGAMO DEBS BRAND FOR SHOES MADE IN THE USA. MUSEO FERRAGAMO, FLORENCE

intriguing mixes of cellophane thread, leather ribbons, and bright-colored metallic strips that created striped effects, or else more intricate, tone-on-tone designs that gave rise to relief textures or interplays of gloss and matte finishes, which also appeared on refined sandals and pumps.[155]

In 1954, Ferragamo's experimentation and affinity for simpler materials prompted him to revisit marine leopard skin, which he had used during the war years, albeit with subpar outcomes: the skin's tanning produced an unpleasant odor after wearing the shoe for a while. Ferragamo partnered up with the Sipo Trading Company of Denmark, which distributed these skins. Actually called wolf fish (*anarhichas lupus*), this fish with spots all over its body lived in North Sea waters. In the 1950s, it was caught off Thule, offloaded at the Royal Greenland Trading Quay, and then shipped by train to the tanneries in Strib, which not only managed to eradicate all odor, they devised a method for dying the skins with bright colors that did not fade over time. This combination of a Danish national product with an internationally acclaimed fashion brand received extensive media coverage, especially in the local press and television, after its February 1955 launch in Copenhagen, with support from the government and Queen Ingrid herself. The Queen ordered marine leopard shoes from Ferragamo in various styles and colors for herself and her daughters Margrethe and Anne-Marie. Ferragamo organized an event at Rome's Open Gate Club to present this latest trend in Italy, with guest of honor Sophia Loren endorsing and representing the new fashion.[156]

In the mid-1950s, Salvatore Ferragamo thought of new footwear brands with evocative names—*Teen-age*, *Vagabondo*, *Vacanza*, *Pic nic*—redolent of the new developments of a carefree lifestyle and leisure time in Italy. One of these was *Leonardo by Ferragamo*, accompanied by a label designed like a painter's tablet, used for heel-free, Capri-style flip-flop sandals.[157]

Made in Italy's growth and advancement on international markets, rising domestic demand, and wide-ranging transformation of the Italian economy and industry prompted Salvatore to reorganize his distribution company's production and administration. Centralizing control and manage-

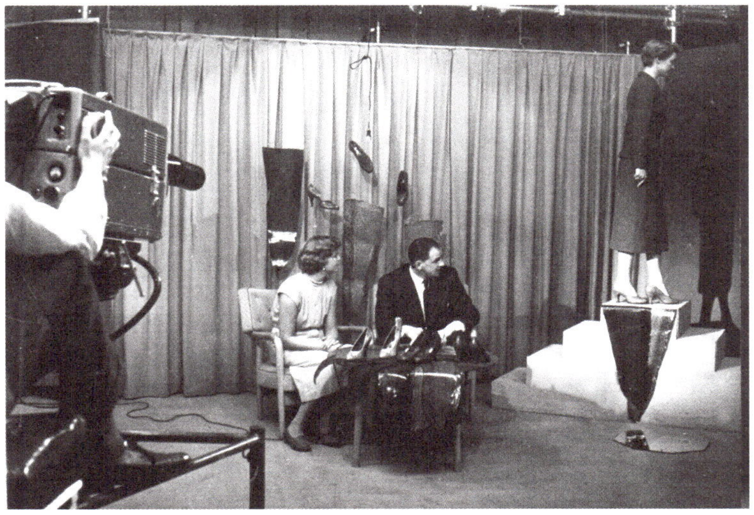

PRESENTATION
OF SEA LEOPARD
SKIN IN DENMARK

ment within the family, he acquired a large proportion of shares previously held by external partners. In 1955, a new corporate structure saw the involvement of Salvatore's wife Wanda, to whom 500 shares were registered, and appointment of Salvatore's nephew Girolamo, known as Jerry, to the Board of Directors. Jerry had come from the United States in 1950 at his uncle's invitation, joining the company to manage footwear quality control. This particular corporate restructuring was part of Salvatore's broader design—he was keen to expand and diversify company output toward a total look, dressing customers, as he liked to say, "from toe to head."

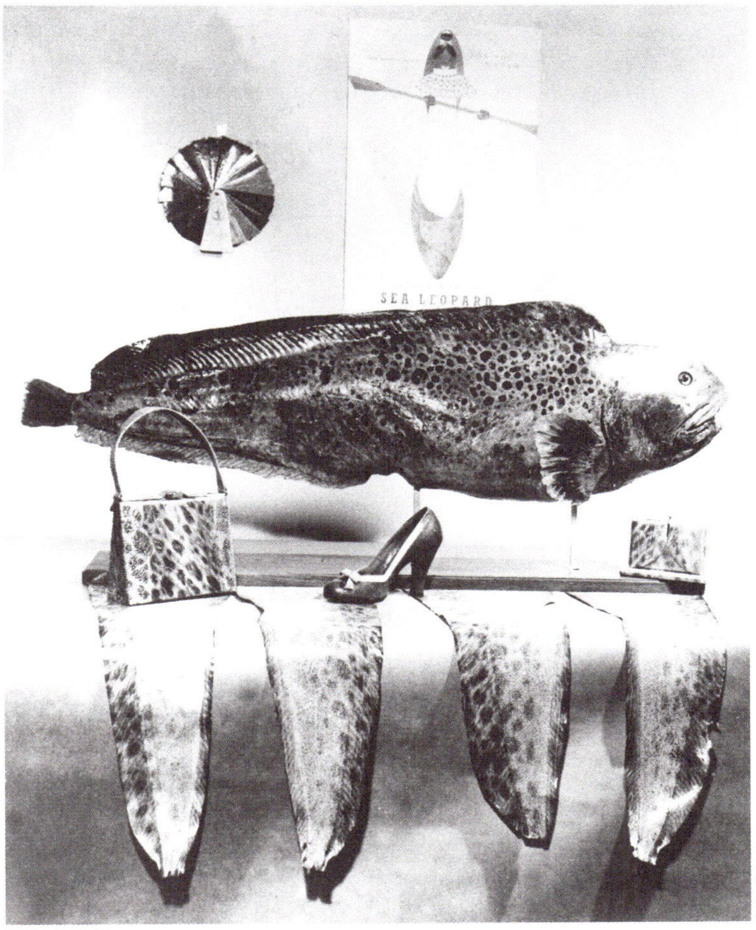

On March 18, 1954, Ferragamo signed an agreement set to last until May 30, 1959 with the John Flautt Shoe Company Inc. of Lynn, Massachusetts, exclusively granting the right to machine-produce and sell directly in the United States, Canada, Mexico, Cuba, Puerto Rico, Panama Canal, and Hawaii shoes and other accessories, such as bags and belts, under the name Ferragamo Debs, a trademark Salvatore Ferragamo would register for Flautt with the intention of using it for the duration of the contract. In the role of designer only, Salvatore committed to providing all necessary information for production, in addition to ideas, designs, and even components like heels, soles, and wedges. Flautt undertook to pay a percentage on every pair of shoes and on every accessory sold, maintaining a predetermined annual turnover. However, Ferragamo reserved the right to continue selling shoes from his line, the one with his signature, on US territory through the Esercizi Ferragamo company. Within two years, the Ferragamo Debs brand was manufacturing a thousand pairs of shoes daily.[158]

Late 1950s adverts in international press listed numerous sales outlets in the Ferragamo name. In addition to those in Italy, to which the one in Capri was recently added, stores were in Stockholm, Munich, Melbourne, Paris, Dallas, Rio de Janeiro, and Mexico City even if not directly managed by the company. In Switzerland, the brand was in Geneva, Lausanne, St. Moritz, Basel, and in Zurich at Bleichweg Straße 8, where it had been operating for several years; in the United States, in addition to New York, it was at 323 Rodeo Drive in Beverly Hills and at 290 Post Street (Union Square) in San Francisco.

THE FERRAGAMO STORE IN FLORENCE DESIGNED BY ARCHITECT PAOLO MALCHIODI, PUBLISHED IN *ARCHITETTI* MAGAZINE, FEBRUARY 6, 1951. THE ARMCHAIRS WERE SPECIALLY CONCEIVED FOR THE STORE

Firenze

Architetto Paolo Malchiodi

Particolari di negozi e appartamenti realizzati a Firenze

Negozio di Salvatore Ferragamo in Palazzo Ferroni

Sala di accesso al piano terreno.

La pianta.

VIA TORNABUONI

L'ingresso.

SALVATORE FERRAGAMO

Foto Barsotti

37

INTERIOR OF THE FERRAGAMO STORE AT 424 PARK AVENUE, NEW YORK

In London, after the Old Bond Street store, Ferragamo opened a sales outlet on Brompton Road designed by architect Leonard Masseh with a rigorous and straightforward interior conceived to showcase product as successfully as possible. Ferragamo's shoe distribution continued to expand in the United States: he added E. Dick & Co. Inc. stores in New York (a company led by Edward D. Schwartz, with whom Ferragamo maintained a long-term, collaborative relationship) to the department stores with which the company already had long-standing relationships.

In 1957, at the peak of his success, Salvatore released his autobiography in English. The book conveyed his life's core message: mastering the craft of making the perfect shoe, and refusing to associate his name with anything inferior.[159]

By 1958, Salvatore was working on expanding into new product categories, extending the product range from shoes to clothing, silk prints, and other leather goods. His eldest daughter, Fiamma, quit high school to join her father's company and help create and manufacture women's footwear. After a fashion design course in Florence at the Lucrezia Tornabuoni school, second-eldest daughter Giovanna was gearing up to launch her first sportswear and beachwear collection at the Plaza Hotel in New York in 1959, to be sold on the first floor of Palazzo Spini Feroni and in a Beverly Hills boutique under the patented name, "Giovanna Ferragamo Florence Italy."[160] Still a minor, Giovanna required Juvenile Court authorization for her name to be on the storefront.

In September 1958, *American Women Weekly* invited Salvatore to Australia. He embarked on the lengthy trip, stopping along the way in Mumbai, Calcutta, Hong Kong, Tokyo, and Manila. On the way back, he visited Honolulu and California. At each stop, he sent a letter to his beloved wife, discussing work progress, relationships and, most prominently of all, telling her how much he loved her. It was

THE FERRAGAMO STORE IN NAPLES, PIAZZA DEI MARTIRI 59–60, DESIGNED BY ARCHITECT ROBERTO MANGO

SALVATORE FERRAGAMO
DURING HIS TRIP TO
AUSTRALIA, 1958

COVER OF ISSUE NO. 21
OF *TREND* MAGAZINE,
DEDICATED TO SALVATORE
FERRAGAMO, 1958

SALVATORE FERRAGAMO
IN TOKYO, 1958

distressing for him to be away from her. He would return with news, fabric samples for his daughter, ethnic shoe prototypes, family gifts, and most importantly, valuable contacts for expansion onto Asian markets.

Salvatore's Australian tour took in Sydney, Brisbane, Queensland, Adelaide, and Melbourne. He met the press, gave radio interviews, appeared on the *Meet the Press* TV show on Sydney's TCN Channel 9, and held fashion shows of his designs. Articles report that he forged business ties with Dunlop Rubber Australia Ltd. to produce a casual line of footwear and with the David Jones department store chain for shoe sales. In Australia, where he was seen as a star, as the "Dior of shoes," Ferragamo displayed models crafted for actresses Sophia Loren, Gina Lollobrigida, and Princess Soraya. The greatest clamor was for a new project, a magnetic shoe that clung to the sock via a magnet, with no upper at all.[161]

His wife was there to greet him when he landed at Rome airport on October 17, 1959. Salvatore seemed unwell, visibly tired from the trip. Wanda persuaded him to rest up at their Capri house for a few days before returning to their children in Florence. Rather than tiredness, however, Salvatore was suffering from the first symptoms of what turned out to be a terminal illness, one that medical diagnostics was unable to detect in a timely manner.

Salvatore remained optimistic about the future. His Via Aretina workshop in the outskirts of Florence employed 750 artisans and produced 350 handcrafted pairs of shoes daily. Industrial-scale production was already starting up in the US and the UK. He felt he had so many ideas left to explore, the most significant of which was an entire shoe collection in a single pair of shoes: a foundational shoe with six uppers, offering a complete wardrobe for the cost of two-and-a-half regular pairs of shoes.

Salvatore's health, however, began deteriorating rapidly. In July 1960, he delegated broader management responsibilities to his wife. The company's share capital was increased from 3.5 million to a whopping 49 million lire, and the majority of shares transferred to her. The amazing shoemaker who transformed shoes into works of art died on August 7, 1960, in the locality of Fiumetto, in Versilia. He was buried in the family chapel at the San Domenico cemetery near Fiesole. Until then merely a wife and mother to their six children, Wanda took over the company, proving herself to be a sharp and adept entrepreneur supported by her elder daughters, Salvatore's faithful collaborators, and his cherished shoemakers.

At the end of his book, which was published in 1957, Salvatore wrote: "I have plenty of time. I know I am going to do it. If it is not done with this body it will be done with another. We are all flowing with the eternal tide, and of the eternal tide only is there no end."[162]

Prophetic words indeed, as the Ferragamo company continues to add new chapters to its story, and as its founder's story continues to exert an extraordinary fascination.

GIOVANNA FERRAGAMO WORKING WITH HER FATHER, 1959

THE FERRAGAMO FAMILY IN 1959. FROM LEFT: GIOVANNA, FULVIA, FIAMMA, LEONARDO, WANDA, FERRUCCIO, MASSIMO, SALVATORE

[1] In 2020, director Luca Guadagnino made a documentary on Salvatore Ferragamo, *Salvatore: Shoemaker of Dreams*, 120 minutes. Scripted by Dana Thomas, edited by Walter Fasano, and produced by Francesco Melzi d'Eril and Gabriele Moratti, it premiered at the 77th Venice Film Festival.

[2] The audio recording is conserved at the Ferragamo Archive. The audio files, henceforth referred to as *SF Memories*, vary in length between *SF Memories no. 1*: 1 hour, 3 minutes, 10 seconds; *SF Memories no. 2*: 1 hour, 5 minutes, 46 seconds; *SF Memories no. 3*: 47 minutes, 39 seconds; *SF Memories no. 4*: 48 minutes, 57 seconds; *SF Memories no. 5*: 31 minutes, 3 seconds.

[3] Elvira Valleri, "The 'Autobiographical Pact' of Salvatore Ferragamo," in *Italy in Hollywood*, exhibition catalogue (Museo Ferragamo, Florence, May 28, 2018 – March 10, 2019), ed. Stefania Ricci (Milan: Skira, 2018), pp. 338–79.

[4] Salvatore Ferragamo, *Shoemaker of Dreams. The Autobiography of Salvatore Ferragamo* (London: George Harrap & Co. Ltd, 1957). The English version was the first edition to be published. It came out in Italy in 1971.

[5] Only limited information is available on John Desmond Currie and Elizabeth Warner. We know that, under the pseudonym Douglas Warner, they wrote the novel *Death of a Cop* (1962), which was adapted into a screenplay for an episode of *The Alfred Hitchcock Hour* (1963). We may infer they were film industry writers; their novel *Death of a Snout* (1961) inspired the movie *The Informers* (1963). The UCLA archive's list of their novels includes *Ghana and the New Africa* (1960), *Death of a Bogey* (1962), and *Death on a Warm Wind* (1968).

[6] The audio recording is at the Ferragamo Archive. Henceforth named *SF Radio Interview Australia*, it consisted of 14 audio files in total: *SF Radio Interview Australia 1*: 4 minutes, 55 seconds, interview conducted in Brisbane by Allan Brant for the *Monitor* program, broadcast at 21:45 on September 24, 1958; *SF Radio Interview Australia 2*: 4 minutes, 31 seconds, interview conducted in Brisbane by John Nash for the *Radio Newsreel*, broadcast at 00:30 on September 25, 1958; *SF Interview Radio Australia 3*: 9 minutes, 33 seconds, interview conducted in Brisbane by David McGovern for the Courier Mail Station, broadcast at 22:15 on September 26, 1958; *SF Radio Interview Australia 4*: 16 minutes, 27 seconds, interviewer unknown, for the *Town Tonight* show on Radio 4KQ, Brisbane, broadcast at 21:00 on September 29, 1958; *SF Radio Interview Australia 5*: 10 minutes, 27 seconds, no further information available; *SF Radio Interview Australia 6*: 8 minutes, 39 seconds, no further information available; *SF Radio Interview Australia 7*: 3 minutes, 34 seconds, interview conducted by Allan Sandlers for the *Monitor* program on Central Radio in Adelaide; *SF Radio Interview Australia 8*: 11 minutes, 32 seconds, for a Melbourne radio station, no other details available; *SF Radio Interview Australia 9*: 5 minutes, 54 seconds, interview conducted by an unknown female journalist, the audio file cuts out; *SF Radio Interview Australia 10*: 15 minutes, 19 seconds, interview conducted by a journalist for a Melbourne radio station; *SF Radio Interview Australia 11*: 6 minutes, 32 seconds, interview conducted by an unknown female journalist, no other details available; *SF Radio Interview Australia 12*: 12 minutes, 49 seconds, interview conducted for the *Here the Traveller* show; *SF Radio Interview Australia 13:* 11 minutes, 43 seconds, interview conducted in Melbourne for the *The Voice of the Voyage* show; *SF Radio Interview Australia 14*: 2 minutes, 15 seconds, no further information available.

[7] The Ferragamo Archive owns the films. Restored and converted into digital files, they are labeled *Filmati SF*. The journey on the *Roma* ocean liner, his return to Bonito in the 1920s, and Florence in the 1930s and 1940s feature in *Filmato SF01*, which lasts 19 minutes, 7 seconds. *Filmato SF02*, which lasts 5 minutes, 28 seconds, captures moments of life in Bonito in the 1920s and at the factory on Via Mannelli in Florence before and during bankruptcy. Wanda and Salvatore's honeymoon and their family life shortly after the wedding are documented in *Filmato SF03*, which is 4 minutes, 3 seconds long. *Filmato SF04*, which lasts 10 minutes, 28 seconds, documents various family moments between 1940 and 1960. Many other historical films, from the Istituto Luce and *Incom Week*, are conserved at the Ferragamo Archive.

[8] We wish to thank historian and scholar Valerio Massimo Miletti for his assistance over the years in obtaining valuable information and images of Bonito and its surroundings.

[9] Salvatore Ferragamo erroneously wrote his brother died at the age of 19.

[10] Salvatore Ferragamo, *Shoemaker of Dreams. The Autobiography of Salvatore Ferragamo* (Milan: Electa, 2020), pp. 8–10; first ed. London: George Harrap & Co. Ltd, 1957.

[11] Carlo Graziano, Franco Molinaro, A. Raffaele Beatrice, Gaetano Di Vito, Emanuele Grieco, and Valerio Massimo Miletti, *Bonito e i suoi figli nel mondo* (Flumeri, Avellino: Grafiche Lucarelli, 2008).

[12] Secondino arrived in the United States in 1905, as did Teodolinda and Clotilde, Alfonso in 1911, Girolamo in 1912, and Rosina in 1922. Arrivals in America are documented at The Statue of Liberty – Ellis Island Foundation, New York. Although Eliodoro was not mentioned, his time in Santa Barbara is documented in the Santa Barbara City Directory (1917–18), in which his profession was stated as "tailor."

[13] Sergio Risaliti and Luca Scarlini, "The magical shoemaker: Symbolic representations and allegories of a mythic figure," in *The Amazing Shoemaker. Fairy tales and legends about shoes and shoemakers*, exhibition catalogue, Museo Ferragamo, Florence, April 19, 2013 – March 31, 2014, ed. Stefania Ricci (Milan: Skira, 2013), pp. 18–63.

[14] *Shoemaker of Dreams*, pp. 13–14.

[15] In his autobiography, Salvatore claimed he was ten years old when his father passed away. In actual fact, he was 14 (*Shoemaker of Dreams*, p. 22). Discrepancies like this crop up elsewhere in the book. They can occur when comparing autobiographical accounts with actual biographies: memory has the ability to distort facts.

[16] *Grand Tour Italiano. 61 film dei primi anni del '900*, ed. Andrea Meneghelli (Bologna: Edizione Cineteca di Bologna, 2016).

[17] *Shoemaker of Dreams*, p. 25.

[18] Ibid., p. 26.

[19] Valleri, "The Autobiographical Pact," pp. 346–47.

[20] *Shoemaker of Dreams*, p. 30.

[21] *Shoemaker of Dreams*, p. 38.

[22] Valleri, "The Autobiographical Pact," pp. 344–45, with reference bibliography.

[23] *Shoemaker of Dreams*, p. 38.

[24] Salvatore erroneously spelled his brother-in-law's surname, which was Coviello not Covelli. The sister who hosted him was Clotilde not Alessandrina: another oversight prompted by the passage of time.

[25] *Shoemaker of Dreams*, p. 40.

[26] On Italians in California, see the previously cited catalogue *Italy in Hollywood*.

[27] Santa Barbara City Directory (1912/13–1922). First cited as a source by Edward Maeder, "The California Experience: Salvatore Ferragamo in Santa Barbara and Hollywood, 1914–1927," in *Salvatore Ferragamo The Art of the Shoe 1898–1960*, exhibition catalogue, Los Angeles County Museum of Art, April 12 – June 7, 1992 (New York: Rizzoli International Publications Inc., 1992), pp. 13–19. See Santa Barbara Historical Society, Sanborn Map, 1903, p. 19.

[28] The deposit book is at the Ferragamo Archive in Florence. Located at 500 State Street in San Francisco, the Fugazi Banca Popolare Operaia Italiana was founded in 1906 by Italian-American John Fugazi to help immigrants recover from the tragedy of the great earthquake. The son of a cart driver and a factory worker from Lodi, Fugazi emigrated to America from Genoa on October 27, 1854. After various stopovers in New Orleans, Memphis, Cincinnati, and New York, he settled in San Francisco where he sold hair dye and started his own travel agency, representing the White Line Star. He began safekeeping and transferring money for his fellow countrymen, and then opened his first savings bank, the Columbus Savings and Loan Society, in 1893. He left the bank in 1903.

[29] He subsequently lived at 423E Micheltorena Street, 312W Figueroa, and 1014 Chapala Street.

[30] "Southern California ideal for pictures and Our Billion Dollar Film Industry," in *The American Cinematographer*, vol. 1, no. 1, November 1, 1920. On movie-related development in the area around Los Angeles, see Roberta Ferrazza, "Italian Know-how in Hollywood," in *Italy in Hollywood*, pp. 80–115.

[31] In his autobiography, Salvatore credits Alfonso (*Shoemaker of Dreams*, pp. 44–45); however, as Edward Maeder suggests in "The California Experience" (p. 14), it was more likely Girolamo, who had been working as a tailor for longer.

[32] *Shoemaker of Dreams*, pp. 44–45.

[33] I thank Virgilio Panarese for his valuable information on his great-grandfather, son of Nicola Ferragamo and brother of Mariantonia Ferragamo.

[34] Deborah Nadoolman Landis, "Hollywood Begins 1908–1929: Clothes, Costumes & Couture," in *Italy in Hollywood*, pp. 410–35, esp. p. 412.

[35] *Shoemaker of Dreams*, p. 67.

[36] Originally founded in 1885, USC Medical School ran evening courses between 1917 and 1922. Research in the institution's archives did not reveal any information on Ferragamo, but, according to the university, the names of evening class students were not noted down. However, the USC Alumni Magazine (2010) published a photo of Salvatore Ferragamo under the caption: "Faced with the challenge of creating shoes that were as comfortable as they were beautiful, Ferragamo turned to USC, where he studied human anatomy." I thank Claude Zachary, USC Libraries Special Collection, for this information. Secondino's daughter, Virginia Ferragamo Schilling, gave an interview in June 1991 (see Edward Maeder's essay, "The California Experience," p. 15) in which she recalled that Uncle Salvatore frequently sketched shoes in the margins of his Human Anatomy coursebook. Santa Barbara City Directories show that Salvatore and Secondino Ferragamo shared a home. See Valleri, "The Autobiographical Pact," p. 378, note 60.

[37] *Shoemaker of Dreams*, p. 68.

[38] Ibid., p. 69.

[39] Ibid., p. 71.

[40] *SF Memories no. 4*, 26:00–29:00, quoted in Valleri, "The Autobiographical Pact," p. 361.

[41] Records of students on courses at the University of Scranton and Berkeley International Correspondence Schools are no more available. We cannot be certain whether Salvatore's reference to correspondence studies refers to this period or a later one. The certificate of attendance for the Scranton correspondence school, today in the Ferragamo Archive in Florence, is dated February 11, 1955; the course payment receipts are undated.

[42] "Auto Races Train. Accident results: one dead and three injured," in *Los Angeles Times*, February 5, 1920.

[43] *Shoemaker of Dreams*, p. 82.

[44] M. A. J. Schoenefeld, "Orthopedic Surgery in the United States Army: An Historical Review," in *Military Medicine*, no. 176, 2011.

[45] Patent for "orthopedic apparatus" no. 1,399,606, issued in the US on December 6, 1921 (application no. 427,740 of December 2, 1920) and patent no. 1,479,536, issued in the US on January 1, 1924 (application no. 512,612 of November 3, 1921). The invention consisted of a cylinder several centimeters longer than the leg. Once the leg had been inserted, one end of the cylinder pressed against the pelvic joint; limb tensioning could be achieved through a screw device located at the foot end, which could either be tightened or loosened. Once it was set, it maintained constant traction.

[46] *Shoemaker of Dreams*, pp. 82–83.

[47] "Announcing that Salvatore Ferragamo has bought The Hollywood Boot Shop from J. M. Bohannon and will run it under the same high-class management which proved so successful in his Santa Barbara shop for the last seven years," in *Holly Leaves*, April 6, 1923. On April 15 that year, the change of ownership was reported in an article entitled "Shoe Store in Hollywood is in New Hands" in the *Los Angeles Times*.

[48] Maeder, "The California Experience," p. 16.

[49] *Shoemaker of Dreams*, p. 92.

[50] "A Passion for Shoes," in *Holly Leaves*, February 20, 1925; *Holly Leaves*, April 6, 1923.

[51] Salvatore Ferragamo, *Document Applications*, http//:ancestry.com (last accessed August 28, 2017). He was naturalized on February 19, 1926. Presumably, his initial applications for American citizenship were rejected because of the February accident in Ventura in 1920; investigations were conducted into Eliodoro Ferragamo's death.

[52] *Holly Leaves*, February 20, 1925.

[53] Elisa Camporeale, "Visioni americane d'interni del Rinascimento italiano: dalla Gilded Age agli anni Venti," in *Archivio Storico Italiano*, III, 2015 and Regina Soria, *Fratelli lontani. Il contributo degli artisti italiani all'identità degli Stati Uniti (1776-1945)* (Naples: Liguori, 1997). Valleri cites both texts in "The Autobiographical Pact," p. 378, notes 97 and 98. On the store, see "Interior of New Hollywood Boot Shop Elaborately Finished," in *Boot and Shoe Recorder*, March 28, 1925; "A Passion for Shoes," in *Holly Leaves*, February 1925. The Ramey Company designed the store's architecture to a plan by architect Black; Lewis & Coules Decorator Designer (634 South Western Hollywood) handled the interior decoration; Doran's Electrical Shop (located at 7515 Sunset Boulevard) the lighting.

[54] See *Italy in Hollywood*.

[55] Ferragamo staged two contests at the Hollywood Boot Shop. The first, "The Perfect Ankle," ran over a six-week period in March–April 1925. Thirteen hundred women took part; 19-year-old Patsy Gribble was declared winner. The second contest was "Miss Los Angeles," a beauty pageant. As part of the judging panel, Salvatore awarded custom-made reptile skin shoes valued at $50 (or $75, as reported in another article) to the winner, who was crowned Miss Los Angeles. All finalists won one of three pairs of shoes worth $15. No cash prizes were on offer. On August 15, the jury awarded Marcella Arnold first place, Marjorie Williamson and Rose Luetzsinger were second and third respectively. However, Ferragamo's personal choice was a young woman with beautiful legs, eager to make her mark in cinema: a certain Joan Crawford, one of Ferragamo's most loyal customers ever after.

[56] A postcard from Rosina addressed to their mother, kept at the Ferragamo Archive, features an image of the Hollywood Bowl. She writes of her frequent visits to the theater with her brother, Salvatore. An article titled "Vibraciones de Hollywood" appeared in *El Heraldo de México* on June 4, 1926, describing the Hollywood atmosphere and notable figures like Salvatore Ferragamo and Maestro Cimini. A note Pietro Cimini wrote to the Remington typewriter manufacturing company, mentioning his satisfaction with the purchase, as warmly advised by his friend Salvatore Ferragamo, is in the Ferragamo Archive.

[57] Victor Coules, "S. Ferragamo's fine new home is credit to entire Southland," in *Hollywood News*, February 20, 1925, p. 1.

[58] In his autobiography, Ferragamo mentions an Indian princess. However, an article dated March 6, 1928 in the "New York Ins and Outs" column of *The New York Evening World* reveals that in an interview Ferragamo spoke of an American actress. This article is today at the Ferragamo Archive.

[59] Stefania Ricci, "Salvatore Ferragamo and Women's Fashion in the 1920s," in *1927. The Return to Italy. Salvatore Ferragamo and Twentieth-century Visual Culture*, exhibition catalogue (Museo Ferragamo, Florence, May 19, 2017 – May 2, 2018), eds. Stefania Ricci and Carlo Sisi (Milan: Skira, 2017), pp. 115–73, esp. pp. 119–20.

[60] Nadoolman Landis, "Hollywood 1908–1929," p. 424.

[61] *Los Angeles Times*, August 11, 1926.

[62] Documents for founding the new Ferra-Gamo Inc. company were officially signed on April 29, 1926. The agreement was filed on May 4, 1926. Catalogue # GC 1145.1–23–35995 1926 Incorporation Record for shoe manufacturers Ferra-Gamo Inc. Seaver Center for Western History Research, Natural History Museum of LA County.

[63] Stefano Luconi and Guido Tintori, *L'ombra lunga del fascio: canali di propaganda fascista per gli "italiani d'America"* (Milan: M&B Publishing, 2004), p. 12.

[64] Salvatore was reported to have left the US around the middle of September 1926: see *La Parola*, September 9, 1926. His return to Europe is widely mentioned in the press: "Europe calls Hollywood's shoe creator of fashion," in *Coast Shoe Reporter*, October 1926; "Salvatore Ferragamo. Le iniziative italiane in California," in *California del Sud*, October 1926, pp. 10–11, which hints at Ferragamo's desire to open a store in Paris.

[65] An order in the Ferragamo Archive shows the shoe factory on Via Mannelli was up and running by February 1927.

[66] Archivio Storico del Comune di Firenze, *Cartelle di casa* collection, Via Mannelli. The building is still standing. Its street number is today 109.

[67] *Guglielmo Vita (1876-1995)*, exhibition catalogue, Florence, January 11 – February 8, 2014 (Rome: Lantana Editore, 2014).

[68] Silvano Fei, *Le vicende urbanistiche del quartiere di Santa Croce dalle origini ai nostri giorni*, City of Florence, Councilor's Office for Town Planning, 1986.

[69] Orders at the Ferragamo Archive in the years leading up to the company's bankruptcy (1933) show that other companies, such as Ferra-gamo & Co. and the Ferragamo Shoe Mfg company, also operated in Italy.

[70] *Shoemaker of Dreams*, p. 110.

[71] Ivi, p. 116.

[72] The Ferragamo Archive in Florence has documented orders with Gimbel Brothers, Saks's parent company, from 1928.

[73] Sommer and Kaufmann of San Francisco sent an invoice dated December 11, 1928 to Ferra-Gamo Inc., regarding returned defective shoes. This invoice is in the Ferragamo Archive.

[74] According to this 1949 memoir, Ferragamo apparently first formed a company with Ugo Squartiti and then the Lorenzi Brothers. Neither of these ventures were particularly successful.

[75] Archivio Storico del Comune di Firenze, *Fogli di famiglia* collection nos. 81864, 79094, and 97996, showing Ferragamo registered in Florence on January 24, 1929, having arrived from Bonito. He later chose to adopt Italian citizenship.

[76] On this topic, see *1927. The Return to Italy*.

[77] The patent application for this brand was made in April 1933. Patent no. 47473 was issued on April 6, 1934. See *Ideas, models, inventions*, exhibition catalogue, Museo Ferragamo, Florence, January 9, 2004 – August 31, 2006, ed. Stefania Ricci (Livorno: Sillabe, 2004), p. 222. It was nevertheless advertised in 1928 by artist Lucio Venna.

[78] Shoe orders flowed in from top stores and department stores, not just in the US but the UK, Switzerland, and France.

[79] *Rascello* was made from poplar bark, soaked in chrome.

[80] Ricci, "Salvatore Ferragamo and Women's Fashion in the 1920s," pp. 147–55.

[81] Stefania Ricci, "Italian Artists at the Panama-Pacific International Exposition in San Francisco," in *Italy in Hollywood*, pp. 66–79.

[82] Lucio Venna (Venice, 1897 – Florence, 1974) moved to Florence aged 15. In 1913, artist Emilio Notte introduced him to painting and the Futurist movement. Venna fervently supported the Futurists in *L'Italia Futurista* revue. On October 21, 1917, he and Notte co-published *Fondamento lineare geometrico. Al genio ed ai muscoli degli incrollabili pittori futuristi*, a tardy if significant contribution to propagating the movement's ideals. Venna worked as an illustrator in the 1920s and opened an advertising studio, Venna-Innocenti. After the partners separated in 1928, he began a new venture, "Nuove Creazioni Venna." In the early 1930s, Venna crafted numerous magazine covers, including for *Gran Sport* (1930–32) and *Corriere musicale dei piccoli* (1930–34). In 1934, he was in charge of the "Poster Artists and Advertising Graphics" section at the VII Fascist Syndicate of Fine Arts art exhibition in Florence. Showcasing his works from 1925 to 1934, the event demonstrated his wide range of graphic expertise over the decade. Venna designed an extraordinary composition for US department store Saks, presumably for shoebox closure-related purposes, in a composition that closely reflected work he was doing for Ferragamo. There is some speculation that the Italian craftsman acted as an intermediary for the American department store. Lucio Venna's works and documents are housed at the Fondazione Primo Conti in Fiesole. Marco Fidolini's book, *Lucio Venna: Dal Secondo Futurismo al cartellone pubblicitario* (Bologna: Grafis Edizioni, 1985), is the essential reference on his works for Ferragamo. Two seminal advertisements from 1928 he created for Salvatore Ferragamo were found at an antiques market in the run-up to this exhibition.

[83] The brand was registered in 1949 under patent no. 91956, October 3, 1949, following application no. 671 of January 23, 1947. A Ferragamo Archive document reveals Venna's design for Ferragamo's first store in Rome, which opened in 1938.

[84] Silvia Grandi and Alessandra Vaccari, *Vestire il ventennio* (Bologna: Bologna University Press, 2004), p. 83.

[85] See the *Ideas, models, inventions* catalogue.

[86] Patent no. 6971, November 27, 1929.

[87] "Fine Italian hand for shoes," in *Vogue* USA, July 15, 1937.

[88] Payments to Francesco Ciardiello for furniture purchases, dated October 10, 1931.

[89] Archivio di Stato di Firenze, *Tribunale di Firenze. Atti in Materia di Commercio, Fallimenti, Sentenze*, decree deposited on August 18, 1933. Throughout the year, a number of businesses of different size filed for bankruptcy. The bankruptcy proceedings continued until January 20, 1936.

[90] Ferragamo changed residence multiple times in this period. In 1931, he lived at Via Maffei 79. By February 1934, he was staying with his sister Rosina and brother-in-law Giuseppe Schiavone at Piazza Nazario Sauro 1, before moving to Via della Piazzola 20 in September 1935, and then to Lungarno Vespucci 40, where he was registered as living in the 1936 census. By 1939, he resided at Via Lamarmora 5A.

[91] Kept at the Ferragamo Archive in Florence, the agreement was terminated due to the outbreak of World War II.

[92] Dating from 1930 on Israel & Oppenheimer agency letterheaded stationery, numerous shoe orders on behalf of store chains in London and on British territory may be found at the Ferragamo Archive.

[93] After being set up in 1931, the partnership company rapidly opened stores in Turin, Genoa, and Venice. A 1949 Italian advertisement lists Italian store locations in Florence, Rome, Milan, Turin (Piazza Castello 113, closed down January 21, 1959), Sanremo (Via Matteotti 2), Genoa (Via Luccoli 61), Viareggio (Viale Marconi 39), Pisa (Corso Italia 112), Naples (Via Chiaia 145), and Palermo (Via R. Settimo 89-95).

[94] No. 194 today. Salvatore Ferragamo memoir from January 29, 1945, preserved at the Ferragamo Archive in Florence.

[95] Agreement letter from April 24, 1939, stored at the Ferragamo Archive in Florence.

[96] *Shoemaker of Dreams*, p. 148.

[97] Ibid., p. 149.

[98] On the building's history, see *A Palace and the City*, exhibition catalogue, Museo Ferragamo, Florence, May 8, 2015 – April 3, 2016, eds. Stefania Ricci and Riccardo Spinelli (Milan: Skira, 2015). Francesco Ciardiello's antique gallery was on the first floor, overlooking Via Tornabuoni. The Alinari print shop also occupied a space on the premises, on the Lungarno Acciaiuoli corner.

[99] This historical reconstruction of the purchase of Palazzo Spini Feroni is based on documents from Studio Tecnico Meucci and its *Libro dei soci, Giornale 1923–1963*.

[100] *Shoemaker of Dreams*, pp. 148–57.

[101] Ferragamo acquired the entire shareholding on January 29, 1942.

[102] Gianni Toniolo, *L'economia dell'Italia fascista* (Rome and Bari: Laterza, 1980).

[103] Grazietta Butazzi, "Gli anni Trenta. La moda italiana si mette a confronto, tra autarchia e nuove prospettive," in *Moda femminile tra le due guerre*, exhibition catalogue, Galleria del Costume di Palazzo Pitti, Florence, June 21, 2000 – March 21, 2001, ed. Caterina Chiarelli (Livorno: Sillabe, 2000), pp. 12–19, esp. p. 18.

[104] Natalia Aspesi, "Gli eleganti sandali di carta" and Stefania Ricci, "Alla ricerca delle calzature autarchiche," in *Lusso & Autarchia. 1935–1945. Salvatore Ferragamo e gli altri calzolai italiani*, exhibition catalogue, Museo Internazionale della Calzatura, Vigevano, September 18 – November 20, 2005, eds. Natalia Aspesi and Stefania Ricci (Livorno: Sillabe, 2005), pp. 11–21 and pp. 23–38.

[105] The wedge patent: no. 354889, December 13, 1937 (application no. 7,496 of September 17, 1937).

[106] *Shoemaker of Dreams*, pp. 145–46.

[107] Ferragamo shoe advertisements for Saks appeared in newspapers like *The New York Times* on December 12, 1937 and May 1, 1938. On January 1, 1938, a lovely article titled "Uplift the sole" appeared in American *Vogue*, pp. 58–59 (even if it had, apparently, been published previously, on December 1, 1937). On August 4, 1941, claiming to have invented the wedge, Florentine shoemaker, Edoardo Frattegiani brought a lawsuit against Salvatore Ferragamo. The final ruling was in favor of Ferragamo. Frattegiani had to pay legal costs and compensation for alleged fault (10 1941, Civil Judgments 601 to 660). Another dispute arose between the two designers in 1951 regarding paternity of the *Kimo* (Ferragamo) or *Pinturicchio* (Frattegiani) models, which looked very similar.

[108] On materials, see *Materiali per la fantasia*, exhibition catalogue, Museo Ferragamo, Florence, June 20, 1997 – January 3, 2000, ed. Stefania Ricci (Florence: Museo Ferragamo, 1997); on patents, see *Ideas, models, inventions*.

[109] *Shoemaker of Dreams*, p. 210.

[110] "Creazioni italiane a traverso il mondo," in *Novus*, XVII, Summer 1940, pp. 4–5.

[111] "La calzatura italiana vista da Ferragamo," in *Documento-Moda*, year II, XX, Summer 1942.

[112] In 1939, Ferragamo attended the Florence Crafts Fair.

[113] *Italy at the World's Fair New York 1939* (Florence: Vallecchi Editore, 1939). Ferragamo shoes illustrated the articles "Calzature italiane e francesi alla Esposizione di New-York," in *Rivista Italiana Calzature*, no. 7, July 1939, p. 32, and "Calzature di

tutto il mondo all'esposizione universale di Nuova York," in *Rivista Italiana Calzature*, no. 8, August 1939, p. 33.

[114] Tommaso Fanfani and Alberto Bianchi, *L'azienda Salvatore Ferragamo: passato, presente e futuro*, report written for the 2010 *A regola d'arte* exhibition at the Museo Ferragamo.

[115] *Shoemaker of Dreams*, pp. 185–91.

[116] Melania G. Mazzucco, "Introduzione," in G. Visconti, *Tà's Red Book. The Life of Wanda Ferragamo* (Milan: Electa, 2022), pp. 4–22.

[117] "Disciplina della produzione e della vendita delle calzature e degli altri articoli in cuoio," in *La Conceria*, 18 January 1941, pp. 3–5.

[118] *Disciplina della produzione e della vendita delle calzature ad usi civili* (Rome, 1942).

[119] Documentation on this Bonito factory, including a list of orders and workers' salaries, was found in Fulvio Miletti's archive; his grandson Fulvio meticulously preserved this material. Work continued in Bonito until at least the early 1950s.

[120] Oral interviews with shoemakers employed by Ferragamo during the war years, recorded and archived at the Ferragamo Archive in Florence.

[121] See *Ideas, models, inventions*.

[122] Patent 405472, filed on February 8, 1942 and granted on August 14, 1943, for an offensive and defensive anti-aircraft system. Patent 405527, filed on February 9, 1942 and granted on August 18, 1943, for construction of a sea fortress, namely an autonomous element located in water with the ability to submerge or function semi-submerged. Patent 405769 followed in 1943, filed on February 9 and granted on September 7, 1943, for a multiple-launch torpedo.

[123] *Shoemaker of Dreams*, p. 194.

[124] Documents at the Ferragamo Archive in Florence confirm that, as late as 1953, Salvatore was still seeking compensation from the Italian State for damage to his palazzo.

[125] *Shoemaker of Dreams*, pp. 194–95.

[126] Salvatore Ferragamo documented these events in his memoir from 1949, cited multiple times here.

[127] "Ferragamo ci scrive," in *Bellezza*, November 1945, pp. 63 ff.

[128] Archivi delle Imprese della Toscana, 1982.

[129] Patent no. 25505, November 16, 1946 (application no. 524 of March 12, 1946).

[130] *Shoemaker of Dreams*, p. 222.

[131] "What Price Foreign Trade," in *Look*, December 9, 1947, pp. 68, 71.

[132] Sheila Gould, "Meet Mr. S. Ferragamo-shoesmith," in *Cavalcade*, December 6, 1947, p. 18.

[133] Trademark patent no. 95294, requested on July 14, 1949, issued on March 27, 1950.

[134] *Shoemaker of Dreams*, p. 231; "Ferragamo fashions for Australia," in *Australian Women's Weekly*, September 24, 1958, pp. 32–33.

[135] Orders dating back to between 1958 and 1961. See also *Marilyn*, exhibition catalogue, Museo Ferragamo, Florence, June 20, 2012 – April 1, 2013, eds. Stefania Ricci and Sergio Risaliti (Milan: Skira, 2012).

[136] *Shoemaker of Dreams*, p. 225.

[137] Ibid., pp. 229–31.

[138] Ibid., p. 212.

[139] Ibid., pp. 213–15. See also *Greta Garbo. Il mistero dello stile*, exhibition catalogue, La Triennale di Milano, February 28 – April 4, 2010, ed. Stefania Ricci (Milan: Skira, 2010).

[140] *Shoemaker of Dreams*, p. 204.

[141] "A Palazzo Strozzi grande ballo storico. 'La donna italiana nei secoli' (dal 1300 in poi)," in *Grazia*, July 10, 1948, p. 21; "La donna nei secoli," in *Corriere Tridentino*, June 20, 1948; "Sogno di una notte di giugno tra costumi e vestiti che ballano," in *Il Mattino dell'Italia Centrale*, June 13, 1948, p. 3.

[142] O. F. (Oriana Fallaci), "Per i colori Dior attende la primavera ma prepara a Firenze un colpo di scena," in *Il Mattino dell'Italia Centrale*, December 8, 1948; Giorgio Gigli, "Dior chiama a Firenze l'Internazionale della moda," in *Oggi*, December 19, 1948, p. 15; Giordano Goggioli, "Quasi storico l'incontro Ferragamo-Dior," in *La Voce*, January 10, 1949; Giorgio Gigli, "A Firenze l'Alta Moda per il Maggio Musicale," in *Gazzetta Sera*, March 25, 1949; Giorgio Gigli, "Per maggio Dior all'ombra del Boboli," in *Momento Sera*, April 23, 1949, p. 3; Giorgio Gigli, "Christian Dior non viene a Firenze in qualità di 'Quinta Colonna'," in *Libertà*, April 23, 1949; Giorgio Gigli, "Allarmati i sarti italiani perché Dior viene a Firenze," in *La Voce Adriatica*, April 26, 1949.

[143] Paolo Colombo, "Il mestiere d'arte e il Made in Italy, tra un passato lontano e un futuro assai prossimo," in *Quaderni di ricerca sull'artigianato*, 60, 2012, p. 54; Elda Danese, "Alto artigianato," in *Bellissima. L'Italia dell'Alta Moda 1945-1968*, exhibition catalogue, MAXXI, Rome, December 2, 2014 – May 3, 2015, eds. Maria Luisa Frisa, Anna Mattirolo, and Stefano Tonchi (Milan: Electa, 2014), pp. 53–55.

[144] Pietro Annigoni met Ferragamo when exhibiting at the Galleria Bellini in Palazzo Spini Feroni during the 1930s. Through Salvatore and his connections with the British elite, he met the English royal family, and went on to paint a renowned portrait of Queen Elizabeth II.

[145] Renato Venturini, "Firenze centro di orientamento per lo stile e la moda d'Italia," in *Il Mattino*, May 21, 1950, p. 3.

[146] Meyric R. Rogers, *Italy at Work. Her Renaissance in Design Today* (Rome: Compagnia Nazionale Artigiana, 1950). The name "Salvatore Ferragamo" appears on the list on p. 65.

[147] The *Kimo* patent application was no. 31163, dated October 2, 1950. The patent was granted as no. 36644 on January 8, 1951.

[148] Nietta Veronese, "Il 'kimo', guaina e sandalo," in *Il Tempo*, February 2, 1951, p. 2; R. V., "Kimo e Pinturicchio scendono in campo in singolare tenzone," in *Il Mattino dell'Italia Centrale*, March 2, 1951, p. 3; "Per una calzatura in due 'tempi' in lite due noti artigiani fiorentini," in *La Nazione*, March 1, 1951, p. 1; *Grazia*, March 1, 1951, p. 2; Erti, "Scarpe uno e due," in *Grazia*, March 10, 1951, pp. 11–12; *Ars Sutoria*, Fall–Winter 1951, p. 39; "Trent'anni ai piedi delle dive," in *Annabella*, January 23, 1956, pp. 26–27.

[149] Patent application no. 3396, dated October 25, 1950. Patent issued as no. 36937 on February 15, 1951.

[150] Patent application no. 1252, dated April 4, 1952. Patent issued as no. 41888 on July 7, 1952.

[151] Two patents: no. 546657 dated July 28, 1956 (application no. 111 of January 4, 1956) and patent no. 546658, dated July 28, 1956 (application no. 112 of January 4, 1956). Both were invention patents.

[152] Invention patent no. 2199, dated February 10, 1956, issued as no. 549050 on October 4, 1956.

[153] Ferragamo had several patents for shell-soled designs. The overall patent was no. 578173 of June 20, 1958 (application no. 13373 of October 31, 1957).

[154] The patent was no. 559719, dated March 27, 1957 (application no. 14459 of September 27, 1956).

[155] *Elda Cecchele: in forma di tessuto*, exhibition catalogue, Spazio Espositivo Lanificio Conte, Schio, December 5, 2010 – February 20, 2011, eds. Maria Luisa Frisa and Gabriele Monti (Venice: Marsilio, 2010), pp. 68, 83–87. The letters are conserved in Venice, at Palazzo Mocenigo; a portion of Elda Cecchele's archive is at the "Pietro Selvatico" Art Institute, Padua.

[156] *Shoemaker of Dreams*, pp. 226–27. All documentation on this output comes from Rex Greatrex, expert footwear buyer for Lillywhites, London, who was at the event in Copenhagen with Miss Greenland. On the Rome event: "Anche Sophia Loren tra le visitatrici al salone in cui sono esposti modelli di calzature femminili," in *La settimana Incom* newsreel, no. 01217, March 3, 1955, Istituto Luce-Cinecittà Historical Archive, Rome.

[157] The brands mentioned above date from 1955 to 1957. See *Ideas, models, inventions*, pp. 225–26. Specifically, the patent for *Leonardo by Ferragamo* is no. 124987, September 10, 1955 (application no. 2234 of April 30, 1955).

[158] The contracts are at the Ferragamo Archive in Florence. More information from *Shoemaker of Dreams*, pp. 234–36.

[159] *Shoemaker of Dreams*, Preface.

[160] Patent no. 155332, filed on June 14, 1961 (application dated November 17, 1959). Another patent, *GiòFer Florence Italy*, no. 152183, dated November 22, 1960 (application no. 1141 of July 10, 1959).

[161] "Magnetic shoe gets TV preview," in *Star*, September 25, 1958; "Magnetic shoe on TV Show," in *The Daily Telegraph*, September 22, 1958.

[162] *Shoemaker of Dreams*, p. 238.

CHIARA
FAGGELLA

THE NEW RENAISSANCE IN ITALIAN FASHION: FERRAGAMO AND THE POST-WAR ERA

In the late 1940s, American fashion magazines and newspapers became enthralled with Italian craftsmanship. Immediately after the war, Italy was associated with and perceived as undergoing a new Renaissance, driven by Italian craftsworkers' innate expertise and skilled creative endeavors. After the shame of fascism, seen according to Benedetto Croce's interpretation, Italy was rehabilitated in magazines such as *Vogue* and *Harper's Bazaar*, major city newspapers, and trade magazine *Women's Wear Daily*. The country's disastrous involvement in the war had been supplanted by a rhetorical celebration of the nation's high-end industriousness, one that was reminiscent of the Renaissance era. Salvatore Ferragamo's personal and professional journey, combined with the ongoing acknowledgment of the excellence of his creations, was a perfect expression of the craftsmanship narrative in the US press. His voyage from Bonito to Hollywood was veritable rags-to-riches stuff, culminating in a return to Italy, to Florence—a city known as the cradle of the Renaissance and regarded as the "most artisanal city in Italy."[1]

At the end of World War II, Ferragamo was one of a handful of Italian firms with a long-established reputation in the United States. Although Italy lacked significant heft in high fashion—Parisian haute couture houses still ruled the roost—exemplary figures like Salvatore Ferragamo were showing buyers all about emerging Italian style. In particular, Ferragamo's footwear offered a shrewd compromise between the exoticism of European exports and adaptability to the US market.

Building on Salvatore's knowledge of American consumer tastes, Ferragamo footwear distribution in the US ramped up dramatically after expert input from at least two specialist organizations. The first was Gimbel Brothers, which sourced products for its Saks chain of department stores and others. Gimbel Brothers' Florence buying office was also at Palazzo Spini Feroni, and its network of relationships with luxury stores facilitated distribution of Ferragamo footwear across the US, including in Texas, where Neiman Marcus operated. In 1947, Ferragamo received the Neiman Marcus Award for Distinguished Service in the Field of Fashion. The press release cited his ability to blend "Italian classicism and age-old craftsmanship with prophetic creativity."[2] This award followed the highly publicized "return" of Ferragamo footwear, which dominated the US fashion press that

THE NEIMAN MARCUS AWARD CEREMONY, SEPTEMBER 8, 1947. FROM LEFT: SALVATORE FERRAGAMO, NEIMAN MARCUS VICE PRESIDENT STANLEY MARCUS, AND IRENE OF HOLLYWOOD

year, confirming the company's stronghold on the American market despite significant war-related distribution issues disrupting supplies since 1940. This is where the second organization came in, a non-profit association set up to help Italian companies specializing in artistic craftsmanship export their goods: the Commissione Assistenza Distribuzione Materiali Artigianato di Firenze (CADMA) was the Italian counterpart to Handicrafts Development Inc. (HDI), founded by academic Max Ascoli in New York to revive Italian craftsmanship after major war-related challenges.[3] Appointed CADMA President by Ascoli, Carlo Ludovico Ragghianti chose Mario Vannini Parenti of Florence to serve as his vice president and main liaison with artisans. A personal friend of Salvatore Ferragamo's, in early 1946 Vannini Parenti secured two leather import licenses from the Ministry of Foreign Trade for the Ferragamo firm. One of these licenses specifically sourced the leathers needed to produce footwear samples for the Saks Fifth Avenue New York department store.[4] After its intermediation successfully culminated in the Neiman Marcus Award, Salvatore was feted at the House of Italian Handicrafts, the HDI and CADMA showroom in the heart of Manhattan.[5]

Ferragamo was involved in HDI and CADMA's promotion of Made in Italy and continued to assist after these organizations merged to form the Compagnia Nazionale Artigiana (CNA), an entity established to hand out non-repayable loans of over four and a half million dollars to Italian artisan

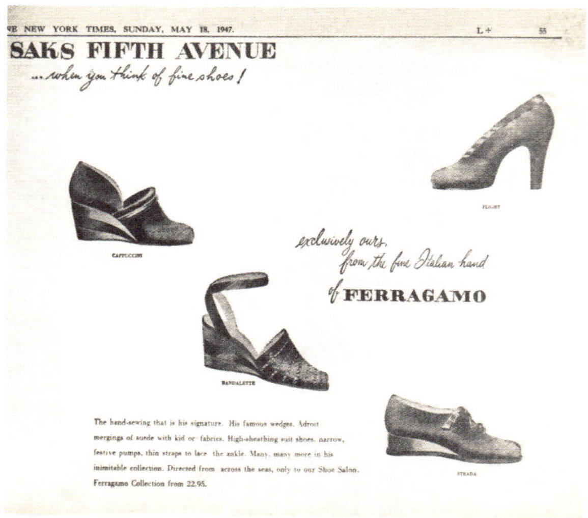

FERRAGAMO ADVERTS IN *VOGUE*, FEBRUARY 15, 1938; *HARPER'S BAZAAR*, APRIL 1947; *THE NEW YORK TIMES*, MAY 18, 1947

ADVERT IN *THE DALLAS MORNING NEWS*, SEPTEMBER 9, 1947

MEYRIC R. ROGERS, *ITALY AT WORK. HER RENAISSANCE IN DESIGN TODAY* (ROME: COMPAGNIA NAZIONALE ARTIGIANA, 1950)

VASES AND OTHER OBJECTS BY DESIGNER GIO PONTI ON SHOW AT *ITALY AT WORK*

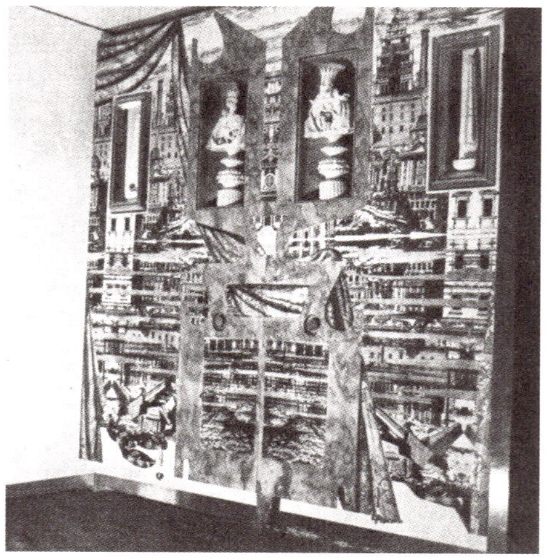

ENRICO BERNARDI, ON THE RIGHT, SHOWS SOME MODELS TO MEMBERS OF THE SELECTION COMMITTEE. FROM LEFT: WALTER DORWIN TEAGUE, CHARLES NAGEL, MEYRIC R. ROGERS AND RAMY ALEXANDER

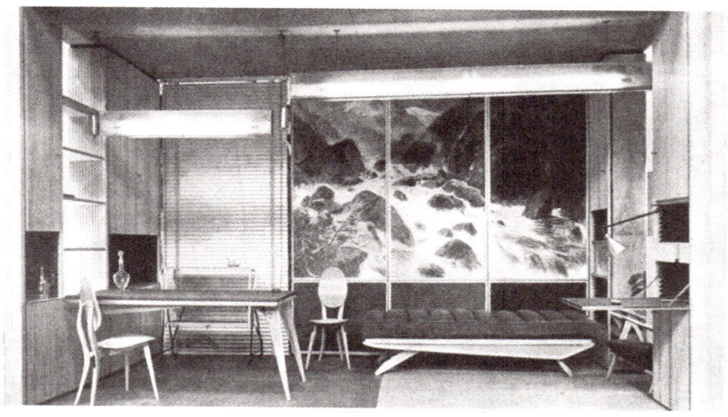

SOME WORKS BY ITALIAN ARCHITECT AND DESIGNER CARLO MOLLINO ON SHOW AT *ITALY AT WORK*

companies, funded by the Marshall Plan. The organization played a key role in organizing the *Italy at Work* exhibition, which traveled through the United States between 1950 and 1953: the final stage of Ascoli's Italian artistic craftsmanship rehabilitation project. The inclusion of Ferragamo's footwear in the exhibition attracted visitors and helped exposing other less-known fashion companies, such as Rome-based boutique Myricae and Valentino Bolognesi's leathers, to the general American public, and introducing them to the finest Italian products of the day.[6]

Curator Meyric R. Rogers specifically decided not to include detailed information in the exhibition catalogue: creating an exhaustive overview was not feasible owing to the vast number of items—some 2,500—on display.[7] So, the catalogue does not offer information on what Ferragamo footwear was displayed, but by the time *Italy at Work* ended in 1953, a number of exhibits, including nine pairs of Ferragamo shoes, remained in the United States and today form part of the Metropolitan Museum of Art Costume Institute.[8] Here, in addition to leather footwear in a more or less classical style, the standout pieces were sandals, slippers, and shoes crafted from unconventional materials such as raffia, straw, and hemp, not commonly seen on the US market. Inclusion of these items in the exhibition aligned with CNA's loan criteria for companies processing animal, plant, or synthetic textile fibers.[9] Highlights were the black *Booty* ankle boot featuring a cotton lace upper, the straw *Mercury* sandal, and the *Valle* slipper.

BOOTY, TAVARNELLE LACE, 1948

EXHIBITS ON DISPLAY AT *ITALY AT WORK*, M. H. DE YOUNG MUSEUM, SAN FRANCISCO, JUNE 18 – JULY 31, 1951

RAFFIA AND CALFSKIN LACED SHOE WITH WEDGE HEEL IN COVERED CORK, 1948

The exhibition was likely updated with new Ferragamo models for each venue, as chosen by the museums or dependent upon local department store availability. In parallel with the exhibition, stores put on promotional events for Made in Italy, generally with a stronger commercial emphasis. Three photographs from the *Italy at Work* installation at the M. H. de Young Museum in San Francisco show Ferragamo shoes other than the ones at the Costume Institute today.[10] The photos were taken in the summer of 1951 and depict several notable Ferragamo shoes: a pair of sandals with an "F"-shaped wedge and Tavarnelle lace upper; heeled sandals with a raffia ankle strap; lace-up shoes with a raffia upper; and, finally, a pump with circular decorations.[11] Some of these shoes may have been supplied by The White House department store in San Francisco, where the summer sale coincided with closure of the *Italy at Work* show at the de Young Museum and included some Ferragamo models among those seen in the installation photographs.[12]

From 1950 onward, the American press extensively covered post-war Italian fashion, fueled by the wide variety of items on display at *Italy at Work*, including fetching Ferragamo pieces. This exhibition confirmed the widespread narrative that the legacy of the Renaissance added credibility to the originality of emergent Made in Italy—an idea of which Ferragamo was the perfect embodiment. Despite war-related disruption, the Ferragamo company went from strength to strength, demonstrating refined creativity, implementing innovative design, and using unconventional materials. Most importantly, Salvatore's creations catered to US customers' style preferences.

FERRAGAMO PUMP IN TAVARNELLE LACE (RIGHT) DISPLAYED AT *ITALY AT WORK*, M. H. DE YOUNG MUSEUM, SAN FRANCISCO

FERRAGAMO SANDALS WITH DECORATED PLATFORM (CENTER) DISPLAYED AT *ITALY AT WORK*, CHICAGO ART INSTITUTE, MARCH 15 – MAY 13, 1951

FERRAGAMO ADVERT IN *THE NEW YORK TIMES*, APRIL 17, 1949

[1] Anna Pellegrino, *La città più artigiana d'Italia. Firenze 1861-1929* (Milan: Franco Angeli, 2012).

[2] "Invitation to the Tenth Annual Fashion Exposition Show at Neiman Marcus including a list of honorees," 1947. Stanley Marcus Papers, DeGolyer Library, Southern Methodist University.

[3] Lorenzo Mingardi and Davide Turrini, "Il Made in Italy come atto politico. HDI CADMA, Max Ascoli e Carlo Ludovico Ragghianti (1945-1948)," in *LUK*, no. 27, 2021, pp. 85–95.

[4] Archivio della Fondazione Ragghianti, FR-CADMA, Correspondence 1945–1949. Letter from Mario Vannini Parenti to Max Ascoli, February 23, 1946. Document 1923b. 39/17–1923b.

[5] "Italian Handicrafts Honor Ferragamo," in *Women's Wear Daily*, September 23, 1947, p. 3.

[6] Chiara Faggella, "Prima della couture: la promozione della moda italiana in Italy at Work," in *L'Italia al Lavoro. Un lifestyle da esportazione*, eds. Paola Cordera and Chiara Faggella (Bologna: Bologna University Press, 2023).

[7] Meyric R. Rogers, *Italy at Work. Her Renaissance in Design Today* (Rome: Compagnia Nazionale Artigiana, 1950), p. 12.

[8] Confirmed in Marcella Martin, "Fashion in the Art Museum: A Case Study of Salvatore Ferragamo Shoes," in *L'Italia al Lavoro*.

[9] Paola Cordera, "Lo 'stile italiano' in viaggio alla conquista degli States," in *Un oceano di stile. Produzione e consumo di Made in Italy negli Stati Uniti del dopoguerra* (Milan: Mimesis Edizioni, 2023).

[10] Paola Cordera tracked down these photos in her research for FARB 2021 VO Project "La voce degli oggetti. Il Design italiano dal museo alla casa" at the Politecnico di Milano. On this topic, see Faggella, "Prima della couture."

[11] The first two models may be traced back to Ferragamo patents no. 28482 and no. 35850.

[12] Advert from *The San Francisco Examiner*, August 30, 1951.

PATENT NO. 28482: LADIES' SHOE IN MESH, MAY 20, 1948

TAVARNELLE LACE AND KIDSKIN SANDAL, 1948

FERRAGAMO ADVERT IN *THE DALLAS MORNING NEWS*, JUNE 15, 1949

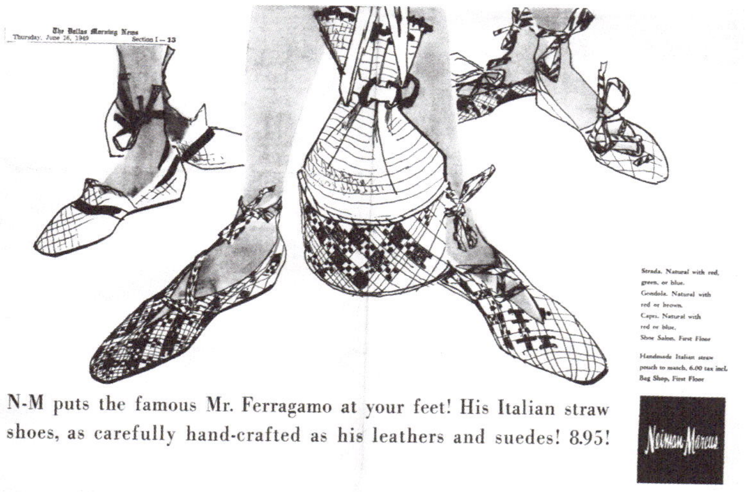

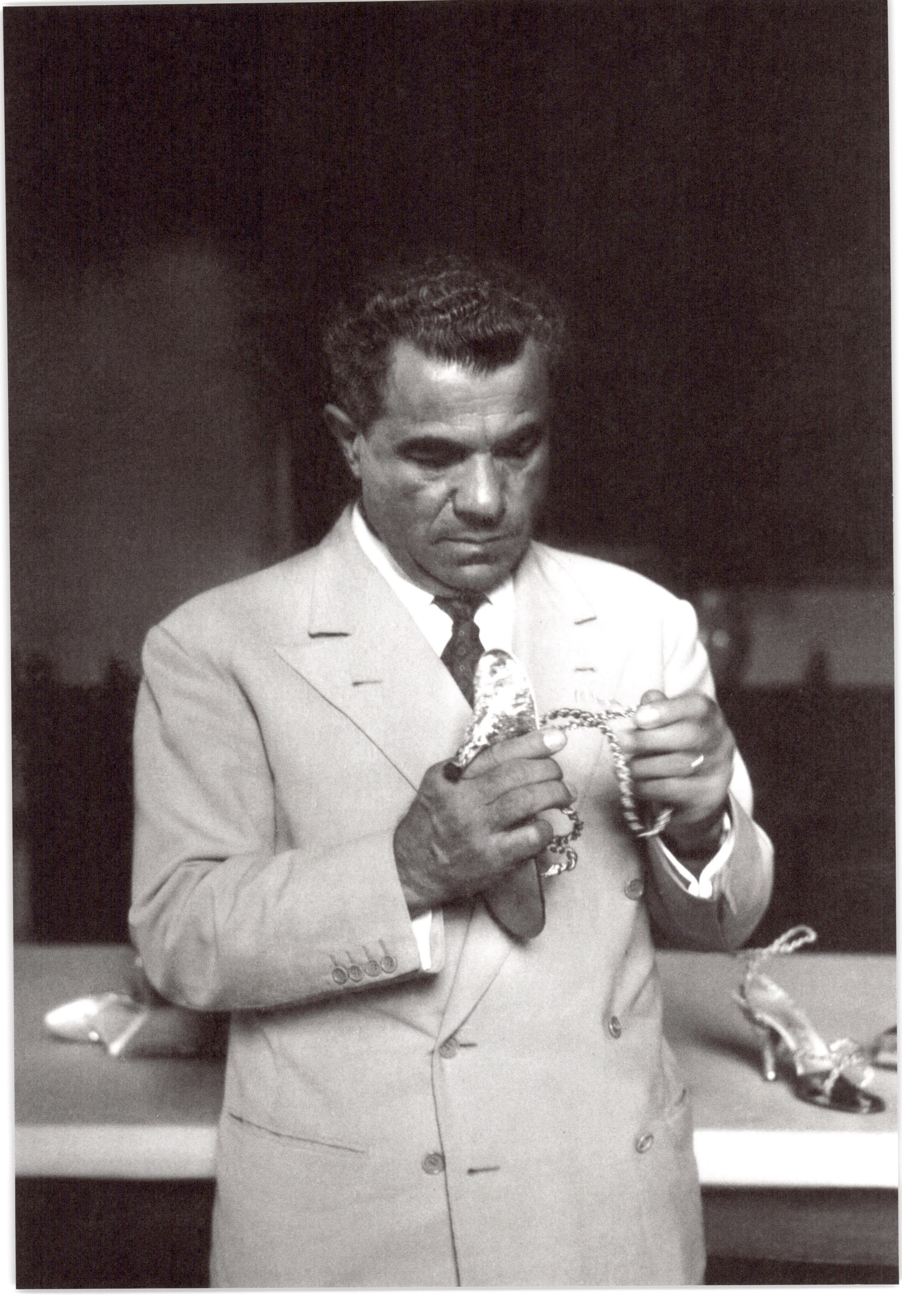

ELISABETTA
NARDINOCCHI

FROM THE GOLDEN *PRIMAVERA* FOOTWEAR TO SALVATORE FERRAGAMO'S GOLDEN SANDALS

On February 18, 1939, a select group of Italian artworks embarked on the transatlantic ocean liner *Rex* on a long journey for display to the American public in an exhibition organized by the Mussolini government at the Golden Gate International Exposition in San Francisco.[1] The Italian government's propaganda aims were clear, as was its hope of improving diplomatic relations between Italy and the US. Despite the title *Masterworks of Five Centuries*, most of the artworks on display were Florentine Renaissance masterpieces such as Masaccio's *Crucifixion*, Verrocchio's *David*, Botticelli's *The Birth of Venus*, Raphael's *Madonna della seggiola*, Michelangelo's *Pitti Tondo*, as well as works by Beato Angelico, Filippo Lippi, and Ghirlandaio.

As memories of the war receded, in 1956 a number of Italian and American museums started planning another major exhibition of Italian Renaissance works to be held in Washington and New York. Although the risks involved on the long journey turned out to be too serious for the project to be realized, it nonetheless drew attention to the deep interest among the American rich upper-middle class in Florentine Renaissance style, which they perceived as ennobling, a signal of social prominence, cultural depth, knowledge, and beauty.

Boosted by Italy's contributions to international expositions in Philadelphia (1876) and Chicago (1893), this historically alluring template had received an enthusiastic reception in the US since the late nineteenth century.

In 1879, an American newspaper wrote: "Our merchant princes, industrialists, money-maker mine owners, railway magnates, and financiers are far more inclined to emulate the Medici family's vast expenditures than to conform to their own frugal ancestors' habits."[2] The leaders of the "American Renaissance," the Morgans, Rockefellers, and Vanderbilts saw themselves reflected in the history and fortunes of the Medicis, Albizis, and Peruzzis.

One particularly celebrated artist was Sandro Botticelli; as Francis Haskell noted, Botticelli was not just rediscovered but recreated.[3]

SALVATORE FERRAGAMO WITH HIS GOLDEN SANDAL, 1956

At *Primavera*'s feet

We are unable to say whether the wealthy American lady for whom Salvatore Ferragamo crafted magnificent gold sandals in 1956 had visited the 1939 Golden Gate International Exposition in San Francisco, or its subsequent stops in Chicago (closed January 9, 1940) and New York (closed April 7, 1940). Regardless, she would certainly have been aware of the lingering echo these works had stirred in the American public. Such was their impact that, years later, alongside Marilyn Monroe and Liz Taylor, Andy Warhol featured the face of Botticelli's *Venus* among his screen prints.[4]

This brings us to the *Primavera*'s footwear. Inspired by classical culture and reminiscent of Greek, Etruscan, and Roman *sandalia*, they had insoles shaped to the foot and tied around the ankle with thin golden straps. We may find a potential cross-reference in Salvatore Ferragamo's golden creation, suggesting an even more evocative conception. While *Primavera*'s footwear appears to crush the meadow flowers on which the various characters stand, the Ferragamo shoes display flowers, carved delicately along the insole and blossoming over the heel, evoking the sensation of going barefoot, in direct contact with lush nature. The flowers' design echoes a Florentine goldsmithing tradition that, particularly in the late fifteenth century, often depicted open corolla inflorescences, their centers marked by perpendicular engravings.

Salvatore Ferragamo's penchant for revisiting models and themes of antiquity was nothing new. It is common knowledge that he worked for major Hollywood directors in the 1920s, creating footwear for the historical spectaculars

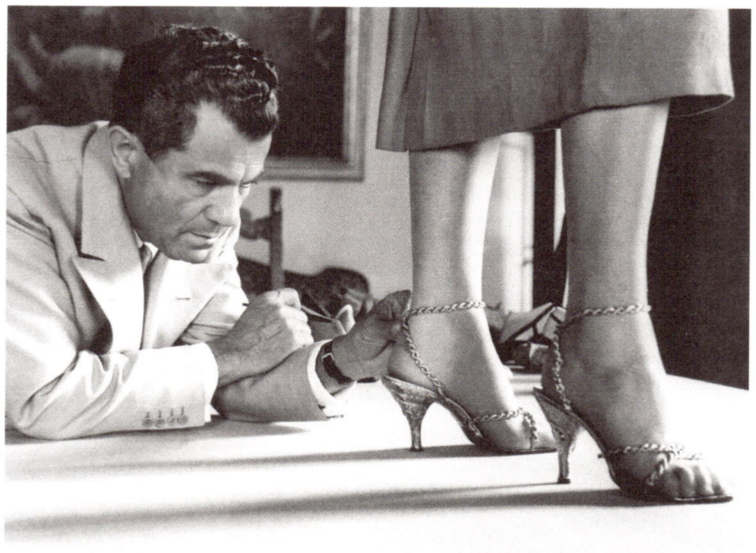

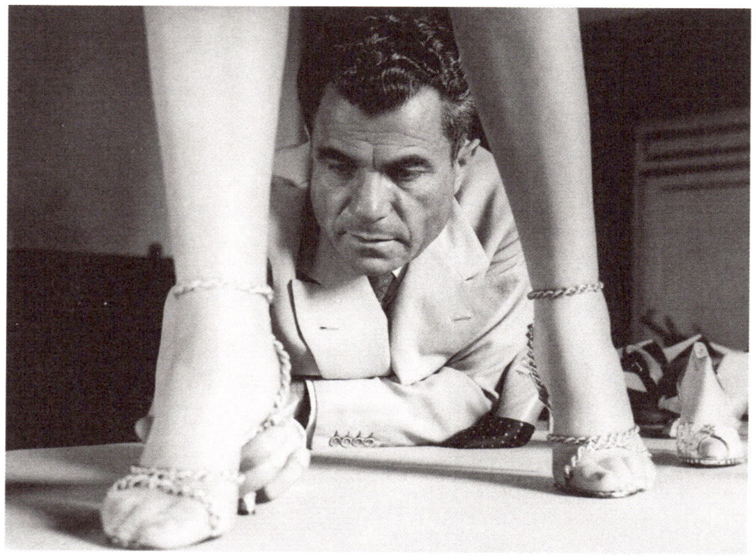

SALVATORE FERRAGAMO TESTING THE GOLDEN SANDAL ON A MODEL'S FEET, 1956

SANDRO BOTTICELLI, *LA PRIMAVERA*, 1482, TEMPERA ON PANEL. GALLERIE DEGLI UFFIZI, FLORENCE

of the day. "In 1930, he patented a sandal tied at the ankle, which he called the *Coturno Ferragamo*. Throughout his career, he frequently drew inspiration from Roman models depicted in books or displayed in museums."[5]

Our shoemaker's ability to absorb a variety of inspirations from the past is well documented.[6] His creations often hinted at Roman *coturni*, Renaissance *pianelle*, and motifs from the Mediterranean, the Orient, and the Americas. In this, Ferragamo was not alone. Emilio Pucci's atelier was renowned for its Botticelli-inspired collection created in 1959. Drawing heavily on the artist's works,[7] in particular it referenced four chest panels the Florentine master painted in 1483, commissioned by Lorenzo il Magnifico as a wedding gift for Giannozzo Pucci and Lucrezia Bini. This implied a parallel between that ancient marriage and Emilio Pucci's 1959 wedding to young baroness Cristina Nannini di Casabianca, offering at the same time a tribute to the bride's resemblance to the young girls the artist painted.[8]

All this had significant resonance with the American market: "To be successful in the United States, an Italian product necessarily had to leverage Italy's artisanal tradition, refined detail, the allure of the country's historic and artistic culture, its thriving design and vitality reflecting the country's sun-kissed landscape. Such elements allowed a product to stand out from high-quality local clothing along the California or Florida coasts."[9]

DETAIL OF THE FOOTWEAR IN BOTTICELLI'S *LA PRIMAVERA*

18-KARAT GOLD SANDAL CHISELED BY GOLDSMITHS FROM THE PALAZZO DELL'ORO IN FLORENCE FOR AN AMERICAN CLIENT, 1956

Flowers and dragons as decorative motifs

Master goldsmith Antonio di Salvi, a contemporary of Botticelli's who learned his craft at Antonio del Pollaiolo's workshop, probably offered the template for Ferragamo's gold sandal decorations. Most of his surviving works are refined religious artifacts in which one recurring motif is open corolla flowers with a checkered button inside plant-like spirals. Soon an integral part of the Florentine tradition, these models were revived in the twentieth century and bear a close resemblance to the ones on Ferragamo's gold sandals. One technique Antonio di Salvi used in his work was a clear-cut distinction on crafted surfaces between flowers, racemes, and the background, giving his artifacts a sense of depth that later became another defining feature of Florentine goldsmithing.[10]

Wrapped around the heel, monstrous figures reminiscent of snakes and dragons seem to intertwine with flowers and grasses. There is no contradiction between the two, for the Latin word *draco* denotes both snake and dragon. As with all symbols, ambivalent values are a dragon hallmark; however, in mythology and classical culture, the dragon most often embodies vigilance, a trait closely associated with wisdom, guardianship, and loyalty. So much so that the Garden of the Hesperides, the golden fleece, the fountain of Thebes, and the cave of Delphi all have dragon guardians. Even Filippo Strozzi chose dragons to safeguard his Florentine palazzo and those who lived there. Vigilantly watching and protecting from every corner, the more homely-looking dragons on the sandal augur our wealthy lady safe passage.

Models for these designs hail from distant lands. Notwithstanding the incorporation of Oriental elements, they hark

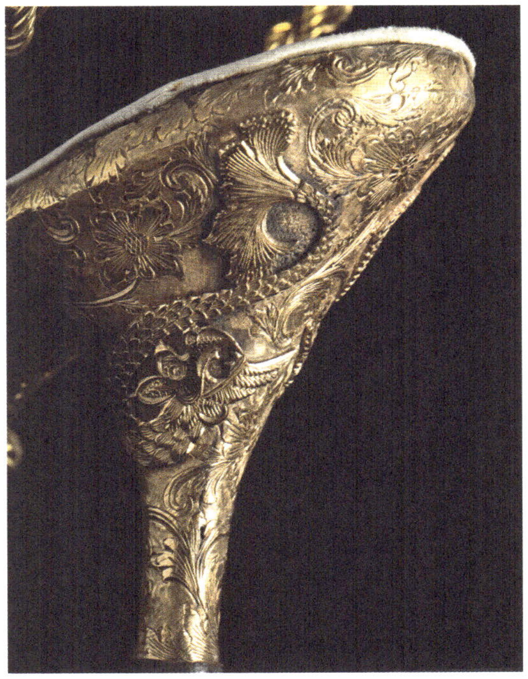

SARACCHI WORKSHOP, *CUP WITH DRAGON-SHAPED LID*, LAST QUARTER OF THE SIXTEENTH CENTURY, GRAUBÜNDEN JASPER, CAST, ENGRAVED, AND ENAMELED GOLD, PEARLS, AND RUBIES. GALLERIE DEGLI UFFIZI, TESORO DEI GRANDUCHI, FLORENCE

GRAND DUCAL WORKSHOPS, GIOVAN BATTISTA CERVI, *SHELL-SHAPED GOBLET*, 1576, LAPIS LAZULI, CAST, CHISELED, AND ENAMELED GOLD. GALLERIE DEGLI UFFIZI, TESORO DEI GRANDUCHI, FLORENCE

back to the dragons on exquisite vases and flasks crafted by the Saracchi brothers. Working at the Casino di San Marco in Florence in the late sixteenth and early seventeenth centuries, the legacy of these Milan-born brothers is amply represented in Florentine museums. A vase shaped like a fantastical creature crafted from jasper is among the Grand Dukes' treasure at Palazzo Pitti,[11] as is a 1576 sea snake whose gold and enamel coils entwine around a lapis lazuli cup made by goldsmith Giovan Battista Cervi.[12]

Form and structure

Cristina Morozzi looked at Salvatore Ferragamo's research into metal soles to ensure foot comfort, notwithstanding their apparent rigidity.[13] In 1955, he had already designed a light, airy sandal with a steel-cage heel, but the apogee for this material came with the gold sandal in 1956, when it defined the shoe's entire structure without in any way compromising adaptability to foot movements. Patent no. 546657, dated July 28, 1956, reveals the whole system's complexity in the title: "Shoe sole system, with metal heel and waist, and front part of the shoe let loose on it."

Essentially, the system replaced the shank (the steel plate Ferragamo had started using as support for the arch in women's heeled shoes) with a single rigid element that ran fully along the rear of the sole, from heel to waist (the recessed part between the heel and the front sole). As illustrated in the plethora of technical drawings submitted with the patent, a flexible surface, allowed for hinging and enabling the foot to move freely, joined the waist and the front part of the sole. The front part of the sole could also incorporate rigid components, "increasing strength without altering lightness." The rigid components were perforated to anchor ribbons and straps (on these particular shoes, golden cords) to form an open upper. All this, of course, was "capable of

ANTONIO DI SALVI, *"PACE" REPRESENTING THE LAMENTATION OVER THE DEAD CHRIST*, LATE FIFTEENTH CENTURY, CHISELED, ENGRAVED, AND GILDED SILVER, TRANSLUCENT ENAMEL, AND NIELLO ON SILVER. MUSEO NAZIONALE DEL BARGELLO, FLORENCE

ANTONIO DI SALVI, *"PACE" REPRESENTING THE CRUCIFIXION*, 1515, GILDED SILVER, ENGRAVED AND CHISELED, TRANSLUCENT ENAMELS. MUSEO DEL TESORO DELLA BASILICA DI SANTA MARIA DELL'IMPRUNETA, IMPRUNETA (FLORENCE)

PATENT NO. 546657: SHOE SOLE SYSTEM, WITH METAL HEEL AND WAIST, AND FRONT PART OF THE SHOE LET LOOSE ON IT, JULY 28, 1956

FERRAGAMO - Caso 1°

1 1 1 1956

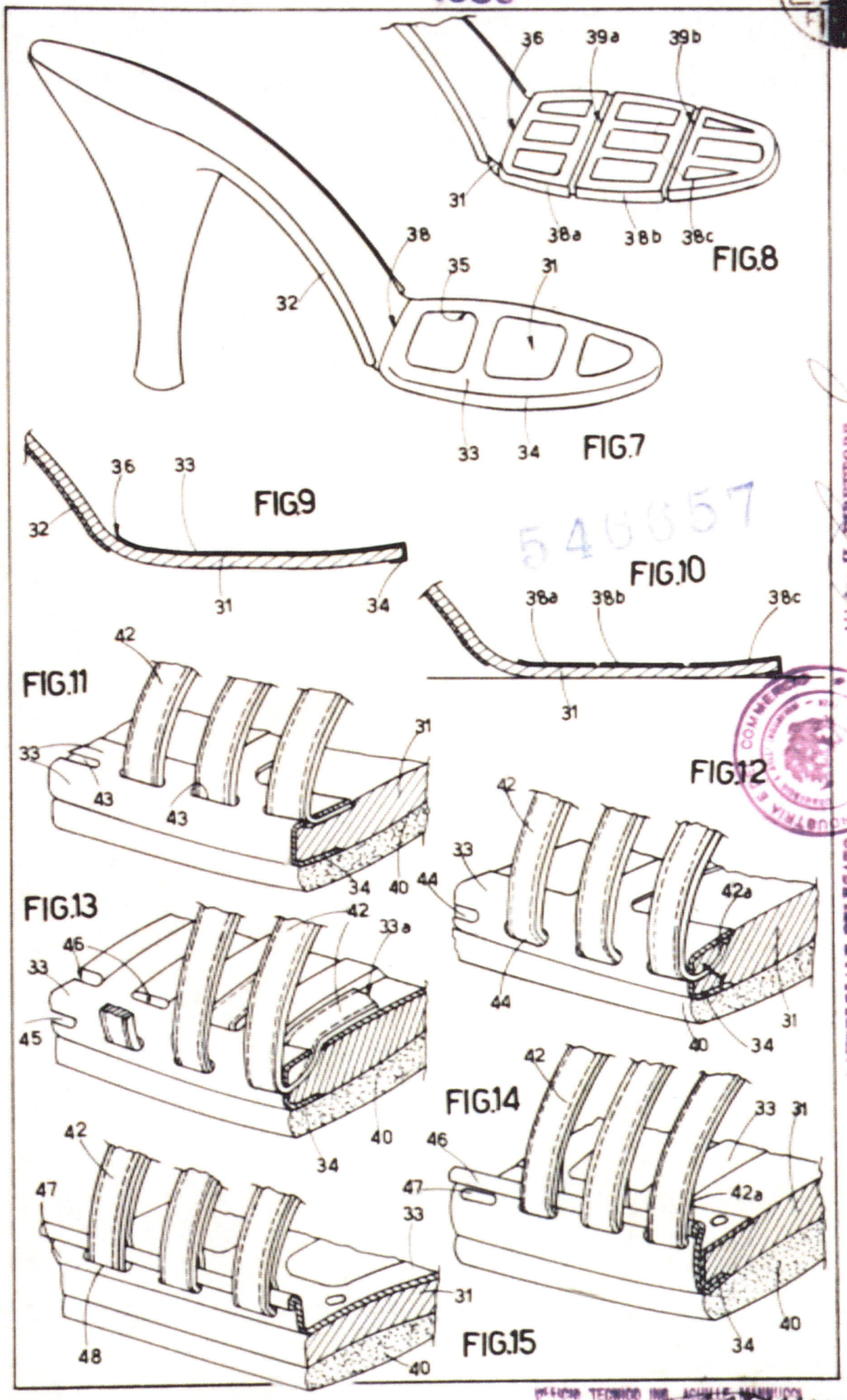

546657

Visto: IL DIRETTORE

L'UFFICIALE DELEGATO

PER PROCURA

undergoing surface treatments to achieve a particular aesthetic in the finished shoe."

Close collaboration between master shoemaker and master goldsmith was essential for making the18-karat gold variant; by this time, Ferragamo was more or less completely unintimidated.

The involvement of goldsmiths

Documentation on these sandals' manufacture does not reveal the name of the goldsmith involved. Doubtless, it was Ferragamo who designed the structure and decorative motifs, making the goldsmith's identity a lesser detail. It is, however, unfortunate that we are unable to provide more information on this detail; it might help us understand the relationship Salvatore had with local Florentine artisans. A note in the Ferragamo archive names craftsmen from the Casa dell'Orafo as working on one particular design.

Located at Vicolo Marzio 2, close to Ponte Vecchio, Casa dell'Orafo became—and still is—a hub for goldsmith shops after World War II, in a former Augustinian monastery linked to the church of Santo Stefano al Ponte. Although Ponte Vecchio was the primary showcase for Florence's goldsmiths and silversmiths, its limited space meant production sites were often located elsewhere; indeed, much crafting moved to areas near the old Augustinian monastery.

Ferragamo considered this an ideal place to find the skilled craftsmen he sought, since every store had expertise in both "traditional and modern" goldsmithing.

In the 1950s, the most notable shops at the Casa were Eugenio Franchi's, a "goldsmith and jeweler in both traditional and modern styles,"[14] the Angelo Mannucci and Enrico Grazioli partnership,[15] and the Nasali & Romiti firm.[16] The master goldsmith responsible for work on the gold sandals was likely one of these, even if, given the consistent high-quality craftsmanship and shared knowledge and tradition of that period's goldsmiths, a specific name may not add much to our knowledge.

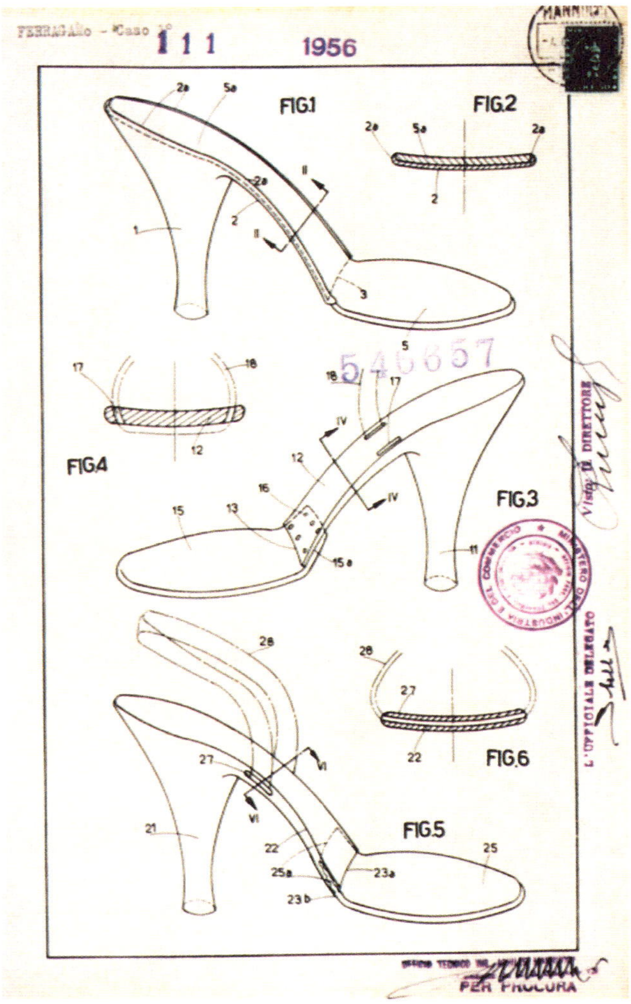

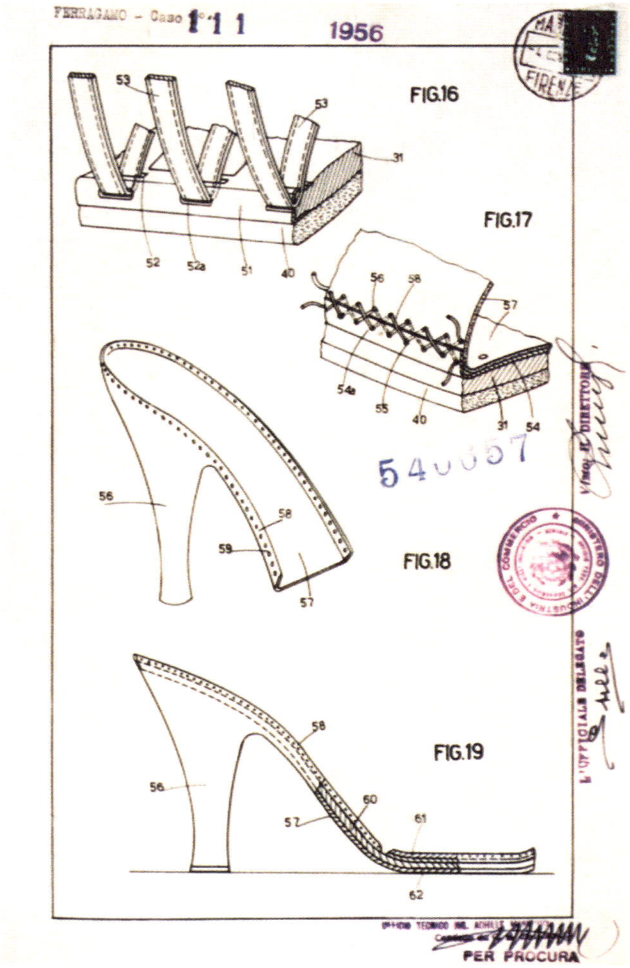

PATENT NO. 546657:
SHOE SOLE SYSTEM,
WITH METAL HEEL AND
WAIST, AND FRONT PART
OF THE SHOE LET LOOSE
ON IT, JULY 28, 1956

"Whether they worked in some long-established workshop—a place where, perhaps, Donatello's relentless strivings for innovation were still in the air—or toiled tucked away in a Ponte Vecchio attic, or in some obscure *fondaco* in one of the narrow streets that converge there and then lead toward the city center, or even across the river, Florentine goldsmiths gloriously upheld a centuries-old tradition with pride, skillfully handling precious metals and stones, solely crafting items for which they took full responsibility, regardless of whether the customer was Italian or foreign."[17]

[1] See Lorenzo Carletti and Cristiano Giometti, *Raffaello on the Road: reintegrazione e propaganda fascista in America (1938-40)* (Rome: Carocci editore, 2016).

[2] Peter Thornton, *Il gusto della casa. Storia per immagini dell'arredamento. 1620-1920* (Milan: Arnoldo Mondadori Editore, 1985), p. 308. On this topic, see also Alexis Gregory, *Families of Fortune. Life in the Gilded Age* (New York: The Vendome Press, 1993) and Claudio Paolini, "American Renaissance," in *MCM*, no. 57, 2002, pp. 26–30.

[3] Francis Haskell, *Rediscoveries in Art: Some Aspects of Taste, Fashion and Collecting in England and France* (Oxford: Phaidon, 1976), pp. 177–78; Carletti and Giometti, *Raffaello on the Road*, p. 81.

[4] See *The Botticelli Renaissance*, exhibition catalogue, Gemäldegalerie, Berlin, September 24, 2015 – January 24, 2016, eds. Stefan Weppelmann and Marc Evans (Berlin: Hirmer, 2015).

[5] Stefania Ricci in *Ai piedi degli dei: le calzature antiche e la loro fortuna nella cultura del Novecento*, exhibition catalogue, Museo della Moda e del Costume, Florence, December 17, 2019 – April 19, 2020, eds. Lorenza Camin, Caterina Chiarelli, and Fabrizio Paolucci (Livorno: Sillabe, 2019), p. 254.

[6] *Salvatore Ferragamo. Inspiration and Vision*, exhibition catalogue, Museo Ferragamo, Florence, May 27, 2011 – March 12, 2012, eds. Stefania Ricci and Sergio Risaliti (Milan: Skira, 2011), pp. 129–35.

[7] Stefania Ricci, "L'artigianato della moda," in *La grande storia dell'Artigianato*, VI: *Il Novecento*, ed. Gloria Fossi (Florence and Milan: Giunti Editore, 2003), pp. 228–55, esp. p. 250.

[8] Alessandra Arezzi Boza, *Emilio Pucci und Botticelli: Kunst, Inspiration und Mode von den Hochzeitstruhen bis zur Couture*, lecture held at the Italian Institute of Culture in Berlin, November 2015.

[9] Stefania Ricci, "L'artigianato della moda," p. 250.

[10] Dora Liscia Bemporad, "Il tramonto dell'oreficeria rinascimentale," in *Argenti fiorentini dal XV al XIX secolo: tipologie e marchi*, ed. Dora Liscia Bemporad (Florence: Spes, 1993), I, pp. 1–55, esp. p. 36. On this artist, see also Liscia Bemporad, "Una nuova attribuzione ad Antonio di Salvi: le due paci smaltate di Santa Maria dell'Impruneta," in *Scritti di storia dell'arte in onore di Roberto Salvini*, ed. Cristina De Benedictis (Florence: Sansoni, 1984), pp. 355–62.

[11] See Paola Venturelli, *Il tesoro dei Medici al Museo degli Argenti. Oggetti preziosi in cristallo e pietre dure nelle collezioni di Palazzo Pitti* (Florence and Milan: Giunti Editore, 2009), p. 96, no. 49.

[12] Ibid., p. 70, n. 28.

[13] Cristina Morozzi, "The Circularity of Ideas: Parallels between the Creations of Salvatore Ferragamo and Research in Design of his own Time and Today," in *Salvatore Ferragamo. Inspiration and Vision*, pp. 129–35, esp. pp. 134–35.

[14] *Dizionario degli Artigiani d'Italia*, I: *Toscana* (Siena: Edizioni Emilio Frullani, 1958), p. 24.

[15] Ibid., p. 26. In the 1970s they moved to Via di Capaccio and worked for Bulgari.

[16] Ibid., p. 27.

[17] Ibid., p. 15.

ELVIRA
VALLERI

ON IMMANENCE AND TRANSCENDENCE: THE SALVATORE FERRAGAMO LIBRARY

Memory as an exercise in knowledge

Adopting the reader's perspective, in *If on a Winter's Night a Traveler*, Italo Calvino emphasizes that every new work is created in relation to other books.[1] This very perspective helps us understand the checkerboard of philosophical and literary references in Salvatore Ferragamo's private library, in a web of diverse suggestions. One shelf in the library houses a number of books from the Anglo-American Theosophical tradition and a collection of texts from Western scientific and philosophical culture, as well as others from further afield. For the most part originally written in English, in the library these writings are mainly in Italian translation; in all likelihood, Ferragamo purchased them after his return to Italy.[2] This essay offers an initial inventory of these texts; without claiming to be exhaustive, it sheds further light on Ferragamo's worldview, on the ideal and cultural references that inspired the art and creativity of the amazing shoemaker.

The texts we have examined reveal an interesting framework of references that might have inspired and nourished Ferragamo's imaginative flair, which was always closely bound up with his attempts to understand aspects of anatomy, physiology, and science in a broader sense. Ferragamo left us a number of notes about this in his "autobiographical agreement,"[3] which, read in concomitance with this small bibliographic collection, take on clearer outlines. Conversely, anyone who reads *Shoemaker of Dreams*, a seminal text for understanding key aspects of the process of piecing together and reconstructing the story Ferragamo wished to tell and share, will benefit from new interpretations and points of view disclosed by some of the books in his library. In one chapter of his autobiography, Salvatore wrote that, from his earliest days, he had no need to learn anything. Rather, he simply had to "remember," to allow knowledge to flow into his mind.[4] He jotted down that all he had to do was focus and the solution would emerge "from the memory of a past life." He concluded these reflections with an intriguing note, a theoretical insight that may potentially be read in multiple ways: "Ever since I've been able to reflect and meditate, I believe in reincarnation and the constant evolution of man toward perfection. It feels that ideas from a past life spring to mind, riding the cosmic flow, already evolved and cleansed of former error." Ultimately, he was wondering whether some other explanation might

SALVATORE FERRAGAMO WITH HIS CHILDREN FIAMMA, GIOVANNA, AND FERRUCCIO WHILE LOOKING AT THE SKY WITH A TELESCOPE IN THEIR HOUSE GARDEN, 1949

account for his "inborn creative ability." As well as being essential to grasping some of the significance Ferragamo likely attributed to the concept of memory, these considerations help interpret his reference to meditation and, ultimately, frame the cultural context that led him to believe in reincarnation and "cosmic tide."[5] We may now cross-reference these observations and evocations with other information from his library, and use that information to re-interpret his autobiography, making it not just a narrative about the life of this artist, businessman, husband, and father, but a cultural and spiritual testament, highlighting the man's human and professional cultural backdrop.

The philosophy of touch.
Toucher le corps… avec l'incorporel du sense

The body of writings, variously referenced and annotated, in Salvatore Ferragamo's library allows us to come up with some potential answers, starting with John Locke's classic of English thought, *An Essay Concerning Human Understanding*. Ferragamo's collection contains the 1941 Italian edition, *Saggio sull'intelletto umano*, featuring extensive annotations using the English empiricist's Italianized baptismal name.[6] It is common knowledge that, when it began circulating, this book fired up enlightened minds of the day, and that Locke paved the way for the birth of Illuminism, with the stars of its philosophical firmament. However, what's of interest here is the significant perspective shift this essay ushered in, in that men of science moved from their specific frame of mind to adopt the viewpoint of the layman, having realized that it was counterproductive to distance themselves from everyday reality, that they should be ready to forgo abstraction if it failed to resonate with the masses. It's no coincidence that John Locke has been called the first "pop thinker" in the history of philosophy. For our purposes, the issues run deeper than this, especially if we consider Chapter XIX in Locke's *Essay*, which was, apparently, the main focus of Salvatore's interest in the copy found in his library. In this chapter, the author delves into the various modes of thinking (memory, reminiscence, contemplation, attention, application or study, dream, ecstasy, reasoning, and judgment), to which he refers as modes of operation that the mind observes within itself. Expressing no undue preference to any one mode over the others, Locke's insightful observations unveil a new conception of mental activity. In his view, far from being dismissed as worthless, daydreaming has a special place as a crucial working of the mind; indeed, he dedicated a specific treatise to visionary daydreaming.[7] Seeking to grasp the human mind's deeper activities, Locke begins his reflections from an experiential standpoint, appearing to establish a dialogue with other scholars of physics and astrophysics found in Ferragamo's library. One notable such writer was Sir Arthur Stanley Eddington, an acute and brilliant man who pioneered popularizing the concepts of modern physics, fearlessly discussing the philosophical value and meaning of his theories in an accessible manner. Eddington's work[8] likely appealed to Ferragamo for its insights into the invisible world embedded in our minds' structure, an unseeable realm aligned with "non-material entities … an ultimate reality that encapsulates the universe as we know it."[9] The library also houses a work by controversial engineer and physicist Georges Lakhovsky, a Russian who was later naturalized French; the book in question is *Science and Happiness*, translated into Italian as *Longevità e immortalità per mezzo delle vibrazioni* and printed by the Fratelli

Bocca publishing house in Milan. Lakhovsky advocated a theory of cellular oscillation, maintaining that human body cells possess a kind of "antenna" capable of being stimulated by electromagnetic waves. According to the physiologist, diseases stem from the "disharmony" of electromagnetic waves within our body cells.[10] During the 1920s, Lakhovsky worked with doctors at the Salpêtrière hospital in Paris to develop experimental treatments using a multi-wavelength oscillator he invented and patented.

It is irrelevant to discuss here the scientific worth of these experiments; for us, the interesting thing is Salvatore Ferragamo's interest in a nuanced and original reflection on the body, one that explored the value and significance of tactile sensitivity, to which he attributed a key role. Many photographs depict Ferragamo in the pose of a man listening intently as he examined his clients' feet, resembling a chief physician who, with all due respect, makes a diagnosis and determines a treatment. Indeed, in his autobiography Salvatore writes: "I love feet. They talk to me. As I take them in my hands I feel their strengths, their weaknesses, their vitality or their failings. A good foot . . . is a masterpiece of divine workmanship."[11] Elsewhere, he describes a kind of "electric shock" passing from the client's foot to the palm of his hand, emphasizing how he feels it directly and instantly, like "the sun when it is warm and the wind when it blows cold."[12]

These comments seem to encapsulate one of the most fascinating aspects of Empiricist reflection, namely, sensation as the result of mutual movement between the perceived object and sense organ: knowledge thus becomes motion, moving from inside to outside in response or reaction to external objects exerting pressure on the sense organs.

BOOKS ON THE SCIENCE OF THE MIND IN SALVATORE FERRAGAMO'S COLLECTION

THE TEXT BY AMERICAN WRITER UPTON SINCLAIR PROPOSING A RATIONAL CONCEPTION OF RELIGION

Salvatore Ferragamo's notes on the relationship, through tactile sensation, with the body evoke the interesting subject of interaction between our upright posture, anchored in our extremities (feet), and our states of mind and mood, a theme on which the amazing shoemaker wrote words of great interest even to this day.[13] Several pages of his autobiography are taken up with ongoing annotations on the physical constitution and pathologies that afflict the feet of people of various ages, from childhood to adulthood. This digression shows how Ferragamo's concern for comfort and respect of the foot's anatomy formed the cornerstones of his work, leading to the "healing shoe" that went on to become the touchstone for his success. The quest for glamour, combined with the "Ferragamo method" of shoe construction, made him not just a successful businessman but, building on his wide-ranging reading and thought, a great innovator. Among other things, he studied the work of Sir Oliver Lodge, a research pioneer into radio and electromagnetic waves and member of the Royal Society,[14] who delved into philosophy and metapsychics and extensively explored relationships between science and religion.

Reflections between sky and earth

The books in the family home library reveal Salvatore's interest in astronomy; among them, *Le più belle pagine di astronomia popolare* by Giovanni Schiaparelli.[15] Director of the Brera Astronomical Observatory, Schiaparelli was the first person to map Mars: his cartography, undertaken as part of proceedings at the Accademia dei Lincei before spreading across the globe and reaching the United States, where the Italian astronomer's work gained traction, is to this day still used to name Martian locations. In the US in particular, people began talking about "little green men" living up there, intelligent beings who had erected megalithic structures to distribute water across the surface of Mars. To further investigate Schiaparelli's findings, American scientist and magnate Percival Lowell built a sophisticated private observatory in Flagstaff, Arizona. The facility was equipped with an impressive 450-millimeter (later upgraded to 600) diameter telescope, arguably the world's largest. Not until NASA's 1965 Mariner 4 space probe and its later mapping did we finally see the true surface of Mars: arid, desert-like, pockmarked with impact craters, deep trenches, and volcanic structures. Prior to that, for many decades Mars had inspired an array of fantastical literature.

Salvatore's collection included an English work on amateur telescope-making,[16] and an essay on the stars and planets[17] by Giorgio Abetti, director of the Arcetri Astrophysical Observatory in Florence.

Salvatore's years in the New World and his evening anatomy courses at the University of Los Angeles[18] played a pivotal role in his personal and professional development, introducing him to a whole realm of cultural and scientific pursuits that shaped his later personal and work-related research—concepts and knowledge he went on to transform into shoe prototypes and studies. As he explains extensively in his autobiography, extraordinary intellectual curiosity nourished his ambition. He was particularly interested in applying "abstract theories"[19] of an anatomical nature, which enabled him to grasp the pivotal role of the human foot and its morphology, to his own research that, through a blend of theory, experimentation, reflections, and applications, led to the discovery of shoemaking's "secret." His research pathway was driven by doubt and unstinting efforts to "unlatch the last door that would lead me . . . into the promised land where shoes would always fit."[20] The culmination of his research and his reference to the "last door" and "promised land" denote his deep comprehension and empathy with this part of the body, encapsulating the essential features of his art and success within a spiritual framework. Indeed, he believed that, left to its own devices, nature heals every wound and "gives us ample warning of everything that is wrong with our bodies."[21] When Salvatore Ferragamo shared these thoughts in his autobiography, respect for nature and its laws was a topic still largely under the radar of cultural discourse, especially in Italy, at that time.

Our initial research is yet to reveal whether Salvatore had heard of plantar reflexology, a discipline in which the foot is viewed as a kind of second heart, a microcosm that internally reflects the entire organism. The medical practice of reflexology, based on traditional Chinese and Indian knowledge, first gained popularity in the United States in the 1920s.[22] What our investigation of Salvatore's library does allow us to infer is an intertwining of anatomical texts and early homeopathic studies, for example by Frenchman Léon Vannier, who set up several specialized labs to manufacture homeopathic medicine,[23] and Horace Fletcher, who back in the 1930s questioned the relationship between food and fasting.[24] Much like Vannier, Salvatore was keen to understand how to maintain or in some cases restore our physical balance: after identifying a person's "distinctive type," and after grasping and analyzing their anatomical structure, temperament, and behavior, suitable remedies were prescribed if necessary.

Analysis of these texts confirms a kind of framework, an intertwining of scientific and anatomical texts with philosophical and cultural ideas in order to achieve a balance between man and the laws of nature.

The laws of physis and a search for the transcendent

Another important and vital aspect of Ferragamo's library is interesting to dwell on: texts associated with Eastern religions and Theosophical thought. Significantly, from World War I through the Roaring Twenties, California was one of the Theosophical Society's flagship locations. The Society had been founded in New York at the end of the nineteenth century,[25] after the discovery of electrical energy and, later, radiation, suggested that the universe was animated by still unknown invisible forces that, studies indicated, might soon become knowable. It is possible that the very invention of the light bulb was in part influenced by Thomas Edison's membership of the Theosophical Society and avid belief in spiritualism.[26]

The Theosophical Society was established without an official doctrine, even if, from the very start, it pursued a form of universal eclecticism as a means of integrating all forms of religious tradition and different confessional frameworks. Promising to answer fundamental questions about human life along a path that was both spiritual and scientific, Theosophy attracted widespread interest from the European and American cultural elites, including artists Wassily Kandinsky (author of a famous treatise on the spiritual dimension in art[27]) and Piet Mondrian, and writers Hermann Hesse, Antonio Fogazzaro, and Luigi Pirandello. It also appealed to members of Italy's scientific community and Maria Montessori.[28]

The Theosophical Society's widespread, multifaceted influence was deeply intertwined with two charismatic figures: founder Helena Blavatsky and her successor, Annie Besant.[29] At least until the 1920s, the latter managed to extend the Society's appeal to an ever-growing number of people. Only in passing do we have the scope to examine how pivotal these two women blessed with charismatic appeal and intellectual authority were to creating a new and successful model of womanhood.

SOME BOOKS FROM FERRAGAMO'S COLLECTION ON PHILOSOPHY, THE HUMAN INTELLECT, AND SCIENCE

MANUAL ON HOW TO MAKE A NON-PROFESSIONAL TELESCOPE AND ASTRONOMY BOOKS IN FERRAGAMO'S COLLECTION

BOOKS ON MEDICINE AND ALTERNATIVE TREATMENTS IN FERRAGAMO'S LIBRARY

SOME BOOKS FROM FERRAGAMO'S LIBRARY ON THE PRACTICE OF YOGA, EASTERN PHILOSOPHIES, AND THE RELATIONSHIP BETWEEN BODY AND MIND

During her time leading the Theosophical Society, Annie Besant identified Jiddu Krishnamurti as the new Messiah, bringing the young Indian to England to be educated at prestigious schools. Besant lived for many years in India, working tirelessly to support the nation's independence. She was elected president of the All-India Congress in 1917, before Gandhi took over that role in 1920. When, in 1929, Krishnamurti disavowed the claim that he was the Messiah, the Society was thrown into crisis.

Fascinatingly, Salvatore Ferragamo owned a copy the Italian translation of Besant's *The Power of Thought*,[30] which was published in many editions, some of which including a series of studies on color (an interest evidently widely shared among Theosophical Society members). Ferragamo also had an Italian edition of Jiddu Krishnamurti's *Discourses*,[31] a book that reiterated his lifelong pursuit of freedom through awareness of our relationship not just with others but with ideas, nature, and everything: "We are full of theories, words, knowledge of what others have said, but we know nothing about ourselves, hence we do not therefore know how to live."[32] This awareness enables us to understand our human dimension, our subjectivity on a journey of seeking "balance" that loomed so large in Krishnamurti's speeches, as it did in various ways in Salvatore Ferragamo's thinking and entrepreneurial career.[33]

Cinema and Theosophy

Above and beyond his privileged relationship with Hollywood cinema, Ferragamo's collection of books enables us to realize how important Salvatore's years in California were to his later development. This is well worth exploring further. Hard as it may be to believe, in the 1920s and 1930s, Theosophy held a prominent place in glamourous "Tinseltown." California was known for its openness and for a strong current of non-conformity that prompted men and women to explore spiritual paths other than those offered by traditional religion. Actress Mae West, for example, was attracted to metaphysics and explorations of latent human powers—and she was not alone: Rudolph Valentino and Jean Harlow, and later Greta Garbo also took an interest in these subjects.[34] We may further note that a sprawling Theosophical spiritual center was established on a large, five-hectare plot in Beachwood Canyon, in the hills north of Hollywood,[35] where many wealthy Californians chose to build a home. Christine Wetherill Stevenson, the creator and financier of the large Hollywood Bowl theater,[36] opened in 1922 and primarily dedicated to music and opera,[37] was one of the VIPs interested in construction of this community, named "Krotona Colony."[38] From the 1920s onward, this area of Hollywood became a significant attractor for the entrepreneurial elite, who flocked here to construct buildings and houses suited to a Theosophical way of life: among others, acclaimed singer Marie Russak, vice president of the American Theosophical Society, who had a keen interest in architecture and likely designed Chaplin's[39] house, not far from the building where Salvatore Ferragamo lived in the 1920s, before his return to Italy.

The proximity of so many people in entertainment and cinema to Theosophy spawned movies that put metaphysical and Theosophical themes onto the silver screen (for example, Jean Cocteau's *The Blood of a Poet*); some commentators suggest *The Wizard of Oz* may also be interpreted as a Theosophical allegory.[40]

Further intriguing texts emerge related to this cultural background: a book by Remo Fedi, a linguist, scholar of hermetic philosophy and esotericism, as well as an opponent of fascism and founder of the Anti-fascist Concentration Committee of Piombino,[41] alongside two works by Prentice Mulford, considered the precursor of New Thought, which was also known as the science of the mind.[42] Alongside his academic studies on human anatomy,[43] Ferragamo nurtured an interest in pranic therapy[44] and Eastern hydrotherapy.[45] He also explored the link between sports discipline and yoga via the autobiography of Selva Raja Yesudian (founder of the first yoga school in Budapest), who describes his leaving India and the impact of landing in Europe and Switzerland.[46]

In all these texts, as well as in many other books of the library we have no space to discuss in this brief essay, reflections on the body, the mind, and the concept of psychosocial evolution come to the fore. Julian Huxley described just such a trajectory in *The Science of Life*, a text we find in a 1936 Italian translation titled *Scienza e vita*.[47]

The circular movement between our life experiences and the books we read generates surprises and discoveries: in this perspective, the volumes we have seen offer some interesting jumping off points. They narrate the journey of Italians to America (*Italiani in America*)[48] and offer other evocative paths that intertwine different cultures and worlds: Eastern wisdom, Theosophy, the relationship between science and the mind through a focus on the body

ONE OF MANY BOOKS BY ANNIE BESANT, LEADER OF THE THEOSOPHICAL SOCIETY, IN SALVATORE FERRAGAMO'S COLLECTION

BOOK BY JURIST AND PHILOSOPHER WILLIAM WALKER ATKINSON IN THE FERRAGAMO LIBRARY

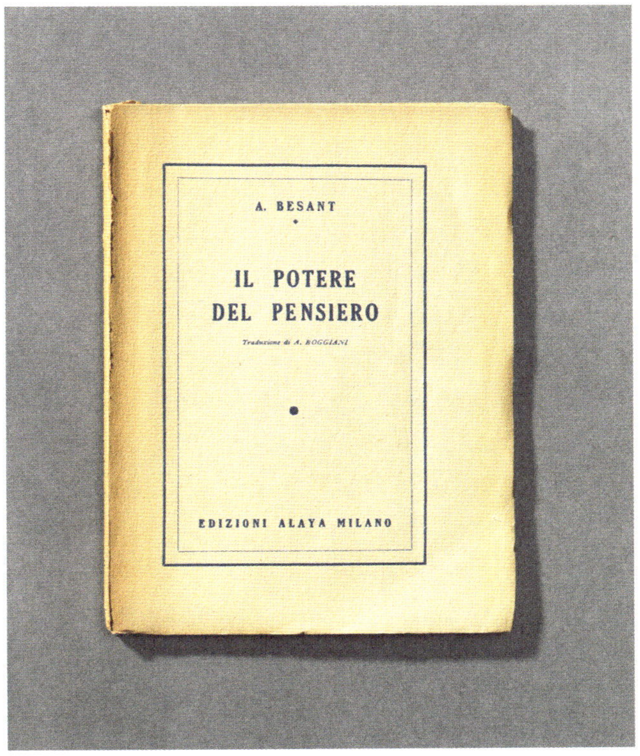

and its vibrations, without forgetting food and its significance: all at a time when such knowledge and thought were likely little known or, in practical terms, ignored.

These many and diverse references allow us to better comprehend Salvatore Ferragamo's human and professional journey in California, where he was known as an elegant, refined "shoe designer,"[49] and the reasons behind his "return to Italy" and discovery of Florence, a city where his creativity was nourished by and intertwined with its long-standing heritage—something the amazing shoemaker could sense from his viewpoint in America. While home decor magazines and opinion-makers were praising the American Renaissance, silent film sets and new world elites increasingly looked to the Tuscan city's fifteenth- and sixteenth-century arts, sciences, mercantile spirit, and luxury.[50]

This brief inventory paints the picture of a man who, upon returning to Italy, not only brought back the creative abilities that had prompted him to cross the Ocean in the first place more than a decade earlier, but numerous, varied intellectual and cultural influences from his extended experience in America: *Lares* and *Penates* that, as many of the books we have examined suggest, would accompany him during the following decades of his life. The books in this initial survey map out the journey of a man who never stopped seeking deeper meanings in the adventure of being human, a man who explored diverse worlds and cultures, creating bridges to foster a deeper understanding of his own essence, in the knowledge that he was "destined" for the "mission" of making shoes. A remarkable narrative of self, Salvatore's autobiography concludes with an observation that confirms his eclectic view of transcendence: "I have plenty of time. I know I am going to do it. If it is not done with this body it will be done with another. We are all flowing with the eternal tide, and of the eternal tide only is there no end."[51]

Such statements conclude the "inner garden" narrative Salvatore Ferragamo was so keen to share. His autobiographical considerations do not reflect just the past he recounts, they were closely bound up with the dialogue he established with objects, human presence, and the emotions that traversed him. "Writing his own life," Salvatore shared his worldview and life perspective, attributing many different meanings to his personal experience, and bearing witness to his existential search.

[1] Italo Calvino, *Se una notte d'inverno un viaggiatore* (Turin: Einaudi, 1979).

[2] Museo Ferragamo dedicated an entire exhibition to Salvatore's decision to return to Italy after his long stay in California: see *1927. The Return to Italy. Salvatore Ferragamo and Twentieth-century Visual Culture*, exhibition catalogue (Museo Ferragamo, Florence, May 19, 2017 – May 2, 2018), eds. Stefania Ricci and Carlo Sisi (Milan: Skira, 2017).

[3] Salvatore Ferragamo, *Shoemaker of Dreams. The Autobiography of Salvatore Ferragamo* (Milan: Electa, 2020); first ed. London: George Harrap & Co. Ltd, 1957.

[4] In his autobiography, Salvatore dedicates an entire chapter to "The Search for a Secret" (ibid., pp. 59–66).

[5] Ibid., p. 60.

[6] Giovanni Locke, *Saggio sull'intelletto umano* (Bologna: Zanichelli Editore, 1941).

[7] British psychoanalyst Wilfred Ruprecht Bion investigated this form of thought activity in detail in the 1960s.

[8] Arthur Stanley Eddington, *La scienza e il mondo invisibile* (Milan: Fratelli Bocca Editori, 1953), p. 2 (original ed. *Science and the Unseen World*, London, 1929).

[9] Ibid.

[10] Georges Lakhovsky, *La scienza e la felicità. Longevità e immortalità per mezzo delle vibrazioni* (Milan: Fratelli Bocca Editori, 1939).

[11] *Shoemaker of Dreams*, p. 67.

[12] Ibid., p. 200.

[13] Ibid., particularly the chapter "The Healing Shoes," pp. 161–73.

[14] Oliver Lodge, *Scienza e Progresso umano* (Milan: Fratelli Bocca Editori, 1953) (original ed. *Science and Human Progress*, London, 1927).

[15] Giovanni Schiaparelli, *Le più belle pagine di astronomia popolare* (Milan: Hoepli, 1945).

[16] Between 1926 and 1953, *Scientific American* magazine published three volumes of *Amateur Telescope Making*, edited by Albert G. Ingalls.

[17] Giorgio Abetti, *Le stelle e i pianeti* (Turin: Einaudi, 1945). Giorgio Abetti facilitated construction of a solar tower near the Florence Observatory, based on one at Mount Wilson, California.

[18] I take the liberty to mention my essay titled "The 'Autobiographical Pact' of Salvatore Ferragamo," in *Italy in Hollywood*, exhibition catalogue (Museo Ferragamo, Florence, May 28, 2018 – March 10, 2019), ed. Stefania Ricci (Milan: Skira, 2018), pp. 338–79.

[19] *Shoemaker of Dreams*, p. 65.

[20] Ibid., p. 66.

[21] Ibid., p. 164

[22] In the 1930s, American therapist Eunice Ingham published two books, *Stories the Feet Can Tell Thru Reflexology* and *Stories the Feet Have Told Thru Reflexology*, building on the work of Boston doctor William Fitzgerald and of Edwin F. Bowers, another doctor interested in spirituality and alternative medicines. In Italy, professor Giuseppe Calligaris, a neurologist and lecturer at the University of Rome until 1939, and doctor Nicola Gentile advanced studies in this field, both publishing research that was highly innovative for the day.

[23] Léon Vannier, *Omeopatia. Medicina umana* (Milan: Fratelli Bocca Editori, 1952).

[24] Orazio Fletcher, *L'arte di mangiar poco* (Milan: Giovanni Bolla Editore, 1930).

[25] The Theosophical Society was founded in New York on November 17, 1875, by Helena Blavatsky and American Colonel Henry S. Olcott. Blavatsky came from a noble Russian family; a great traveler in search of the invisible laws of nature and an enthusiastic student of philosophy, religions, and metaphysical sciences, she pondered on and wrote about the relationship between the visible and invisible. Decorated army officer Colonel Olcott was a scientist, journalist, and a renowned lawyer in late nineteenth-century New York. The Theosophical Society's first president, he left behind his successful careers in his homeland and moved to India to set up and live in a Theosophical community. His legacy is remembered to this day in the Buddhist world.

[26] Lucetta Scaraffia and Anna Maria Isastia, *Donne ottimiste Femminismo e associazioni borghesi nell'Otto e Novecento* (Bologna: il Mulino, 2002), p. 41.

[27] Wassily Kandinsky, *Dello spirituale nell'arte*, 1910 (original ed. *Über das Geistige in der Kunst*, Munich, 1911; English ed. *On the Spiritual in Art*, New York, 1946). See Alain Besançon's thoughts in *L'image interdite. Une histoire intellectuelle de l'iconoclasme* (Paris: Gallimard, 1994).

[28] Another significant portion of this library concerns texts connected to Eastern religions and Theosophical thought. On Maria Montessori, see Valeria P. Babini and Luisa Lama, *Una "donna nuova." Il femminismo scientifico di Maria Montessori* (Milan: Franco Angeli, 2000), p. 18.

[29] Anne Taylor, *Annie Besant. A Biography* (Oxford and New York: Oxford University Press, 1992); René Guénon, *Il teosofismo*, ed. Calogero Cammarata, 2 vols. (Turin: Delta Arktos, 1987).

[30] Annie Besant, *Il potere del pensiero* (Milan: Ed. Alaya, undated). The book is stamped "PROMETEO. Rappresentanze editoriali Esoterismo occultismo spiritualismo, Via Borgo Pinti 8, Firenze" (other books in Salvatore Ferragamo's library come from this same repository). Nobel laureate Luigi Pirandello's library also contained a copy of this text. See Giovanni Macchia, "Luigi Pirandello," in *Storia della letteratura italiana*: *Il Novecento*, eds. Emilio Cecchi and Natalino Sapegno (Milan: Garzanti, 1987), pp. 489–97.

[31] Jidddu Krishnamurti, *La via della vita. Discorsi* (Milan: Fratelli Bocca Editori, 1949); Mary Lutyens, *Krishnamurti. Gli anni del risveglio* (Milan: Armenia, 1979).

[32] Krishnamurti, *La vita della vita*, p. 123.

[33] On these issues, it is de rigeur to reference *Equilibrium*, exhibition catalogue (Museo Ferragamo, Florence, 19 June 2014 – 12 April 2015), eds. Stefania Ricci and Sergio Risaliti (Milan: Skira, 2014), and in particular essays by Stefania Ricci, "Feet Don't Lie" and Duccio Demetrio, "Walking. A Philosophy and Lifestyle."

[34] Moon Laramie, "La Teosofia e l'età dell'oro di Hollywood," in *Rivista Teosofica Svizzera/Ticinese*, November 2020.

[35] Alfred Willis, "A survey of surviving buildings of the Krotona Colony in Hollywood," in *Architronic*, vol. 8, no. 1, January 1999.

[36] Sam Watters, "Utopia in Hollywood," in *Los Angeles Times*, February 6, 2010.

[37] Salvatore Ferragamo used to attend the Hollywood Bowl, as we know from a postcard from his sister Rosina to their mother Mariantonia dated January 1924; see my essay, "The Autobiographic Pact," p. 374.

[38] In the article cited, Watters describes why they chose Hollywood to set up a Theosophical community: "With its cheap land for private paradises, California was home to more utopian colonies than any other state... picked up 11 acres west of Beachwood Canyon and north of Franklin Avenue, below where the Hollywood sign stands today, to create an Adyar settlement. He called it Krotona, after the Greek school founded by Pythagoras, who applied musical theory to harmonizing the body, mind, and spirit."

[39] Watters, *Utopia*.

[40] Laramie, "La Teosofia e l'età dell'oro di Hollywood."

[41] Remo Fedi, *Nel tempio dell'io* (Milan: Fratelli Bocca Editori, 1941). The fascist regime's racial laws policy included an order to dissolve the Italian Theosophical Society in 1939, after the Society officially refused to change the wording of its brochure on universal brotherhood, "without any distinction of religion or race."

[42] Prentice Mulford, *Le forze che dormono in noi* (Milan: Fratelli Bocca Editori, 1949) (originally a series of essays published between 1886–92); by the same author, *I doni dello spirito* (Milan: Fratelli Bocca Editori, 1952) (original ed. *The Gifts of Spirit*, London, 1919). The influence of Eastern thought on Mulford is evident in his emphasis on the importance of the power of thought as an essential premise for the quality of words and actions. Owing to their power to act on interpersonal relationships even at great distance, he wrote that "thoughts are things." According to his philosophy, "It is less important to seek helpful forces than to keep our spirit and mental construction in tune with our own desires." His conclusion was that it was necessary to let the silent and persistent power of the mind unconsciously activate such hidden forces.

[43] Antonio Pensa and Giuseppe Favaro, *Anatomia umana e sistematica* (Turin: Unione tipografica, 1944).

[44] Pierre Saint-Yves Cassac and G. Girod, *La guarigione con l'imposizione delle mani* (Milan: Fratelli Bocca Editori, 1949).

[45] Yoghi Ramacharaka, *La cura dell'acqua. Idroterapia orientale col sistema Hindu-Yoghi* (Milan: Fratelli Bocca Editori, 1946). Likely, a text by William Walker Atkinson, who often wrote under the pseudonym Ramacharaka, an Indian philosopher who traveled to Chicago in the mid-nineteenth century. The yogis of India practice and teach many methods and different aspects of Hatha Yoga, a system for physical well-being. Associated harmoniously with mental therapy, this discipline is India's natural medicine. By the same author, see *La suprema sapienza inana yoga* (Milan: Fratelli Bocca Editori, 1950) and, edited by him, a classic text of Hinduism, *La Bhagavad Gita* (Milan: Fratelli Bocca Editori, 1947).

[46] S. R. Yesudian and Elisabeth Haich, *Sport e yoga* (Milan: Fratelli Bocca Editori, 1952).

[47] Biologist and geneticist Julian Huxley studied at Eton and Oxford in the 1930s. He was a member of a commission set up in London in 1931 to lay out the British government's health, financial, and agronomic plans for Great Britain and the colonies. Huxley was the first director of UNESCO and one of the founding members of the WWF. Moreover, he won an Oscar for a scientific documentary he directed. Huxley was a multi-talented figure, who met Virginia Woolf in the 1930s. He coined the term "transhumanism" to express his belief that the entire human species is capable of "transcending." However, even if humans remained humans, they were still "realizing new possibilities suited to their nature."

[48] Amerigo Ruggiero, *Italiani in America* (Milan: Treves, 1936).

[49] *Los Angeles Times*, October 22, 1926.

[50] Elvira Valleri, "1927. The Return to Italy," in *1927. The Return to Italy*, p. 90.

[51] *Shoemaker of Dreams*, p. 238.

LIST OF CONTENTS

www.electa.it

This volume was printed by Electa S.p.A.
at Errestampa s.r.l., Orio al Serio (BG), in 2024